Preventing the Use of Weapons of Mass Destruction

Editor

ERIC HERRING

(University of Bristol, UK)

FRANK CASS
LONDON • PORTLAND, OR

First Published in 2000 in Great Britain by
FRANK CASS PUBLISHERS
Newbury House, 900 Eastern Avenue
London, IG2 7HH

and in the United States of America by
FRANK CASS PUBLISHERS
c/o ISBS, 5804 N.E. Hassalo Street
Portland, Oregon, 97213-3644

Website: www.frankcass.com

British Library Cataloguing in Publication Data

Preventing the use of weapons of mass destruction
  1. Weapons of mass destruction 2. Security, International
  I. Herring, Eric
  327.1'74

  ISBN 0-7146-5044-7 (cloth)
  ISBN 0-7146-8097-4 (paper)

Library of Congress Cataloging-in-Publication Data

Preventing the use of weapons of mass destruction / editor Eric Herring.
    p. cm.
  Includes bibliographical references and index.
  ISBN 0-7146-5044-7 (cloth) – ISBN 0-7146-8097-4 (pbk.)
    1. Weapons of mass destruction. 2. Nuclear arms control. I. Herring, Eric.

JZ5665 .P74 2000
327.1'747 – dc 21   00-031504

This group of studies first appeared in a Special Issue on
'Preventing the Use of Weapons of Mass Destruction'
of *The Journal of Strategic Studies* (ISSN 0140 2390) 23/1 (March 2000)
published by Frank Cass.

Printed in Great Britain by Antony Rowe Ltd., Chippenham, Wiltshire

Contents

1

Introduction

ERIC HERRING

The bulk of the literature on weapons of mass destruction (WMD) concentrates on preventing their spread. While that is an important subject, the aim of this collection is to contribute to the literature on preventing their use. A common argument runs through all of the contributions: that, while complacency must be avoided, much of the post-Cold War focus among Western governments on the threat posed by weapons of mass destruction (WMD) is excessively alarmist. Beyond this shared ground, the authors are diverse in their approaches and in many of their conclusions:

The first three authors provide critiques of Western, especially NATO and US, policy as in some ways having the unintended effect of increasing rather than reducing the chances of the use of WMD, especially nuclear weapons:

- In his assessment of US policy, James Wirtz argues that the Clinton administration has failed to face up to the potential for escalation to nuclear use by an opponent forced into a 'use it or lose it' situation should the United States use conventional forces to attempt to destroy its nuclear weapons. He is sufficiently concerned to want to call conventional counterforce to destroy nuclear weapons a form of nuclear war as a means of drawing attention to that escalation potential.

- NATO's twin track policy of support for non-proliferation regimes and nuclear deterrence as a means of preventing the use of WMD is analysed by Henning Riecke. He develops two competing hypotheses. The first is a neoliberal institutionalist one that these two approaches are compatible and contribute to reinforcing the norm of WMD non-use. The second is a social constructivist one that the two tracks send rather mixed signals, and thus are not very effective in reinforcing the norm of WMD non-use. Riecke sides with the social constructivist hypothesis. On the one hand, NATO's support for anti-proliferation regimes send out a signal suggesting the norm of delegitimisation of WMD use. On the other hand, NATO's military policies which include plans for the use of nuclear use in a variety of circumstances imply the legitimacy, and military and diplomatic utility, of nuclear weapons. Furthermore, Riecke sees no evidence of a shift towards a norm of WMD non-use in several countries in NATO's vicinity such as Iraq, Iran, Libya and Israel.

- Focusing specifically on Iran and Iraq, Carolyn James considers the implications should they acquire 'mini-arsenals', namely, nuclear arsenals big enough to inflict a great deal of damage but too small to ensure the destruction of the opponent's state or society. She sees mini-arsenals as being associated with the following hierachy of preferences: unilateral use without nuclear retaliation from the enemy, then mutual nuclear use, then mutual nuclear restraint and then unilateral use by the enemy without nuclear response. In contrast, she sees Mutually Assured Destruction (MAD) as associated with a less dangerous hierarchy of preferences: mutual nuclear restraint, then unilateral use without nuclear retaliation from the enemy, then unilateral use by the enemy without nuclear response and then mutual nuclear use. Instead, of hyping the threat posed by Iran and Iraq by labelling them 'rogue states', she argues that the West should treat them as rational actors. A controversial option she considers is that, if they acquire nuclear weapons, the West should assist them to move beyond the mini-arsenal stage as quickly as possible to reach a capability for MAD. However, she prefers to advocate conventional strength, regional alliances and alternate energy options as policies aimed at reordering their preferences to safer ones.

The next three authors address themselves to the various contexts which may influence the use of WMD:

- The cultural context is the concern of Beatrice Heuser, who considers principally Britain, France and the Federal Republic of Germany, but also touches on a wide range of other countries. Her aim is to assess the beliefs decision-makers have had about why nuclear weapons in particular are worth acquiring, about the nature of the world, about their own identity and about the identity of potential enemies. Through this approach, she argues, one can gain some insights into their propensity to actually launch a nuclear attack. She shows that nuclear weapons have use value beyond launching attacks - they also have mythic, symbolic and status value. Heuser spells out the similarities and differences between various countries considered. She argues that many countries are culturally predisposed to avoiding the use of nuclear weapons as an instrument of war, but cautions that even they may nevertheless find that predisposition to be altered by circumstance.

- The systemic context is scrutinised by Yannis Stivachtis for its possible impact on the probability of nuclear use. He offers an analysis of the post-Cold War relationships between motives for acquiring WMD, deliberate and accidental use, the power structure of the international system, the decline of ideological competition between major powers, increasing interdependence and globalisation, and the development of international rules and norms, especially the norm of WMD non-use. He concludes that, taking into account these conditions, nuclear use ranges from least to most likely as follows: between major powers; between major and minor powers; and between minor powers. He also argues that the more powers are entangled in interdependence and globalisation processes, the less likely WMD use becomes.

- The technological context in the form of an information-based Revolution in Military Affairs (RMA) involving a shift from mass destruction to precision disruption is considered by Patrick Morgan. He argues that we do appear to be heading for an RMA, even if seen restrictively as involving a combination of new technology, new social and organizational systems, and new conceptions (which actually reshape practice) of how to use force and threats effectively for political purposes. He considers the possible impact of the information RMA on the previous RMA brought about by the development of nuclear weapons deployed on long-range delivery systems: it may supersede, stimulate, deter, pre-empt or become a new version of the use of WMD. Morgan concludes that, on balance, the information RMA will make the use of WMD less likely, although it cannot guarantee that WMD will not be used and is a long way off eliminating the desire to acquire or maintain WMD.

The last two authors challenge widely-held assumptions among many of those worried about the threats posed by WMD:

- The labelling of chemical and biological weapons and related delivery systems as WMD is seen by John Mueller and Karl Mueller as something to be avoided because it is very difficult to actually inflict mass destruction with them. They prefer to restrict the label WMD to nuclear weapons and point out that little attention is paid to the mass destruction inflicted by economic sanctions. When economic sanctions do inflict mass destruction, they prefer the term 'economic warfare'. They argue that Western decision-makers are excessively worried about the threat posed by terrorists and rogue states, and that this is true even of fears about the dangers of such actors acquiring a small nuclear arsenal. Western decision-makers, they maintain, should rely on low-key measures to control the scale of terrorism and on deterrence and containment rather than economic warfare to deal with rogue states. They also argue that the limited threat posed by terrorists and rogue states has declined considerably with the end of the Cold War because they have lost their principal backer, the Soviet Union.

• The labelling of some states as 'rogue states', supposedly the most worrying kind of state when it comes to the potential for WMD use, is assessed sceptically by Eric Herring. He critiques three social science perspectives on the label 'rogue state': it is appropriate for the very serious threats to the West which exist (the conservative perspective); it exaggerates the threats to the West from certain states (the liberal perspective); and it exaggerates the threats to the West and is applicable also or even primarily to the United States and some of its allies (the perspective of the left). He points out that those writing from the conservative and liberal perspectives simply ignore the left. Ironically, he finds the left's position to be the most persuasive of the three. The also argues that one's position on this issue is driven less by the facts than by one's own values and identity underlying one's construction and interpretation of the facts (the interpretivist perspective). He concludes by proposing the development of 'radical security studies', not only as an approach to the issue of rogue states but also as an approach to the study of security generally. Radical security studies aims to engage seriously with the left as well as more mainstream perspectives, while trying to integrate social science and intepretivism.

2

Counterproliferation, Conventional Counterforce and Nuclear War

JAMES J. WIRTZ

US policymakers and analysts are increasingly pre-occupied by the problem of nuclear proliferation, once considered, in the parlance of the Pentagon, to be a 'lesser included threat' covered by the nuclear policies of the United States and its allies. Several factors, probably the least of which was the 1995 Nuclear Non-Proliferation Treaty Review Conference, have sparked this interest. The end of the Soviet empire has highlighted the potential proliferation of nuclear technology, materials, expertise and even weapons as a superpower-sized nuclear infrastructure is divided among several states, including some that are hard pressed to safeguard a nuclear arsenal or materials.[1] The concerted efforts of several nations – Iraq, Iran and North Korea – to acquire nuclear weapons serves as a continuous reminder of the dangers of proliferation. The confrontation between Baghdad and the UN Special Commission repeatedly threatened to end in war, while the termination of UN inspections marked the complete militarization of the US effort to contain Iraq's nuclear ambitions. Doubts also linger about whether or not the 1994 Agreed Framework has contained North Korea's nuclear program. The May 1998 series of Indian and Pakistani nuclear tests suggests that both states are determined to deploy modest nuclear arsenals, thereby adding the prospect of a nuclear arms race to their already troubled relations.[2]

The Clinton administration has made stopping the spread of nuclear weapons a priority by developing a broad range of initiatives, often referred to as the 'Eight Ds'.[3] Four of these initiatives – dissuasion, denial, disarmament and diplomatic pressure – resemble traditional approaches to stemming the spread of nuclear weapons. For example, the administration has worked to strengthen the international legal regime against the spread of nuclear weapons, has supported supplyside activities to prevent states from acquiring nuclear technology, and has addressed the demand side of the proliferation problem by taking steps to reduce states' incentives to acquire nuclear weapons.[4]

However, the administration also has embarked on a relatively new path best described as counterproliferation: initiatives labeled defense, deterrence, defusing and destruction. The United States is taking steps to use force to stop the spread of nuclear weapons and to prepare its forces to meet and defeat new nuclear powers on the battlefield. According to a Defense Department report, the United States is pursuing several initiatives to neutralize the military advantages gained by potential opponents from deploying, threatening to use or actually using Weapons of Mass Destruction (WMD):

> [1] Ensuring that the US has the ability to destroy WMD with a high degree of assurance at acceptable costs; [2] Maintaining the US capability to deter credibly any state that would threaten the use of WMD; [3] effective military power projection with minimum vulnerability; [4] ability to identify origins of attacking WMD; [5] viable decision-making and C3I after WMD attack; [6] ensuring the capability to prevail militarily; [7] enhanced capability for damage limitation and escalation control; and [8] providing the capability for rapid deployment of active and passive defenses.[5]

Counterproliferation policies make reference to nuclear deterrence of successful proliferants, but they emphasize conventional counterforce and defensive capabilities to neutralize emerging arsenals.

Counterproliferation primarily is an effort to use conventional weapons to deny proliferants military benefits from threatening to use or actually using nuclear weapons against US forces or allies. Even among supporters of the administration's efforts to slow the spread of nuclear weapons, counterproliferation now raises the troubling issues of preventive war and preemption.[6] Others have noted that counterproliferation undermines more traditional non-proliferation strategies because it communicates to a global audience the American conviction that the proliferation of nuclear weapons is inevitable.[7]

The aim here, however, is not to offer a detailed critique of the Clinton administration's counterproliferation policies. Instead, this study explores what the emergence of counterproliferation doctrine implies about how the strategic situation facing the United States has changed since the end of the Cold War. In other words, it explains why issues of preemption and preventive war are now emerging in the US strategic debate, mirroring similar interest in these strategies that emerged following the Soviet acquisition of nuclear weapons.[8]

It also explains how the conventional counterforce and defensive strategies embodied in counterproliferation policy rely heavily on US nuclear forces and actually constitute a form of nuclear war. This sort of theoretically informed discussion of the concept of counterproliferation is crucial. To achieve national objectives in a conflict, policymakers must first identify accurately the nature of the war they are about to enter; to treat a nascent nuclear conflict as merely an exercise in conventional precision bombardment would be a recipe for disaster.[9]

This study first describes the logic inherent in the strategic situation that prompted the formulation of counterproliferation doctrine. It then briefly explains why US counterproliferation policy is best viewed as a form of nuclear war by using the concepts of inadvertent escalation and the stability-instability paradox. It then describes how the conventional counterforce attacks envisioned by US counterproliferation policy must be carefully crafted to succeed without prompting the use of nuclear weapons.

THE NEW INTEREST IN COUNTERFORCE

Three factors, produced by a changing global strategic environment, can explain why conventional counterforce and defense are at the center of US counterproliferation policy.[10] First, Mutual Assured Destruciton (MAD) does not characterize the nuclear balance between the United States and likely proliferants. US policymakers now believe that they have a reasonable chance to deny opponents even the most rudimentary second-strike capabilities. Theorists apparently were correct in highlighting the consequences of the nuclear revolution during most of the Cold War: escapes from MAD, at reasonable costs and risks, simply were not available.[11] Now, one probably could distinguish winners from losers, for instance, in a conflict between the United States and North Korea: by definition, MAD does not exist. Strategies to disarm opponents become an option for states that possess overwhelming conventional or, for that matter, nuclear counterforce capabilities.

It would appear that policymakers are willing under extreme conditions to exercise the option of destroying opponent's nuclear capabilities with conventional weapons.[12] Despite a lack of immediate relevance to winning the 1991 Gulf War, Iraq's nuclear infrastructure was attacked during the conflict in an effort to destroy its nascent nuclear capability and these attacks were renewed following the demise of the UN Special Commission.[13]

There also is evidence that the United States is improving its ability to conduct a conventional defense against nuclear attack. American forces are strengthening their ability to conduct the three elements of a 'damage limitation' strategy against ballistic missile attacks launched by nuclear proliferants: counterforce, active defenses and passive defenses are all integral parts of counterproliferation strategies.[14] MAD, after all, was always a situation, not US policy; it should not be surprising that policymakers prefer robust defenses based on counterforce strategies to deterrence.[15]

If the reverse were true, counterproliferation policies, efforts to deny states a nuclear capability, would be of little interest. Policymakers would simply rely on nuclear deterrence to diminish the likelihood that emerging nuclear powers would use their small nuclear arsenals.

A second factor explaining renewed interest in counterforce strategies is the emergence of pressures to fight a war now to avoid the risks of war under worsening circumstances later. Jack Levy has called these pressures, most closely associated with preventive war, 'preventive motivation' for engaging in war. According to Levy:

> The most important factor affecting the strength of the preventive motivation is the preventer's perception of the extent to which military power and potential are shifting in favor of a particular adversary. This decline will have a direct impact on his future bargaining power and the distribution of benefits from the *status quo*, and an indirect impact on the probability of a future war. The greater the expected advantage of the adversary, the greater his relative bargaining position, the extent of the preventer's likely concessions, and the likely costs of a future war; hence the greater the incentive for preventive action now in an attempt to impede the rise of the adversary.[16]

Levy directs his comments toward Great Power rivalry, but he notes that relatively weak challengers could provoke these preventive motivations if critical military thresholds, for example, procurement of nuclear weapons, are involved.[17] The strength of preventive motivation can also be affected by policymakers' views of the probability of future war and the potential costs of fighting now as opposed to fighting later. The offensive/defensive balance plays a part in increasing preventive motivation: 'The greater the offensive advantage', according to Levy, 'the greater the potential advantage for a preventer who chooses to strike first, and hence the stronger the preventive motivation.'[18] Planning to initiate a counterforce strike is a prerequisite in any scheme to destroy an opponent's nuclear arsenal. The only hope of winning a nuclear war lies in firing first; second-strike attacks suffer from obvious limitations as the basis of a strategy to destroy an opponent's nuclear weapons.

One phenomenon that Levy identifies as increasing preventive motivation, however, is absent in US relations *vis-à-vis* would be nuclear powers. War is not yet viewed by US policymakers as inevitable, although at times the situation on the Korean peninsula or between Iraq and the United States appears to be deteriorating inexorably towards war.[19] Once war is considered inevitable, fears of miscalculated escalation would no longer dominate policymakers' behavior in a crisis; instead, defensive preparations are more likely to be undertaken despite the increased risk of provoking an opponent's preemptive attack.[20] Under these circumstances, the catastrophic military consequences of allowing the North Koreans 'to go first' in a nuclear or conventional war would be extremely salient to policymakers. Pre-emption, getting off the first shot against opponents who are generating their forces, would be viewed as a viable option.

Almost by definition, the absence of MAD serves as a necessary military condition for a successful counterforce strategy: if MAD existed, efforts to disarm opponents would be impossible or extraordinarily costly. Similarly, preventive motivations serve as the necessary political condition for the existence of counterforce strategies. Preventive motivations are political judgements about the likelihood and likely outcome of hostilities.[21] Yet, neither preventive motivations or an absence of MAD can explain why policymakers have not turned to nuclear weapons as the basis of the counterforce strategies embodied in US counterproliferation policy. Indeed, counterproliferation objectives could be more decisively, quickly and cheaply achieved if nuclear strikes were employed against the nuclear arsenals and infrastructures of proliferators.

The strength of the nuclear taboo,[22] felt by American elites and citizens alike, is the third factor that has forced US policymakers to concentrate on developing non-nuclear options as the basis of potential counterforce strategies. Indeed, in this instance, logic and politics converge. It would be difficult, if not impossible, to convince an attentive global audience why it was necessary to use nuclear weapons to preserve the international norm against nuclear non-use and non-proliferation. According to Thomas Schelling, 'we can probably not ... ignore the distinction [between nuclear and conventional weapons] and use nuclears in a particular war where their use might be of advantage to us and subsequently rely on the distinction in the hope that we and the enemy might both abstain. One potential limitation of war will be substantially discredited for all time if we shatter the tradition and create a contrary precedent.'[23] In a sense, using nuclear weapons to disarm one state might accelerate nuclear proliferation by providing an example of the utility of actually using nuclear weapons.

Additionally, preventive motivations for war would need to become extremely intense before they reach the point at which the risk of immediate nuclear death and destruction would outweigh the possibility of even greater future nuclear cataclysm. In a crisis, policymakers will hope until the last possible moment that at least nuclear, if not conventional, hostilities can somehow be avoided. As Bernard Brodie argued: 'It is somewhat bizarre to argue that it would be wise to choose now an infinitely drastic and terrible course mostly because the problem that would allegedly be liquidated in that way is one which we or our heirs would be too stupid to handle properly later.'[24]

In sum, counterproliferation doctrine is made possible by the more permissive strategic environment the United States now encounters with the demise of the Soviet Union. The necessary political condition for the execution of the strategy, preventive motivation, has occasionally not reached requisite intensity to prompt an attack. And, paradoxically, the nuclear taboo has greatly reduced the likelihood that the US nuclear arsenal would be used in preemptive or preventive attacks. Conventional weapons are thus viewed as 'weapons of choice' in counterforce strategies directed against nuclear proliferants.

CONVENTIONAL COUNTERFORCE IN A NUCLEAR AGE

Conventional counterforce attacks against proliferants' nuclear infrastructures or weapons are a form of nuclear war. Admittedly, this judgement flies in the face of conventional wisdom, but even the conventional wisdom about nuclear war can appear misguided depending on changing circumstances. For example, it would appear impossible to argue that nuclear war would not occur if one party willingly targeted and detonated a nuclear weapon against another party, creating death and destruction to achieve some political objective. Defined in this way, World War II was the first nuclear war, an observation that Americans often ignore. Michael Mandelbaum, for example, seems to suggest that nuclear war exists primarily in the imagination: 'Nuclear war can be and has been all too readily imagined. It is, however, not more but rather less likely to occur for that reason. The world is well aware that as long as the weapons exist, it will be possible to use them. It is aware that the result of their use would be disaster.'[25] In response, one might say that nuclear war also exists in the realm of history, not the imagination, and that its consequences are not necessarily equally disastrous for those involved. Nuclear war is not some theoretical construct that only exists in the minds of analysts; it is misleading to say, as Ashton Carter does, that we 'have no historical experience of nuclear war to draw upon'.[26] We already have experienced at least one variety of the real thing.[27]

Thus, the most important point in thinking about the relationship between counterproliferation and nuclear war is that the use of nuclear weapons requires no mutual agreement among the combatants to engage in a nuclear war. Since both the course and outcome of a war is determined by a strategic interaction between opponents, one side cannot determine the course of battle on its own.[28]

The exception to this generalization is when one side possesses a 'splendid' first-strike capability: if one party can eliminate its opponent's nuclear capabilities before they are employed, then it would be possible to control at least this aspect of the battle. Clearly, to engage in a perfectly successful (i.e., splendid) preemptive attack is an extraordinarily difficult task.

The more important point is that just because one party has no interest in using nuclear weapons in a conflict does not mean that the other shares a similar interest. Without a splendid conventional first-strike capability, it is impossible to guarantee that nuclear weapons will not be used. Despite what policymakers say or plan to do, counterproliferation policy not only relies on US nuclear capabilities (specifically, the stability-instability paradox), it also directly affects the likelihood that a nuclear war will inadvertently erupt.

Inadvertent Escalation

Despite *ex ante* descriptions of the scope of future war and the nature of one's strategy, it is difficult to control the outcome of war because what the opponent does or does not do has a great impact on the course of battle. Acknowledging that events are not entirely under control of one combatant also raises the issue of inadvertent nuclear war. Inadvertent escalation, especially Barry Posen's definition of the term, is relevant to a discussion of conventional counterforce. In Posen's analysis, conventional operations undertaken against a nuclear-armed opponent's conventional forces can increase the likelihood that the opponent might use nuclear weapons. Even in the electronic age, the fog of war descends quickly on the battlefield: attacks against conventional forces and command and control networks could be interpreted as a prelude to nuclear attack or as the initial stage of a conventional attack against nuclear forces; weapons might go astray hitting nuclear facilities; or individuals facing wartime strain might decide to use rather than lose the nuclear forces under their command.[29]

Conventional counterforce attacks against the nuclear facilities and weapons of a weak nuclear power would only exacerbate the problems identified by Posen. Even if the leaders suffering a conventional counterforce attack choose not to use but to lose their small nuclear forces, their command and control system might 'fail deadly'. Situational stress, organizational malfunction or even the ex ante design of their command and control system might make it impossible for some states to withhold their nuclear weapons once they are attacked by conventional forces.

From the perspective of the weaker party that inadvertently employs nuclear weapons while suffering a conventional counterforce attack, nuclear war would be accidental. Stress, organizational malfunction, or the fog of war would sever the proliferants nuclear forces from political control.

From the perspective of the state actually launching the conventional counterforce attack, however, nuclear war could not be viewed as an accident.[30] By executing a conventional counterforce strategy, leaders would in reality be making the political decision to run a deliberate risk of nuclear war.[31] Policymakers contemplating conventional counterforce attacks might not want to provoke a nuclear war, but their actions will greatly increase the possibility that nuclear weapons might be used in a conflict. Whether or not policymakers recognize this risk, it would still exist.

The Stability-Instability Paradox

The US nuclear arsenal can influence the political or military course and outcome of a conflict without actually being employed in battle.[32] The stability-instability paradox, identified years ago by Glenn Snyder, offers insight into this phenomenon.[33] In Snyder's analysis, stability at the strategic nuclear level of conflict produced by MAD, lead to instability at lower levels of conflict. MAD paved the way for aggression (instability) by making it 'safe' to engage in conventional conflict: states could fight for limited gains without inordinate fear that these small wars would spiral out of control. Even though nuclear weapons are not employed in a conflict, MAD, according to Snyder, exerts an important influence on the occurrence, course, scope and outcome of conventional wars.

Of more contemporary importance is the issue of whether the stability-instability paradox exists when MAD does not characterize a strategic relationship but when nuclear weapons are present in the arsenals of one or both combatants. Clearly, the presence of nuclear weapons has caused militaries to alter battlefield tactics. The Chinese were first to attack deliberately a nuclear armed opponent. To counter the potential threat posed by America's nuclear arsenal, the People's Liberation Army made extraordinary efforts to 'dig in' to protect individuals against the effects of nuclear weapons.[34] The US Army's Pentomic concept, which called for the dispersed deployment of units in a checkerboard fashion, also was a response to the potential battlefield use of nuclear weapons.[35]

In terms of strategy, the connection between the presence of relatively limited nuclear capabilities and the emergence of a stability-instability paradox is more difficult to discern. In retrospect, it is obvious that the United States enjoyed overwhelming nuclear superiority over the Soviets until the mid-1960s. But at the time, uncertainty about the extent of the US nuclear advantage and limited American reconnaissance capabilities led policymakers to take a dim view of the prospects for a first-strike; in a political and strategic sense, the possibility of nuclear retaliation influenced American policymakers years before the Soviets secured an assured destruction capability.[36]

Additionally, factors not related to the stability-instability paradox contributed to early US decisions not to use nuclear weapons. In Korea, a sense of nuclear and conventional inferiority led the Truman administration to decide to husband its limited nuclear arsenal for what appeared to be the coming main event in Europe.[37] During the Indochina War, Eisenhower's political savvy and military expertise stopped a move to use tactical nuclear weapons to relieve the besieged French garrison at Dien Bien Phu. Eisenhower apparently believed that nuclear weapons could not save the French position in Indochina; for Eisenhower, short and long-term political costs to the United States outweighed the potential benefits of using nuclear weapons against the Viet Minh surrounding Dien Bien Phu.[38]

Other events and strategic thinking during the 1950s and early 1960s, however, support the notion that just the presence of nuclear weapons produces a stability-instability paradox. For example, some observers believed that the availability of nuclear weapons made conflict at lower levels of violence more likely. A focal point for this thinking was criticism of the Eisenhower administration's declaratory nuclear strategy of Massive Retaliation and its New Look procurement policy.[39] According to General Maxwell Taylor, an influential critic of Eisenhower's plans, 'the many other [than Korea] limited wars which have occurred since 1945 – the Chinese civil war, the guerrilla warfare in Greece and Malaya, Vietnam, Taiwan, Hungary, the Middle East, Laos, to mention only a few – are clear evidence that, while our massive retaliatory strategy may have prevented the Great War – a World War III – it has not maintained the Little Peace; that is, peace from disturbances which are little only in comparison with the disaster of general war'.[40] Because the new New Look produced large cuts in US conventional forces, Taylor's organizational interests as a senior army officer lay in fighting against Eisenhower's nuclear policies.[41]

Yet, concerns about 'salami tactics', efforts by communist opponents to mount small challenges to US interests, were not confined to army officers. President Kennedy, for example, was alarmed by Khrushchev's 6 June 1961 announcement that the Soviet Union would support 'wars of national liberation' in the Third World.[42] The Kennedy administration's policy of Flexible Response was directed at threats below the nuclear threshold, or at least below the threshold of a full-scale nuclear exchange.

At the time, how did strategists explain the political and military effects produced by what were in some respects highly limited nuclear arsenals? A new school of limited war theorists identified the obvious risk of suffering cataclysmic damage, especially after the development of thermonuclear weapons, as a source of this stability. According to Walt Rostow, both Soviets and Americans acknowledged, following the detonation of a Soviet hydrogen bomb in August 1953, '… that the new weapons of war could, if delivered, by themselves bring about not merely a military decision but also, in some sense, permanent damage to the societies attacked'.[43]

A somewhat less obvious reason for this nuclear stalemate was a widespread perception of the general military and political disutility of actually using nuclear weapons in most circumstances.[44] In Robert Osgood's view, limited wars are, by definition, fought for limited objectives; but the death and destruction wreaked by thermonuclear weapons would be out of proportion to the objectives sought. In circumstances that do not directly and clearly threaten vital national interests, the very destructiveness of nuclear weapons reduces the credibility of nuclear deterrent threats. Osgood thus recommended development of low-yield tactical nuclear weapons and careful target selection to increase the utility of nuclear weapons by actually decreasing their ability to inflict death and destruction on an opponent.[45]

Similarly, Henry Kissinger noted that 'A limited war … is fought for specific political objectives which, by their very existence, tend to establish a relationship between the force employed and the goal to be attained'. Kissinger then built on this reasoning by introducing an important observation that limited war 'reflects an attempt to affect the opponent's will, not to crush it, to make the conditions to be imposed seem more attractive than continued resistance, to strive for specific goals and not for complete annihilation'.[46] For Kissinger, limited war is an exercise in coercion. The threat of a nuclear strike 'fixes' opponents by reducing the likelihood that they will escalate a conflict to escape the destruction produced by conventional attacks.

Thus, nuclear weapons, even one's own nuclear weapons, influence political and military objectives and strategy during a conventional conflict in two ways. In potential nuclear conflicts, one side alone cannot determine if nuclear weapons are used in a conflict. By definition, a splendid conventional first-strike capability would allow one party to determine if nuclear weapons will be employed; but, to achieve this objective, a state contemplating a conventional counterforce strike would have to be prepared to run a risk of inadvertent nuclear war. In other words, there would always be a chance that the opponent's arsenal could fail deadly or that the opponent might launch under attack.

The stability-instability paradox also suggests that the presence of nuclear weapons profoundly influences the scope of war. It is the potential of nuclear escalation that helps to keep limited war (conventional counterforce strikes against nuclear arsenals and infrastructures) limited under these circumstances; the potential for nuclear escalation reduces the possibility that states will choose to use rather than lose their nuclear weapons when subjected to conventional attack.

Before Thomas Schelling's *Strategy of Conflict*, theorists of limited war sometimes overlooked combatants' important mutual interest in keeping limited war limited and the relative ease with which behavior could converge around the norm of nuclear non-use even in very large and deadly conflicts.[47] The side possessing nuclear superiority, for example, has an interest in not using its most destructive weapons: nuclear attacks are likely to be out of proportion to the stakes at hand. Put somewhat differently, counterproliferation makes political and military sense if it only results in a conventional military conflict: in most circumstances, it will be difficult to justify using nuclear weapons to prevent nuclear weapons from being used.

Simultaneously, the weaker or even non-nuclear side has an even more obvious interest in avoiding a cataclysmic nuclear attack in retaliation for some overly provocative activity.[48] As the stability-instability paradox would suggest, even the threat of a few nuclear detonations seems to create the preconditions needed for the thinking about limited war that is currently manifested in calls for conventional counterforce attacks against states' nascent nuclear capabilities. An important reason why states might not adopt a launch under attack strategy in the face of a US conventional counterforce attack against their arsenal is to avoid the almost certain American nuclear response.

CONVENTIONAL COUNTERFORCE AND NUCLEAR WAR

Conventional counterforce attacks against an opponent's nuclear arsenal are thus a form of nuclear war in several significant ways.

First, the presence of nuclear weapons influences political objectives, even if conventional weapons are only used in a conflict. To date, it appears that the political goal of limiting conflict, preventing escalation to the nuclear level, is a high priority of both nuclear and non-nuclear combatants. The potential for massive collateral damage from both large and small-scale nuclear attacks seems to preclude the use of nuclear weapons in a conflict, although they might represent an effective and efficient way to attack a particular opponent or target base.[49]

Second, conventional counterforce attacks increase the risk that nuclear weapons may be used inadvertently. Alternatively, opponents may decide to make the irrational decision to use rather than lose their nuclear weapons.

Third, the threat of nuclear escalation helps to constrain both the nuclear and non-nuclear actors involved in a conflict, creating a stability-instability paradox that lays the groundwork for conventional counterforce attacks in the first place. In a strategic sense, conventional counterforce attacks against an opponent's nuclear arsenal would be nothing more than wishful thinking in the absence of a nuclear deterrent capability. An actor lacking nuclear weapons that contemplates a conventional attack against an opponent's nuclear infrastructure would simply have to hope that the opponent did not decide to use rather than lose its nuclear arsenal.

By contrast, the potential for nuclear retaliation reduces the likelihood that an opponent suffering a conventional counterforce attack will respond by unleashing its nuclear weapons. Thus, the political, strategic and tactical course and outcome of a conventional counterforce attack is influenced by the presence of nuclear weapons. Prudence dictates that conventional counterforce attacks against the arsenals of nascent nuclear powers be considered as a form of nuclear war.

Several observations flow from this characterization of conventional counterforce attacks against nascent nuclear powers. Policymakers apparently tend to ignore or dismiss the risks of nuclear war entailed in conventional military strategies. The chance that policymakers might ignore the nuclear implications of conventional counterforce makes it extremely important that they not forget that battle is a strategic interaction. In all probability, they will be unable to to determine unilaterally the pace and scope of events; they alone will not dictate whether or not nuclear weapons will be used in a conflict. The burden of proof is on those advocating denial strategies to explain how their polices will cope with the nuclear risks that they generate.

Another important observation is that the political and military objectives pursued by counterproliferation strategies must be confined to destroying the opponent's nuclear capabilities with a minimum of collatoral damage. Communicating these limited objectives to an opponent while executing a counterforce strategy, however, would be no small accomplishment. The eruption of counterforce attacks against a nuclear infrastructure would be seen as evidence of America's aggressive intentions by the nascent nuclear power. In other words, the perceptions of threat that motivated policymakers to construct a nuclear arsenal would be confirmed by the execution of a US counterforce strategy.[50]

It would also serve as evidence that small or emerging nuclear arsenals were not a particularly effective deterrent; this might raise proliferants' fear that counterforce strikes are just a prelude to countervalue attacks. Alternatively, counterforce strategies could generate a feeling of resignation and a willingness to negotiate among those subjected to attack because they have just lost the capability to execute their military strategy.[51]

It thus is crucial that counterleadership or countervalue attacks are not launched under the guise of a counterforce strategy. Even though countervalue and counterleadership attacks would be limited in terms of the weapons used to carry them out, in a political sense they would constitute an unlimited assault against an opponent. Similarly, loose talk about negotiating with a successor regime or 'seeing you at the war crimes trial' must be avoided. Instead, negotiations to end the conflict as quickly as possible should be undertaken even as a counterforce strategy is executed.[52] Strenuous efforts should be made to inform the leaders in question that it is their nuclear weapons, not their personal existence or the political independence of their state, that has prompted counterforce strikes against their nuclear arsenal.

Ultimately, policymakers must convince proliferants that it is in their interest not to escalate the conflict because the United States will not take advantage of its ultimate escalation dominance by destroying their regime or country. According to Thomas Schelling, 'To use the threat of further violence against somebody requires that you keep something in reserve – that the enemy still have something to use.'[53] It would be a mistake to kill the hostage gratuitously.

Military requirements, however, might easily undermine efforts to communicate the limited political objectives behind a conventional counterforce strategy. In theory it might be possible to distinguish between a decapitation strategy and an effort to destroy a nuclear infrastructure. In practice, efforts to deny an opponent a militarily useful nuclear arsenal might incorporate a sustained and massive attack on its associated command and control network; but, the proliferant's political and military leadership might be located in command bunkers and complexes subjected to attack.[54] Collateral damage might be kept to a minimum, but the sheer number of targets associated even with a nascent nuclear power's command and control network might produce a massive conventional strike, sending mixed signals to an opponent.[55]

Even more troubling is an observation supported by events during the Cuban Missile Crisis and the 1991 Gulf War: the physical occupation and temporary control of an opponent's territory will be necessary before the US military can hope to determine if a proliferant's nuclear arsenal was destroyed.[56] As a result of the military exigencies involved in counterforce strategies, it will be unlikely that proliferants will take at face value diplomat's descriptions of the limited nature of the instrumentalities and objectives of a US counterforce attack.

A somewhat more counterintuitive observation is that although conventional counterforce strategies appear to be incredibly crisis unstable, in reality they might only contribute marginally to crisis instability. Admittedly, US policymakers during a crisis will face enormous pressures to launch preemptive attacks before a proliferant can generate its nuclear forces. Proliferants also might face enormous pressures to generate their forces to strengthen their deterrent threats, to increase the survivability of the nuclear forces through dispersal or to improve their ability to launch their nuclear forces while they are under attack. However, from the proliferant's perspective, conventional counterforce strategies probably contribute little to perceptions of crisis instability in a technical sense of the term.

Proliferants daily face the fact that the United States possesses a splendid nuclear first-strike capability against nascent nuclear arsenals. It might be apparent to Americans that it is unlikely in the extreme that the United States would initiate nuclear hostilities, but proliferants must plan to meet US capabilities, not US intentions. Until proliferants build a significant secure second-strike capability against Washington, the nuclear and conventional military balance, in a strict technical sense, will remain crisis unstable, regardless of the refinements the United States makes to conventional counterforce strategies.

And, in the political sense of the term, underlying hostility, alternate views of history, and competing political agendas will only serve to fuel competition between the United States and proliferants. Clearly, the states involved believe that war is a real possibility; this perception alone greatly contributes to crisis instability.[57] It would be mistaken to trace crisis instability under these circumstances solely to the creation of a conventional US denial capability.

CONCLUSION

Because MAD does not characterize the strategic relationship between the United States and nascent nuclear powers, American policymakers enjoy a variety of options in selecting a counterproliferation strategy. They must not forget, however, that their efforts constitute a type of nuclear coercion. Whether or not they acknowledge the fact, the US nuclear arsenal poses a deterrent threat to proliferators, 'fixing' them both politically and militarily so that economic coercion or conventional denial can be effective. Policymakers might believe that they have adopted a non-nuclear counterproliferation policy, but their strategies ultimately are supported by the US nuclear arsenal. And from the perspective of a proliferant that lacks a second-strike capability, even the most benign efforts to restrain the spread of nuclear weapons might be seen as part of coherent plan of escalating coercion that terminates in a US nuclear first-strike.[58] The shadow cast by the presence of nuclear weapons is not as pronounced as the dark veil of Armageddon created by the Superpower's Cold War arsenals, but it none the less exists.

Those who champion counterproliferation strategies believe that by reducing the number of nuclear armed states, or by helping to prevent the further spread of nuclear capabilities, the chances that nuclear war will erupt will decrease. Setting aside the debate over whether nuclear weapons are a source of stability or instability in world politics,[59] an unrestrained application of counterproliferation strategies can actually increase the chances of bringing about a nuclear conflict. Because the international struggle to contain or to stop the proliferation of nuclear weapons is a strategic interaction, it is unlikely that counterprolifeation initiatives alone can dictate the scope and pace of events. Counterproliferation advocates might state that they want to reduce the prospects of nuclear conflict; but in this case their intentions in no way guarantee results. In fact, as counterproliferation efforts increase in intensity, producing an international crisis, the effort to stop the spread of nuclear weapons actually evolves into a competition in risk taking. Policymakers might believe that they are simply turning up the political pressure on some hapless pariah regime, but what friend and foe alike are feeling is a distant nuclear heat.

NOTES

1. Statement by Dr Ashton B. Carter, Assistant Secretary of Defense before the Committee on Armed Services, United States Senate, 28 April 1994, pp.12–27; and William C. Potter, 'Nuclear Leakage from the Post-Soviet States', in Barry R. Schneider and William L. Dowdy (eds.) *Pulling Back from the Nuclear Brink* (London and Portland, OR: Frank Cass 1998) pp.107–19.
2. James J. Wirtz, 'Nuclear Weapons in Asia: A Report from ISA-JAIR', *International Studies Notes* 23/2 (Spring 1998) pp.11–16; Jaswant Singh, 'Against Nuclear Apartheid', *Foreign Affairs* (Sept./Oct. 1998) pp.41–52.
3. For a list and description of the 'Eight Ds' see Memo for Robert Gallucci, Assistant Secretary for Political-Military Affairs, Dept. of State and Ashton Carter, Assistant Secretary for Nuclear Security and Counterproliferation, Department of Defense SUBJECT: Agreed Definitions, 18 Feb. 1994, National Security Council.
4. For a discussion of these traditional appraoches to non-proliferation see Barry R. Schneider, 'Nuclear Proliferation and Counter-Proliferation: Policy Issues and Debates', *Mershon International Studies Review* 38/2 (Oct. 1994) pp.216–25.
5. Office of the Deputy Secretary of Defense, *Report on Nonproliferation and Counterproliferation Activities and Programs* May 1994, p.27. As former Secretary of Defense William Perry explained, the administration has established three lines of defense against proliferation: 'The first line is to prevent or reduce the proliferation threat. The second line, if prevention fails, is to deter the threat, And the third line, if deterrence fails, is to defend against the threat.' William J. Perry, 'US Counterproliferation Efforts: Prevent, Deter, Defend', in Schneider and Dowdy *Pulling Back from the Nuclear Brink* (note 1) p.270.
6. David C. Hendrickson, 'The Recovery of Internationalism', *Foreign Affairs* 73/5 (Sept./Oct. 1994) p.34–8. Until recently, few proliferation experts acknowledged that, in the words of Steve Fetter, 'preventive war represent[s] the dark side of nonproliferation policy', see idem, 'Ballistic Missiles and Weapons of Mass Destruction', *International Security* 16/1 (Summer 1991) p.36.
7. Leonard S. Spector, 'Neo-Nonproliferation', *Survival* 37/1 (Spring 1995) pp.66–85.
8. As Bernard Brodie wrote in the late 1950s, 'Preventative war seems today no longer a live issue, though it was that only a few years ago among a small but important minority of American citizens. The pressure in favor of it diminished as the Soviets developed a nuclear capability, and especially as Americans became acclimated to living with those nuclear bombs that had provoked the idea in the first place', Bernard Brodie, *Strategy in the Missile Age* (Princeton UP 1959) pp.227–8. On the issue of preventative war in US strategy see Marc Trachtenberg, *History and Strategy* (Princeton UP 1991) pp.21, 103–7; David Rosenberg, 'The Origins of Overkill: Nuclear Weapons and American Strategy, 1945–1960', *International Security* 7/4 (Spring 1983) p.33; and, Richard K. Betts, *Nuclear Blackmail and Nuclear Balance* (Washington DC: Brookings 1987) pp.161–4.
9. Fred Ikle has expressed a similar thought: '… it can happen that military men, while skillfully planning their intricate operations and coordinating complicated maneuvers, remain curiously blind in failing to perceive that it is the outcome of the war, not the outcome of the campaigns within it, that determines how well their plans serve the nation's interests. At the same time, the senior statesmen may hesitate to insist that these beautifully planned campaigns be linked to some clear ideas for ending the war, while expending their authority and energy to oversee some tactical details of the fighting', see Fred Charles Ikle, *Every War*

Must End (NY: Columbia UP 1991) p.2.

10. Leonard Spector also offers a compelling bureaucratic explanation for the rapidity with which counterproliferation (DoD) efforts have replaced more traditional (State Dept., Arms Control and Disarmament Agency) approaches to non-proliferation see Spector, 'Neo-Nonproliferation' (note 7) pp.77–80.

11. Robert Jervis, *The Meaning of the Nuclear Revolution: Statecraft and the Prospect of Armageddon* (Ithaca, NY: Cornell UP 1989) pp.1–45. For a debate on the behavioral consequences of the Nuclear Revolution see John Mueller, 'The Essential Irrelevance of Nuclear Weapons: Stability', *International Security* 13/2 (Fall 1988) pp.55–79; and Robert Jervis, 'The Political Effects of Nuclear Weapons: A Comment, *International Security* 13/2 (Fall 1988) pp.80–90.

12. This option has rarely been exercised in the nuclear age and attacks have never been conducted deliberately against an opponent's nuclear weapons. According to Schneider, 'Preemptive counter-proliferation attacks have been launched in at least six instances in the past. During World War II, the Allies bombed the Nazi heavy-water plant in Norway and the US bombed Japanese nuclear laboratories. During the first week of the Iran-Iraq War, the Iranian Air Force unsuccessfully bombed the Iraqi Osirak nuclear reactor. Nine months later, on 7 June 1981, the Israeli Air Force bombed and destroyed the Osirak reactor in Iraq on order from Menachim Begin. At the end of the Iran–Iraq War in 1987, the Iraqi Air force bombed and destroyed the Iranian Bushehr reactor. The last time nuclear facilities came under military attack was in Jan. 1991 when the American-led coalition's air offensive struck but only partially destroyed Iraq's nuclear, biological, chemical and SCUD missile assets in the Desert Storm operation', see Schneider, 'Nuclear Proliferation and Counter-Proliferation' (note 4) p.226.

13. Lawrence Freedman and Efraim Karsh, *The Gulf Conflict 1990–1991: Diplomacy and War in the New World Order* (Princeton UP 1993) p.319

14. *Report on Nonproliferation and Counterproliferation Activities and Programs.* This is the classic prescription for damage-limitation strategies see Charles Glaser, 'Why do Strategists Disagree about the Requirements of Strategic Nuclear Deterrence', in Lynn Eden and Steven E. Miller (eds.) *Nuclear Arguments: Understanding the Strategic Nuclear Arms and Arms Control Debates* (Ithaca, NY: Cornell UP 1989) p.135.

15. Ashton Carter makes a similar argument about the US attitude towards these proliferants: 'It seems likely that the United States will pass through a period in the future with most non-Soviet nuclear powers when it has the capability to mount an entirely or nearly disarming strike against them ... Since some of these nations might be quite hostile to the United States, and might have populations that relish their capability to do nuclear damage to this wealthy superpower, America will not willingly relinquish its first-strike advantage', see Ashton Carter, 'Emerging Themes in Nuclear Arms Control', in Emanuel Adler (ed.) *The International Practice of Arms Control* (Baltimore: Johns Hopkins UP 1992) p.256.

16. Jack S. Levy, 'Declining Power and the Preventive Motivation for War', *World Politics* 11/1 (Oct. 1987) p.97.

17. Levy's observation is supported by James H. Schampel's finding that high-speed change in the ratio of material capability between potential combatants is perceived by policymaker's as threatening see James H. Schampel, 'Change in Material Capabilities and the Onset of War: A Dyadic Approach', *International Studies Quarterly* 37/4 (Dec. 1993) pp.395–408.

18. Levy, 'Declining Power' (note 16) p.98.

19. Prior to President Carter's visit to Pyongyang, there was widespread concern over the brewing crisis over North Korea's nuclear weapons program, including Pyongyang's threat that sanctions would be interpreted as a *casus belli* see David Ottaway, 'N. Korea Forbids Inspections', *Washington Post*, 8 June 1994, p.25; and Stewart Stogel and Paul Bedard, 'US Proposes Arms Embargo on North Korea', *Washington Times* 16 June 1994, p.1. Following Carter's visit observers became hopeful that the crisis would end in a negotiated settlement see Jeffrey Smith and Ruth Marcus, 'White House Hails Carter for Efforts', *Washington Post*, 20 June 1994, p.1; and Merrill Goazner, 'North Korea Neighbors Hoping Crisis with US is Really Over', *Chicago Tribune*, 20 June 1994, p.6. Fear of an impending crisis was revived following the death of Kim Il Sung see Thomas Ricks and Steve Glain, 'Death of

Kim May Be Beginning of End for North Korea's Communist Regime', *Wall Street Journal*, 11 July 1994, p.1; and Mark Matthews and Gilbert Lewthwaite, 'Kim's Passing Could Affect World Scene', *Baltimore Sun*, 10 July 1994, p.1.

20. On miscalculated escalation see Richard Ned Lebow, 'Miscalculation in the South Atlantic: The Origins of the Falklands War', in Robert Jervis, Richard Ned Lebow and Janice Gross Stein (eds.) *Psychology and Deterrence* (Baltimore: Johns Hopkins UP 1985); and James Wirtz, *The Tet Offensive: Intelligence Failure in War* (Ithaca, NY: Cornell UP 1991) p.5.

21. From the American perspective, both of these conditions began to fade in the Soviet-American strategic relationship in the 1950s see Warner Schilling, 'US Strategic Nuclear Concepts in the 1970s', in Steve Miller (ed.) *Strategy and Nuclear Deterrence* (Princeton UP 1984) pp.212–14.

22. According to Thomas Schelling, 'nuclear weapons are in a class apart from conventional weapons. They are under a curse, a taboo, despite the awe in which they are held and the prestige that may go with them, Thomas Schelling, 'From an Airport Bench', *Bulletin of the Atomic Scientists* (May 1989) p.30. Also see T.V. Paul, 'Power, Influence, and Nuclear Weapons: A Reassessment', in idem, Richard Harknett and James J. Wirtz (eds.) *The Absolute Weapon Revisited* (Ann Arbor: U. of Michigan Press 1998) pp.19–45.

23. Thomas Schelling, *The Strategy of Conflict* (NY: OUP 1963) p.265.

24. Brodie, *Strategy* (note 8) p.233.

25. Michael Mandelbaum, *The Nuclear Future* (Ithaca, NY: Cornell UP 1983) pp.21–2.

26. Ashton B. Carter, 'Sources of Error and Uncertainty', in idem, John Steinbruner and Charles A. Zraket (eds.) *Managing Nuclear Operations* (Washington DC: Brookings 1987) p.616.

27. John Hersey, *Hiroshima* (NY: Knopf 1946); and Tatsuichiro Akizuki, 'A Doctor at Nagasaki, August 1945', in Lawrence Freedman (ed.) *War* (NY: OUP 1994) pp.41–3. An image of mutual annihilation has long dominated American views of nuclear war, even before the arrival of MAD. According to Herman Kahn, 'The usual image of war today held by many experts as well as most laymen can be summed up in the phrase "orgiastic spasm of destruction", or "spasm war". Many believe that if one single button is pressed all the buttons will be pressed …' see Herman Kahn, *Thinking about the Unthinkable* (NY: Horizon Press 1962) p.59.

28. Edward Luttwak, *Strategy: The Logic of War and Peace* (Cambridge, MA: Harvard UP 1987). For a more specific discussion of how war is unpredictable because of the the the interaction of adversaries see Alan Beyerchen, 'Clausewitz, Nonlinearity, and the Unpredictability of War', *International Security* 17/3 (Winter 1992/93) pp.72–5.

29. Barry Posen, *Inadvertent Escalation: Conventional War and Nuclear Risks* (Ithaca, NY: Cornell UP 1991); Edward Rhodes, *Power and MADness* (NY: Columbia UP 1989); and Jerrold M. Post, 'The Impact of Crisis Induced Stress on Policy Makers', in Alexander George (ed.) *Avoiding War: Problems of Crisis Management* (Boulder, CO: Westview 1991) pp.471–94. For a critique of the notion of inadvertent escalation, based on the notion that SOPs can be designed to either increase and decrease the likelihood of inadvertent escalation see Lewis Madden, 'Irrationality-Based Deterrence Reconsidered', *Defense Analysis* 8/3 (Dec. 1992). Jeffrey Legro makes a similar point about the impact of organizational culture on the likelihood of inadvertent escalation see Jeffrey Legro, 'Military Culture and Inadvertent Escalation in World War II', *International Security* 18/4 (Spring 1994) pp.108–42.

30. In other words, if someone shot themselves in the head playing Russian roulette, the outcome would be inadvertent, but not accidental.

31. Here I am invoking Thomas Schelling's notion of the 'threat that leaves something to chance', see Schelling, *Strategy* (note 23) pp.187–203.

32. Despite the fact that nuclear weapons were not used during the Korean War, for example, they were used by American statesmen to manage the politics and diplomacy of the war, see Roger Dingman, 'Atomic Diplomacy During the Korean War', *International Security* 13/3 (Winter 1988/89) pp.50–91.

33. Glenn Snyder, 'The Balance of Power and the Balance of Terror', in Paul Seabury (ed.) *The Balance of Power* (San Francisco: Chandler 1965) pp.184–201.

34. John English, *On Infantry* (NY: Praeger 1984) p.176 and fn 84.

35. Christopher C.S. Cheng, *Air Mobility: The Development of a Doctrine* (Westport, CT:

Praeger 1944) pp.61–4.
36. Richard Betts, 'A Nuclear Golden Age? The Balance Before Parity', *International Security* 11/3 (Winter 1986–87) pp.3–32.
37. Trachtenberg, *History and Strategy* (note 8) pp.115–32; and Rosemary Foot, *The Wrong War: American Policy and the Dimensions of the Korean Conflict, 1950–1953* (Ithaca: Cornell UP 1985) pp.113–30. On the Truman administration's effort to increase the size and capability of the US nuclear arsenal see Rosenberg, 'The Origins of Overkill'(note 8) pp.22–4.
38. Melanie Billings-Yun, *Decision Against War: Eisenhower and Dien Bien Phu, 1954* (NY: Columbia UP, 1988). On the siege see Bernard Fall, *Hell in a very Small Place: The Siege of Dien Bien Phu* [1967] (NY: Da Capo 1985). Ronald Spector describes two plans for using nuclear weapons to defend Dien Bien Phu, one calling for the use of six 31-kiloton devices. According to Spector, 'The authors of the two studies recognized that employment of atomic weapons risked retaliatory military action by the Soviet Union or China but argued that this risk could be minimized by disguising the US role, for example by using aircraft with French markings', see Ronald H. Spector, *Advice and Support: The Early Years of the US Army in Vietnam 1941–1960* (NY: Free Press 1985) p.200.
39. On Massive Retaliation and the New Look see Lawrence Freedman, *The Evolution of Nuclear Strategy* (NY: St Martin's 1981) pp.81–90.
40. Maxwell D. Taylor, *The Uncertain Trumpet* (NY: Harper 1959) pp.5–6.
41. In Taylor's view, 'the New Look was little more than the old air power dogma set forth in Madison Avenue trappings ... Its implementation assumed the preponderant use of airpower and avoidance of the bloody, exhausting battle on the ground', see ibid., p.17.
42. Leslie H. Gelb with Richard Betts, *The Irony of Vietnam: The System Worked* (Washington DC: Brookings 1979) pp.70–1; and Andrew F. Krepinevich, *The Army and Vietnam* (Baltimore: Johns Hopkins UP 1985) p.29.
43. W.W. Rostow, *The United States in the World Arena: An Essay in Recent History* (NY: Harper 1960) p.309.
44. Certain practical considerations are likely to become important in limited wars fought for limited political objectives. As Martin van Creveld notes: 'an Arab Bomb dropping on Tel Aviv would almost certainly inflict grievous damage on precisely the Palestinian people ... whereas exploding such a weapon on the Golan Heights, only 50 kilometers (30 miles) from Damascus and with the prevailing winds blowing from the west, is an even less attractive proposition', see Martin van Creveld, *Nuclear Proliferation and the Future of Conflict* (NY: Free Press 1993) p.123.
45. Robert Osgood, *Limited War: The Challenge to American Strategy* (U. of Chicago Press 1957) pp.9, 249. After surveying various arguments about the utility of employing nuclear weapons on the battlefield Morton Halperin concluded 'the question of who would gain from the use of tactical nuclear weapons can only be answered by saying that it depends on a host of variables including who uses them first, the geographic area, the terrain, the sympathies of the indigenous population, and the state of technology and production at the time', see Morton Halperin, *Limited War in the Nuclear Age* (NY: John Wiley 1963) pp.68–9.
46. Henry Kissinger, *Nuclear Weapons and Foreign Policy* (NY: Harper 1957) p.140.
47. For example, Osgood, noted that some sort of agreement was needed between combatants to keep limited war limited: 'A feasible strategy of limited war must be based upon a conception of limitation that is acceptable to Americans and to Communist leaders; for unless the major adversaries of the cold war observe the conditions for limiting war, an American strategy of limited war will not be feasible regardless of what the objective interests of the adversaries my require', Osgood, *Limited War* (note 45) p.10. Thomas Schelling's work on tacit bargaining, however, would suggest that Osgood's concerns were not as daunting as they first appear. Nuclear non-use is an extremely salient point of convergence between parties to a conflict; states will probably begin to limit conflict by taking steps to avoid using nuclear weapons or provoking others into using them see Schelling, *Strategy* (note 23) pp.53–80.
48. According to Kissinger, 'It is clear that war cannot be limited unless both sides wish to keep it limited. The argument in favor of the possibility of limited war is that both sides have a

common and overwhelming interest in preventing it from spreading. The fear that an all-out thermonuclear war might lead to the disintegration of the social structure offers an opportunity to set limits to both war and diplomacy', see Kissinger, *Nuclear Weapons* (note 46) p.144.

49. Of course, the clear exceptions to these generalizations are the US attacks on Hiroshima and Nagasaki.

50. Robert Jervis, *Perception and Misperception in International Politics* (Princeton UP 1976) pp.143–55.

51. For an elaboration of this logic see Robert Pape, 'Why Japan Surrendered', *International Security* 18/2 (Fall 1993) pp.154–201.

52. Osgood recommended that during a limited war, policymakers should make 'every effort to maintain an active diplomatic intercourse toward the end of terminating the war by a negotiated settlement on the basis of limited objectives ... This consideration becomes especially important in light of the fact that even a small nation that possessed an arsenal of nuclear weapons might, in desperation, inflict devastating destruction upon a larger power rather than accept humiliating terms', Osgood, *Limited War* (note 45) p.24.

53. Thomas Schelling, *Arms and Influence* (New Haven, CT: Yale UP 1966) p.173.

54. This would obviously reduce the possibility of communicating all but one message (we want you dead) to the opposing leadership. For a discussion of the role of maintaining communication between combatants and the means to communicate with their respective forces in war termination see Paul Braken, 'War Termination', in Ashton B. Carter, John Steinbruner and Zraket, *Managing Nuclear Operations* (note 26) pp.197–214.

55. In the late 1980s, Ashton Carter identified 1577 targets (Command Centers, communication nodes, warning and assessment sensors) associated with the US nuclear command and control network. But, proliferants' command and control networks might actually be larger. For example, during the 1991 Gulf War, the allies struck 32 'leadership targets'. Carter's list, however, only contained about 20 similar targets (11 major US command centers and 7 airborne command posts and alert bases) in the US infrastrucutre see Ashton B. Carter, 'Assessing Command System Vulnerability', in idem, Steinbruner and Zraket (note 26) pp.560–72; and Freedman and Karsh, *Gulf Conflict* (note13) pp.323–4.

56. The 'air-strike' options discussed by the Ex Comm during the Cuban Missile Crisis also called for an invasion to 'ensure no reconstitution of a military threat to the United States – also, of course, disposing of Castro once and for all', see Raymond Garthoff, *Reflections on the Cuban Missile Crisis* (Washington DC: Brookings 1989) p.53; and Richard Betts, 'Wealth, Power, and Instability: East Asia and the United States after the Cold War', *International Security* 18/3 (Winter 1993/94) p.66.

57. Purely, 'technical' assessments of the military balance or imbalance between states are not sufficient to produce instability in strategic relationships. The United States possess a splendid first-strike capability against most nations, yet people do not worry, for example, about what this implies about the future of US-Canadian relations. For an elaboration of this logic see Colin Gray, *Weapons Don't Make War* (Lawrence: UP of Kansas 1993).

58. According to Robert Jervis, policymakers tend to see the behavior of others as more coherent, purposive and centrally directed than it is. Policymakers also have a tendency to ignore the ways that they contribute to international problems; instead they tend to blame the policies of others as the source of international conflict see Robert Jervis, 'Hypotheses on Misperception', *World Politics* 20/3 (April 1968) pp.454–79.

59. Representative of those who acknowledge the potential positive impact of nuclear proliferation are Kenneth Waltz, 'Nuclear Myths and Political Realities', *American Political Science Review* 84/3 (Sept. 1990) pp.731–45; John Mearsheimer, 'Back to the Future: Instability in Europe after the Cold War', *International Security* 15/1 (Summer 1990) pp.5–56; John Mearsheimer, 'The Case for a Ukrainian Nuclear Deterrent', *Foreign Affairs* 72/3 (Summer 1993) pp.50–66; and Stephen Van Evera, 'Primed for Peace: Europe After the Cold War', *International Security* 15/3 (Winter 1990/91) pp.7–57. For critics of this strategy see Steven Miller, 'The Case Against a Ukrainian Nuclear Deterrent', *Foreign Affairs* 72/3 (Summer 1993) pp.67–80; and Scott D. Sagan, 'The Perils of Proliferation: Organization Theory, Deterrence Theory, and the Spread of Nuclear Weapons', *International Security* 18/4 (Spring 1994) pp.66–107.

3

NATO's Non-Proliferation and Deterrence Policies: Mixed Signals and the Norm of WMD Non-Use

HENNING RIECKE

Since early 1994, the North Atlantic Treaty Organization (NATO) and its member states have invested a lot of effort in collecting and assessing information on the spread of weapons of mass destruction (WMD).[1] They adapted the alliance's organisational and force structure to meet the risks emanating from proliferation. The result was a two-track non-proliferation approach, directed toward stronger institutions and deterrence. The US and others want to include a nuclear threat into the latter part of the strategy and refuse to drop the first-use doctrine in NATO. Some member states are reluctant to accept any military component of this policy, embracing both counterforce and nuclear deterrence. The debate has been transferred to a working group.

The visible effects of the NATO campaign are not too impressive, however. Despite the fact that the alliance machinery has run for five years now to stem WMD proliferation and use, there are still WMD programs conducted in the alliance's neighbourhood. There is reason to believe that chemical weapons have been used in Bosnia.

Meanwhile, the regimes on non-proliferation of WMD are gaining ground around the globe. These regimes promote a norm of non-use. They do not only regulate the denial of certain WMD and the relevant verification procedures. They do also point to the hazardous qualities of WMD, through distinct language in the treaties' preambles (the discriminating Nuclear Non-proliferation Treaty, NPT, being an exception). The NPT has been extended indefinitely in 1995 and has been signed by nearly the whole of the international community except India, Pakistan and Israel. In April

1997, the Chemical Weapons Convention (CWC) entered into force. A year later, it had been signed by 169 participants, but some Arab states with alleged Chemical Weapons (CW) programs did not (Iran did under reservations). The Biological Weapons Convention (BWC), in force 1975, has been signed by 147 and ratified by 114 states. Anyway, some of the most discomforting regime outsiders are situated in NATO's vicinity. Usual suspects for ABC programs are Algeria, Iran, Iraq, Egypt, Israel, Syria and Libya. There is no sign that NATO's adaptation has enhanced the support for WMD non-proliferation in those countries. No clear sign of renunciation has occurred (except membership in the African Nuclear Weapon Free Zone by Algeria and Egypt). Accordingly, those states cannot be observed as following a norm prohibiting WMD. They also are likely to defying a norm prohibiting their use.

The alliance's activities are directed against WMD. They are, however, designed to meet an enemy's use of such weapons in combat involving NATO troops – a scenario resembling Operation 'Desert Storm'. An intervention by NATO ground troops in the Kosovo, against hostile opposition by the Yugoslav Army possibly armed with chemical weapons, would have been a case in point. Though a nuclear threat against the Serb army would not have been credible, the alliance's remaining nuclear weapons might dissuade other potential opponents to deploy or use WMD in such conflicts. NATO's nuclear weapons are not thought to deter WMD use in general or in civil wars without NATO involvement. The impact this reliance on nuclear weapons has on a developing norm concerning the non-use of WMD, however, remains foggy.

This study undertakes to analyse the impact of military instruments, most prominently deterrence, but also pre-emption and intelligence, on a norm prohibiting the use of WMD. Since a clearly observable effect in direction of WMD non-use in NATO's neighbourhood seems to be lacking, we have to search for alternative effects the NATO campaign might have. The questions are: How does this set of military strategies influence the situational and normative conditions for the decision to use WMD? What impact has NATO policy on the development of the norm on WMD non-use?

The focus on the use of WMD delimits the choice of theory and methodology. The literature on proliferation theory, looking basically at the strategic, technological or domestic motives underlying the decision to start a WMD program will only be touched shortly. For the *use* of WMD by state actors, the acquisition is a necessary, but not sufficient precondition. Furthermore, the rationale behind the military approach is based on core tenets of deterrence theory. A modified deterrence theory provides a framework to understand the way deterrence against a proliferation country works. A nuclear 'First-Use' doctrine of can be rational to secure a credible deterrence against any use of WMD.[2]

Further clarification is needed in which 'theatres' the use of nuclear weapons is conceivable for NATO. In the ongoing debate, some allies refuse to adopt US calculus of nuclear deterrence to retaliate against the use of B and C weapons for NATO. Since nuclear weapons thus can only be used on battlefields far away from Europe's borders, in thinly populated areas, the question comes down to a decision whether NATO remains a European security organisation or whether it can be utilised for power projection into other areas of conflict.[3] This debate is not yet closed, and the final task of NATO's nuclear weapons has not been agreed upon.

Since we do not look for the deterring effect itself, but for the generation of a norm on restraint, theories focusing on the formation and existence of norms might be more useful. *Neoliberal institutionalism* representing a rationalist view, and a *social constructivist* understanding of the internalisation of norms will guide this analysis.

The *neoliberal institutionalist* understanding about the causes and persistence of norms is a functional one. State actors need norms and verification procedures to make co-operation possible, where it is desirable. By stabilising expectations about an actor's behaviour and by increasing transparency, the fear of cheating will diminish and long term commitments become more likely. States have a demand for institutions to provide functions enabling them to co-operate, like transparency or sanctioning mechanisms. Third party engagement to supplement or complete those functions is under certain conditions desirable. NATO's activities thus stabilise the existing norm on the non-use of WMD.

In *social constructivist* thinking, an actor builds up an identity inside an ideational setting consisting of ideas, principles, values, but also meanings attached available instruments and knowledge about their effects. Knowledge about the qualities of a certain sort of weapon can be regarded as part of this environment as well as the meaning they might have. The norm of non-use rests on a coherent set of ideas about the negative quality of WMD, that has to succeed over more positive perceptions, for example, that nuclear weapons are prestigious, chemical weapons are the "poor man's atomic bomb" and so on. The internalisation of a norm can be interpreted as a process of learning new knowledge about a weapon's qualities. The use of the overarching term 'WMD' for all three types of weapons has equalised their distinct characteristics, as has done the fight against the proliferation of all classes of WMD with equal vigour. Furthermore, the idea that the application of nuclear weapons against B or CW attack might have enhanced this trend. Following from this, the NATO reform can be analysed with regard to the signals it casts out about the significance of WMD and their legitimate use in a just case.

The theoretical arguments generate two competing hypotheses:

(a)   Neoliberal-institutionalist:

NATO's military instruments enhance the norm prohibiting the use of WMD by supplementing or providing institutional functions which enable states to co-operate.

(b)   Social constructivist

Only when it includes signals about the negative ethical value of WMD, NATO's military approach can enhance the norm prohibiting the use of WMD. By sending signals that show the significance of such weapons and which prevent a learning directed against WMD, an opposite effect can be expected.

How do we determine whether a norm is followed or not? Restraint can only be exercised by a state that already has developed WMD. There are states with CW arsenals, which have openly renounced their use and have embarked on a disarmament process. Only two countries have declared CW possession, the USA and Russia, and renounced them in the context of negotiations for the CWC. Those activities are signs that a norm on non-use and restraint is followed. Visible and publicly confirmed renunciation by actors in possession of WMD is seen as a sign that a norm on non-use is obeyed.

A second group of actors is more relevant for our questions: States which embark on or pursue a hidden WMD or missile program. Can such a country be seen as violating the norm not to use WMD? Its endeavour shows a clear sign that it has not accepted the norm as valid. Progressing WMD programs, that show no sign of delay, large arsenals that are upheld despite growing support against WMD and open resistance to participate in non-proliferation regimes will be regarded as signs that a country is probably not clinging to the norm of WMD non-use.

Only NATO activities are in the centre of interest here. Their impact on states such as India or North Korea which are situated outside the NATO's area of operation will be neglected. To look at an actor or alliance with limited geographical range of operations and fewer opponents is an analytical decision to facilitate inference. NATO's military approach reflects the American strategic thinking about how to counter proliferation by counterforce. To analyse the global effects of the US counterforce strategy, however, would be far more complicated.

Applying the two theoretical approaches, the military NATO campaign will be examined with regard to the functions it might fulfil and to the signals it might hold. The non-use of WMD, however, being the dependent variable, can only be observed on the side of the threshold states. A clear-cut outcome does not exist. Neither have WMD been totally abandoned, nor, fortunately, have we seen a significant increase of WMD use. Certain criteria will be used to assess the effects of Western or NATO policy, such as actual behaviour of those states concerning WMD use, public statements of government officials, their position toward the relevant regimes and so on. The number of states suspected of conducting WMD programs in the vicinity of NATO is manageable.

In the next section, the competing theoretical hypothesis will be further discussed. The political and military NATO reform will be analysed in section three, which is followed by a short survey of WMD policy in NATO's vicinity. The concluding section will discuss the effects the alliance's military approach might have had.

COMPETING VIEWS ON NORMS

The main focus here is on the use and not on the possession of WMD. It is obvious WMD cannot be used by a country which is not in control of them. The well examined motives for the acquisition of WMD thus play a secondary role in our argument. What we look for is a norm not to use WMD – whether nuclear, chemical or biological. Our theoretical considerations have to focus on the process of building and upholding a norm in international relations. The motives why states might prefer to acquire WMD instead of conventional weapons are well discussed in proliferation literature.[4]

- WMD are sought to help states to gain a regionally *hegemonic* position once the superpowers have retreated.

- For the same reason, other states might wish to acquire WMD to uphold the *status quo* by deterring a neighbour from using them.

- Having the conventional superiority of the West in mind, as proven during Operation 'Desert Storm', expansionist states (or those who wish not to be disturbed with their illegal activities in domestic conflict) might wish to balance this *asymmetry* with WMD. This motive has become more prominent after the Second Gulf War.

- The *prestige* assigned to certain kinds of armament is important. Especially nuclear weapons are still widely regarded as symbols for technological and industrial superiority. This is not true for chemical or biological weapons, which will be discussed below.

- Decision-makers also have *domestic incentives* for the acquisition of WMD. The prestige attached to nuclear weapons might enhance the public support of the leader who decided to embark on a nuclear weapons program, as was seen in India. Chemical and biological weapons can be used against domestic opposition or ethnic or secessionist groups.

- As for nuclear weapons, the *availability* of nuclear technology and material on the open market or via illicit exports has risen, due to the uncertain control over nuclear complex in the former Soviet Union and the growing number of nuclear suppliers.

- The *technological development* in the threshold states might have a similar effect, increasing the availability of technology and material at home.

- *Bureaucratic inertia* might impede governments to stop WMD programs once they have been initiated.

This contribution focuses not on the decision to proliferate, but at the decision to use WMD, these motives might be kept in mind, but will not guide the analysis. The process leading to the decision to use or not to use WMD is itself shaped by strategic, situational or normative conditions. The latter result from a normative framework about right or wrong behaviour in warfare, part of which can be the norm not to use WMD. What might have an effect on the formation of such a norm?

In the *institutionalist* view, the military campaign can have a positive impact on the long term prevention of WMD use by stabilising the norm prohibiting it. Given the fact that an all-out spread and use of WMD can be considered the worst outcome in every actor's perception, co-operation in form of a collective renunciation of those weapons would be desirable for all.[5] Behaviour according to a norm of non-use would be rational for actors (even those in possession of those weapons), who know that their own breech of this norm would induce others to defect as well. Since a unilateral renunciation of WMD use while others are still prepared to apply such weapons could be disastrous, however, states might wish to overcome uncertainty about the other's conduct. They have a demand for institutions that provide functions to facilitate co-operation.

Transparency measures can help states overcome their insecurity. Monitoring of military activities, multilaterally agreed-upon verification procedures like challenge inspections on the opponents territory or reporting schemes about nuclear energy production can calm down fears about hidden WMD programs. Sanctioning mechanisms that guarantee punishment against a defector can make the opponent's behaviour more reliable by raising the costs of defection. Decision-making bodies can discuss accusations about defiance and put the case on the agenda of a more superior body. Most of all, an institution supervising a set of norms will lower the political and financial costs of coming to an agreement.[6]

A rational actor who benefits from norms which are accompanied by an institutional framework, can accept the involvement of a third party providing or supplementing the institution's functions. To be sure, even a rational actor might be cautious in accepting such an 'assistance' and ask for restrictions, such as a certain degree of multilateral consensus and reference to international law. Especially measures concerning transparency can be applied more effectively by a powerful actor with sophisticated intelligence capabilities (a case in point was the North Korean nuclear crisis, when Washington provided intelligence information to the International Atomic Energy Agency, IAEA). Others might seek ways to keep the powerful actor from utilising is prominent role for espionage.[7] Even the threat of prevention measures or sanctions can be upheld more credibly by a powerful single state than by a politically divided body like the UN Security Council. [8]

In neoliberal institutionalist understanding, institutions work without the dominance of a strong actor, but temporary dominance is not contradictory to the functional demand for a norms and institutions. Thus, deterrence and other military means provided by NATO could indeed enhance the norm of non-use.[9] The hypothesis derived from this argument is that NATO's military instruments enhance the norm prohibiting the use of WMD by supplementing or providing institutional functions facilitating co-operation.

The rationalist approach of the neo-liberals faces similar limitations as the logic of deterrence underlying the alliance's reform. The assumption that all states (in the region) equally deny the possession and use of WMD, and consider using them only under the influence of a *prisoner's dilemma*-like situation, is certainly weak. Also contestable is the concept of rationality, which is applied as a regular pattern of decision-making to all actors. It might be misleading to analyse the use of WMD from this starting point, especially with regard to the damage some actors might be willing to risk on their population or their international reputation.

A third critique would point to the fixed concept most rationalists are coerced to apply when dealing with interests as exogenously given, like state survival. Cultural or historical patterns might, for some states, induce a more belligerent standing toward the Western alliance and might bias the definition of interests and the choice of instruments to secure them. Neoliberal institutionalism cannot account for these variables.[10]

A *social constructivist* paradigm goes beyond the rationalist understanding of norms and actors. International norms are not followed because it is reasonable with regard to a certain objective. Norms are part of an ideational setting in which an actor is situated, and which an actor relies upon to build up identity. Other elements of this setting, that is, sources of identity, are for instance principles about statehood, or values, be they political, cultural or religious.[11]

In this view, the decision to use WMD is not merely one of costs and benefits. Decisions for military operations are shaped by an overarching framework of norms concerning the appropriateness of certain activities in combat, that constitute a sometimes vague but existing codex about right and wrong behaviour. Part of such a framework are norms concerning the use of different kinds of weaponry. These norms rest upon characteristics that are assigned to families of weapons. Weapons can be more or less effective or vulnerable, but they also have differing ethical values or meanings. Throughout the history of warfare, certain categories of weapons have been perceived as depraved, though perceptions changed over time – from the medieval attempts to outlaw crossbows to the ban on landmines in the 1990s. In early World War II submarine warfare was regarded a contemptible military instrument.[12]

This idea about an ethical value is in the core of the norm prohibiting the use of WMD, which carry a very singular and complex character distinguishing them from other categories of weapons. The gruesome consequences of WMD use, especially the separation of use and effect (the last victim of Hiroshima not being born by now), earned them a reputation of being cruel and terrible weapons with a somewhat metaphysical nature. The perception, that nuclear, biological and chemical weapons are equally designed and labelled for "mass destruction" defies their distinctive characteristics.[13]

These characteristics generated different beliefs about the qualities of A, B and C weapons: Nuclear weapons on the one hand, are the most destructive of all weapons. In the 1940s and 1950s, they were developed only by states with an advanced industrial base and great power ambitions – USA, USSR, Great Britain and France. These official nuclear weapons states plus China are permanent members of the UN Security Council (as victors of World War II) or the P5. Since the 1960s, lesser developed threshold countries tried to follow this example. To master the engineering tasks of a nuclear weapons program and to control the nuclear jinn was a symbol for the potential of matching the industrialised states with this regard. Hence, a certain prestige and symbolic value is still assigned to them, leaving aside the tremendous burden of creating and upholding an effective nuclear force.[14] The possession of nuclear weapons is allowed to a small privileged group. Their use is perceived as being allowed, too – under certain conditions.

Chemical weapons, on the other hand, are much easier to construct and not as destructive as their atomic counterpart. They have been used more often with cruel but relatively limited effects. Accordingly, CW acquisition is far from being prestigious, they have the image as being wicked and depraved.[15] Chemical weapons, however, have also been considered as a cheap instrument to balance the P5's nuclear superiority, being regarded as the 'poor man's atomic weapon'.[16]

Biological weapons are even more hazardous, since they carry serious dangers for those who develop and deploy them. BW arouse the most intimate fears about physical intactness. Their effects are limited, compared to nuclear weapons, but they are much easier to apply.

Obviously, these perceived qualities of WMD are contradictory, depicting them as both useful and contemptible. A norm prohibiting WMD use would have to rest on the negative qualities or meanings of a type of WMD. One could write the history of the development of the norm on non-use as a struggle between the positive and negative meanings attached to WMD, or, in other words, as the spread of consensual knowledge in the international arena about the vicious character of such weapons. The process, in which such a knowledge is adopted by state or other corporate actors has been conceptualised by early reflectivists as 'organisational learning'.[17] To look at learning rather than at the national and international discourses reproducing knowledge and meaning[18] is, again an analytical decision. By focusing on the signals of NATO's policy, we observe only one dimension of a certainly mutual and interactive process. The use or deployment of WMD in Europe's vicinity probably has an impact, too, on the Western states' willingness to consider nuclear weapons appropriate means of warfare.

Quite common is a distinction between *simple* and *complex* learning,[19] or *adaptation* and *learning*,[20] that will be applied here. Both terms describe the change of behaviour according to new knowledge. Adaptation (simple learning) is a process of using new knowledge (or newly attached meanings) to redirect instruments without a re-formulation of basic principles and goals. The process of learning (complex learning) is one in which a corporate actor is induced to put fundamental causal beliefs in question, which leads to a re-definition of interests and objectives. It 'involves recognition of conflicts among means and goals in casually complicated situation, and leads to new priorities and trade-offs'.[21]

To use the concept of learning to understand the internalisation of norms, one has to go beyond a narrow understanding of 'common knowledge' to be learned by a corporate actor. In the literature on learning, varying forms of knowledge are mentioned, ranging from scientifically collected and testable experience to a broad understanding of causal relations in the world.[22] For the purpose here, the spectrum will be extended toward learning of beliefs, here about qualities and appropriateness of WMD.[23]

Corporate actors learn from experience, such as the effectiveness of means. But learning, the acquisition of knowledge, is an inter-subjective process. How are values about instruments learned? It is conceivable that ethical values concerning WMD change on the side of a proliferating country, when certain signals from other states' behaviour are experienced, which reflect values they themselves attach to WMD. Given these values are consistent with a broader set of values the proliferating state call its own, the door for learning is opened. Decisions about military operations are taken in a normative framework. This is shaped by the ethical qualities ascribed to the available instruments. When these ethical qualities are seen as more and more negative, a norm might be established or fostered, which guides state behaviour against the use of WMD.

Only if we take beliefs about the ethical quality of WMD into the picture, we can make a difference between *adaptation* (i.e. the cost-benefit ratio a kind of WMD is altered) and *learning* (i.e. WMD are neglected in principle). Only when the second process occurs in the countries suspect of developing WMD, when beliefs are spread like 'WMD are immoral' or, more distinctive, 'nuclear weapons are not only expensive but terrible and dangerous'. or 'Chemical and biological weapons defy the principles of humanity', the use of those terrible weapons can be prevented. Experiences are conceivable which induce states to learn, such as examples given by other states (like South Africa gaining influence in the nuclear non-proliferation debate only after quitting the nuclear option) or the experience of growing isolation, especially when trading opportunities are lost.

Note, that NATO's military strategy might have a deterring effect which only leads to *ad hoc*-adaptation, but not to learning of new principles. NATO's strategy might cause fears of retaliation or detection. It might change the cost-benefit ratio of the WMD instrument and lead to different choices in a given situation. Credible deterrence can thus only prevent WMD use against the deterring country but does not help to promote a new understanding about the negative qualities of WMD.

Only when NATO's military approach includes signals about the negative ethical value of such weapons, the norm prohibiting the use of WMD can be enhanced. By sending signals which show the significance of such weapons and which prevent a learning directed against WMD, the opposite effect can be expected. An analysis of the signals which are held by the violent content of the NATO reform might allow some comprehensive understanding about the way NATO's reform works.[24]

NATO'S NON-PROLIFERATION CAMPAIGN

The risk of WMD proliferation in areas relevant for operations concerning the basic alliance missions had profound repercussions on NATO's strategic planning. Both the traditional task of collective defence and the recently defined functions in crisis reaction, peacekeeping and -enforcing came were affected by these new threat scenarios. The development of WMD programs in areas of conflict in which NATO operations might be expected challenges its ability for crisis reaction. The alliances' Rapid Reaction Forces might be exposed to an attack with nuclear, chemical or biological weapons.[25] The increased vulnerability would not only diminish the Western states' ability to conduct tasks like peacekeeping or humanitarian assistance, but would also touch vital national interests – in case operations under UN mandate, designed to promote stability in neighbouring regions, are impeded. NATO strategy, force structure, deployment, air defence and equipment have been modified with regard to this diffuse proliferation risk. Initiated by the US Counterproliferation program, which served as a model for the NATO reform, the member states built up a consensus about the character of the risk and the best ways to cope with it.[26]

The early understanding, that growing proliferation risks made a re-definition of the alliance's strategic requirements necessary, can already be found in the November 1991 Rome Declaration.[27] In subsequent communiqués, NATO bodies pointed to the growing dangers resulting from

WMD proliferation. The documents focused on the surplus of fissile material generated by the disarmament process in the Soviet Union and later Russia, on the denuclearisation of Ukraine and on the unlimited extension of the NPT due in 1995.[28]

Also in the autumn of 1993, US Secretary of Defence Les Aspin presented the Pentagon's Defense Counterproliferation Initiative (DCI) to his NATO colleagues.[29] Given the expectation that proliferation could not be prevented by export controls and safeguards alone, DCI was thought to impede or reverse proliferation with combined political and military means, such as sophisticated intelligence technology and the procurement of systems able to detect and destroy WMD. A second task was to decrease the vulnerability of US armed forces through an attack with WMD. With the subsequent programs, the Pentagon reacted to the growing risk that the applicability of US armed forces against an opponent equipped with nuclear, chemical, or biological weapons might be limited. Aspin's speech focused on five points[30]:

1. Public announcement of the new aggressive non-proliferation policy; this included information campaigns for the four segments of the military, new guidelines for the Chiefs of Staff and a post for an Assistant Secretary in the Pentagon in charge for the DCI networking.

2. Equipment to localise and destroy WMD (*counterforce*), like earth-penetrating ammunition against subsoil bunkers, programmes for detection and destruction of mobile missile launchers and the development of a *Theatre Missile Defence* against sub-strategic missiles.[31]

3. Development of new strategies to cope with enemies with WMD in hand. The military was ordered to re-evaluate its operational capabilities for such a case and to put forward ideas for improvement.

4. Collection of intelligence information regarding potentially proliferating states. Intelligence capabilities were to be improved and the Central Intelligence Agency was to establish a new Assistant Director. A non-proliferation centre was designed to collect specific knowledge on WMD proliferation.

5. International co-operation to fight WMD proliferation should be co-ordinated and strengthened. This component was directed at NATO and the fellow Western states in the arms control bodies. Bilateral expert meetings were arranged to complete the international networking.

The initiative was also thought to be a model for the adaptation of the NATO force structure. Though the military bias caused some opposition among the allies, its principles were a blueprint for NATO reform. It included measures to replace or supplement transparency functions the International Atomic Energy Agency (IAEA) is responsible but hardly suited to fulfil. This, in neo-liberal perspective, can be regarded a support for the non-proliferation regimes, as long as the findings are made public. The counterforce element of the American strategy tells a different story. Signals cast out by the DCI are (a) we take WMD seriously as one of a few remaining threats to our (that is the US) security, and (b) we are prepared to wage military action in case a program is detected and not reversed afterwards.

The subsequent NATO summit in Brussels in January 1994 initiated the re-orientation of NATO toward a new risk assessment.[32] The heads of state and government declared WMD proliferation to be a threat for international security. In no way did they address the question why a weapons generation, regarded as having pacified the East–West Conflict during the past decades, is a threat today. With this, the NATO members re-stated the significance-signal, this time as 'WMD are dangerous in your hands, but secure in ours'.

The summit agreed to create two working groups dealing with the political and military consequences of the new situation for NATO. A Senior Politico-Military Working Group (SGP), chaired by the Assistant Secretary General for Political Affairs, examines measures to enforce the existing arms control and non-proliferation agreements. A Senior Defence Group on Proliferation (DGP), co-chaired by an American and a European senior official (a Frenchman until 1995, a British MoD official until 1996, until 1997 an Italian), discusses the adaptation of NATO forces and to the new conditions. Both groups convene in a *Joint Committee* where they first formulated a 'Political Framework of the Alliance to the Problem of Proliferation of Weapons of Mass Destruction'.[33]

This document was issued at the NATO summit in Istanbul in June 1994, half a year after the forceful American initiative. The threefold objective was to review the alliance's efforts for the prevention of WMD, to find ways to decrease the risk of proliferation and to maintain security in the face of ongoing WMD programs. The 'Framework' had a much stronger political bias than the American initiative. The document expressed strong support for the ABC non-proliferation regimes and the unlimited extension of the NPT. The core phrase was that existing agreements should be supplemented but not duplicated by NATO activities.

This focus was due to criticism from European allies, notably Germany, who were reluctant to adopt the DCI's military direction for NATO. France and the UK, the other two nuclear weapons states inside the alliance had already reviewed their troops' operability under WMD impact.[34] Germany and others demanded that the traditional non-proliferation policy should not be replaced by a military one. Especially the timing of DCI was considered wrong, with several non-proliferation agreements, like the NPT or the Comprehensive Test Ban, standing at the crossroads.[35]

The procurement decisions necessary to carry out the DCI were not too attractive for the Europeans as well.[36] Hence, the military dimension occupied only a small space in the 'Framework' document. The document included the expectation that proliferation sometimes could not be prevented by traditional instruments, and that NATO's defence capabilities would have to be amended. The defence posture was considered to play some role in coming diplomatic negotiations with proliferating countries. The reiterated call for institutionalisation of non-proliferation issues in the political section contained an idea about the inappropriate qualities of WMD.

Another signal, vague but audible, was that the complete NATO arsenal was considered an instrument for coercive diplomacy, and that NATO embarked to prepare its troops to keep this leverage in hand even against states already in possession of WMD.

The DGP subsequently examined the military implications.[37] The working group adopted a three-stage program for itself. In the first stage, the DGP conducted a risk assessment, with help of intelligence information provided by member states. The second phase was an evaluation how far the new situation affected NATO's existing defence posture. The results were made public in November 1995. 'NATO's Response to Proliferation of Weapons of Mass Destruction' collected the results of the DGP's work to 'address the military capabilities needed to discourage NCB-proliferation, deter threats or use of NBC weapon, and to protect NATO populations, territory and forces'.[38] It enshrined four proposals concerning prevention, deterrence and surveillance.

- 'Alliance military capabilities reinforce and complement international efforts to prevent proliferation'. All capacities – strategic intelligence and 'robust military capabilities' that show NATO's resolve 'should strengthen internationally-shared norms against proliferation'. These capacities would decrease the value of WMD systems. The expectation that norms are enhanced through support of transparency measures meets the neo-liberal concept of regimes.

- A mix of capabilities would provide the basis for deterrence and prevention.

- 'Complementing nuclear forces' with a mix of conventional weapons, passive and active defences 'would reinforce the alliance's deterrence posture'. This point is of special interest, for it reiterates the usefulness and operability of nuclear weapons against other kinds of WMD.

- NATO would need strategic and operational intelligence capabilities, ground surveillance, early warning equipment against attacks with B and C weapons, individual protective equipment, improved C^3I systems and air defence against tactical missiles for troops in combat. With these results in mind, DGP identified shortcomings of the existing force structure and proposed ways cope with them. This referred to new co-operative procurement programs.[39]

Intra-alliance procedures for force planning were thus tightened by order of the Ministers of Defence. DGP developed 39 separate plans for action to improve existing weapons systems, including the R&D and financial requirements of the projects. The group will survey the implementation.[40] The Berlin NATO Council in June 1996 took note of these results.[41] A NATO public relations officer official said during a briefing in early 1997 that the procurement measures were not designed for counterforce purposes, a consensus of the allies on this matter would not be likely. According to this statement, the alliance does not plan to conduct preventive strikes against WMD production or storage sites, like the US did in Sudan.[42]

The demand for an extended air defence (EAD) coincides with a development already underway in NATO and older than the DCI. Between June 1992 and August 1993, NATO-Air Defence Committee (NADC) worked on a framework plan for extended air defence directed at tactical missiles, being the logical extension of the existing integrated air defence. In October 1994, NATO-Headquarters SHAPE issued a procurement plan for tactical defence for Europe, to guarantee the security of the so-called *NATO-Guideline Area*, but also of the troops in conceivable operations. SHAPE, NADC and the Conference of National Air Force Directors (CNAD) put together an eight-member working group under American chairmanship to review co-operation projects. CNAD is in charge for assisting the DGP in the third stage of its work on procurement requirements.

The working group further improved the plan. The Extended Air Defence will rest on four pillars (in order of priority) 1. Improved Battle

Management/C^{3}I 'architecture' for ground surveillance. 2. Active Defence, which would include interceptor systems attacking in high and low altitude and against taking-off or ascending missiles. 3. Conventional Counterforce directed especially against delivery systems carrying WMD on or over an opponent's territory. The alliance regards strict (internal) rules of engagement as precondition for such sensitive operations. 4. Passive Defence, including military and civilian protective shelters, early warning etc.[43] The procurement patterns resulting from EAD reform, especially regarding the counterforce component, might be taken as evidence that scenarios for preventive missions are in NATO's drawer.

The double objective of the program's military component is to impede or reverse the spread of WMD on the one hand and to deter the use of such weapons on the other. NATO promises (a) to retaliate against WMD use, (b) to make its troops less vulnerable under WMD impact, and (c) to use its technology to detect WMD development and to render the acquisition of such weapons more costly. The idea is to change the cost-benefit-ratio of WMD programs: the costs of such programs would be considerably higher, since detection and destruction would become more probable; the benefits, with NATO troops operable and effective even under the impact of WMD use, would be lower.

NATO's nuclear weapons play a vaguely defined but relevant role in this approach, as part of a broader set of deterrence capabilities. The friction about the future of a nuclear first-use in NATO doctrine between Germany and the United States shortly before NATO's 50th birthday shows how important an instrument nuclear weapons are regarded in Washington. In November 1998, the new Foreign Minister Joschka Fischer tried to initiate a re-discussion of this element in NATO strategy, talking to US Secretary of State Madeleine Albright and NATO Secretary General Javier Solana. Fischer cited the coalition contract of his Green Party with the Social Democrats, who had agreed to bring up this question in NATO, and pointed to NATO's changed threat scenario compared to the conventional Soviet advantage in Cold War times. Fischer met heated criticism in the United States, which was calmed down only by German Defence Minister Scharping on his subsequent introductory visit in Washington.[44]

The core argument behind the American opposition, next to the still perceived threat from Russia, was the idea that NATO's remaining nuclear capabilities could be used to meet enemies equipped with WMD. An official was quoted, that adopting a no-first-use doctrine would 'encourage rather than dissuade other countries to go after nuclear weapons'.[45] US Secretary of Defence William Cohen put it more clearly: 'We think the ambiguity involved in the issue of nuclear weapons contributes to our own security, keeping any potential adversary who might use either chemical or biological (weapons) unsure of what our response would be.'[46] This view is shared by the European nuclear weapons states, too, though they remain more ambiguous than Washington.[47]

Bonn and Washington quickly put a lid on the open argument, not to risk irritations at NATO's 50th anniversary summit in Washington in April 1999. Later on, the Kosovo conflict inhibited any strong discussion about the issue. The debate whether a first-use doctrine is needed has crossed the pond and has reached the public in Western Europe.

At the Washington summit, a new strategic concept was agreed upon. A basic principle for conventional force postures is their invulnerability facing WMD use in operations outside NATO territory.

> 56. The Alliance's defence posture against the risks and potential threats of the proliferation of NBC weapons and their means of delivery must continue to be improved, including through work on missile defences. As NATO forces may be called upon to operate beyond NATO's borders, capabilities for dealing with proliferation risks must be flexible, mobile, rapidly deployable and sustainable. Doctrines, planning, and training and exercise policies must also prepare the Alliance to deter and defend against the use of NBC weapons.

On nuclear weapons, the concept reiterates the words from the 1991 Strategic Concept. It thus maintains as core function of nuclear weapons to ensure

> uncertainty in the mind of any aggressor about the nature of the Allies' response to military aggression. They demonstrate that aggression of any kind is not a rational option. (...) These forces need to have the necessary characteristics and appropriate flexibility and survivability, to be perceived as a credible and effective element of the Allies' strategy in preventing war. They will be maintained at the minimum level sufficient to preserve peace and stability.

The ambivalence against what opponent or what kind of attack nuclear weapons are considered appropriate has not been removed. On the one hand, this reflects US preferences for a deliberately ambiguous position regarding the nuclear deterrence against C and BW attack, but might also be the lowest common denominator among the diverging positions of NATO members. Probably to meet the opponents' demands, a paragraph points to the waning value of nuclear weapons and to the new security conditions.

> (...) The circumstances in which any use of nuclear weapons might have to be contemplated by them [the member states, H.R.] are therefore extremely remote.[48]

The document lists several reduction and de-targeting measures conducted by NATO. In peace time, no sub-strategic nuclear weapons will be deployed on surface vessels and attack submarines.

The summit has transferred the discussion about nuclear doctrine and first use to a working group, probably connected to the DGP. Pending a clear-cut decision, the ambiguity, which leads to contradictory non-proliferation and deterrence goals is still there, but on a higher level.

FUNCTIONS OFFERED AND SIGNALS SENT BY NATO'S MILITARY REFORM

NATO and its members, on the one hand, have expressed strong and active support for the non-proliferation regimes. All member states have renounced B and C weapons and the nuclear component of the defence posture has been devalued and is regarded as an instrument of 'last resort'. Furthermore, NATO's intelligence capabilities might be useful to complete the non-proliferation regime's transparency measures – that is, to support the IAEA safeguards-system,[49] to demand challenge inspections from the Organisation for the Prohibition of Chemical Weapons or – since no verification system exists for the ban on biological weapons yet[50] – to offer relevant BW information to the international community. While NATO documents openly stated this purpose, three reservations have to be made.

First, any third party offering sophisticated intelligence information might be accused of following narrow interests and putting a bias into an organisation.

Second, intelligence collected by powerful nation states is not necessarily better than that gathered by an agency entitled to inspect on-site. Washington's problems persuading Russia to drop a nuclear deal with Iran might result from the vague information the US could offer (compared to the high quality information concerning North Korea). India's nuclear tests show that WMD activities can be concealed even from sophisticated satellite supervision.

Third, whether information is credible for all participants is relevant when measures to punish a defection are on the agenda, aiming to stabilise a norm. 'Evidence' such as Washington offered about CW production in

Khartoum – samples of dust from the later destroyed facility – might have been sufficient for the US to decide on the attack, but it would not be enough to provide transparency to mollify collective action problems.[51]

On the other hand, the military side of the NATO reform, especially the counterforce, contains different signals on the qualities of WMD to threshold states in its vicinity, that might consider WMD use. Those signals can be grouped under four headings.

(a) WMD states are important. WMD are taken serious as one of a few remaining threats to Western security. States are taken more seriously, too, when they are willing to use WMD. They are regarded as contemptible, but dangerous enemies. For some states, in which governments utilise anti-western or anti-American sentiments to rally domestic support, this role might be appealing.

(b) NATO is willing to touch your sovereignty with high-tech warfare. The alliance shows itself prepared to wage military action in case a program is thought to be detected. Both nuclear and conventional weapons, equipped with sophisticated targeting technology and guided by advanced C^3I systems, are – vaguely – promised to be applied in preventive operations for this objective.

(c) There are just cases for the use of WMD. The nuclear weapons backing both deterrence and diplomatic endeavours against proliferation give an idea that they are part of a set of appropriate instruments and that their use is still legitimate.[52] In US strategic planning, the use of nuclear weapons as retaliation against chemical or biological weapons is included.[53]

With these signals, an image of WMD might be promoted, that does not rest on their gruesome and corrupt character, but on their significance and usefulness against conventionally superior troops.

CONCLUSION: WMD USE IN NATO'S VICINITY

The countries that will receive a closer examination are the 'usual suspects' for WMD proliferation.[54] Have they changed their position toward WMD and toward the use of such weapons in the past four years?[55] Empirical data is scarce, so we have to rely on the careful estimates made by pundits from the non-proliferation community.

Concerning nuclear weapons, the situation might provoke some optimism.

Iraq has destroyed its nuclear weapons program under observation by the United Nations Special Commission (UNSCOM).

Israel holds a large arsenal (50 – 200 warheads) which is neither confirmed nor denied by Tel Aviv.

Beside the two well known cases, *Iran* is most frequently cited candidate in the Middle East. Washington presumes that the Iranian nuclear program has a hidden military purpose. Iran has a multidimensional civil nuclear program still in its early stage. It has an ambiguous attitude towards a military nuclear option, evoking its NPT commitments on the one hand, while publicly claiming the right to develop a Muslim nuclear bomb against the Israeli threat on the other.[56] There are rumours but no factual evidence for any planned military uses of the nuclear program. The American apprehension is based on intelligence material concerning Iranian procurement policy, pointing for instance to a secret gas centrifuge enrichment program uncovered in spring 1995. Washington's accusations were not matched by findings of earlier IAEA inspections.[57] Since 1998 the US and Iran have slowly moved into a careful form of constructive engagement, but there is no sign that Iran would publicly drop its nuclear ambitions.

Other suspect countries are *Algeria* and *Libya*. Algeria aroused suspicions in the early 1990s, when it secretly constructed a research reactor which was far too big compared to its rudimentary nuclear energy complex. Only when the site was detected, Algeria decided to put the reactor under IAEA safeguards and to sign the NPT (which happened in January 1995). In April 1996, Algeria joined the Africa Nuclear Weapons Free Zone (NWFZ) and can be regarded as having dropped the nuclear option.

The same can be said of *Egypt*, that once pondered a nuclear weapons program, but later was leading the field to establish the African NWFZ.

Libya tried for 25 years to acquire nuclear warheads from others, without success, and has meanwhile entered the African NWFZ (only Algeria, Gambia and Mauritius have ratified the treaty).

Sometimes *Syria* is counted among the would-be nuclear weapons states, but the technological basis is lacking.

As for chemical and biological weapons, the picture looks more discomforting. In *Iraq*, UNSCOM has since 1991 destroyed large amounts of CB weapons and materials in Iraq. The country has unveiled its biological weapons program in summer 1995 (after detection by UNSCOM) and said that in 1991, 190 weapons had been ready to use. Iraq did not use them, which might point to the deterring effect of American nuclear warnings delivered in connection with Operation 'Desert Storm'.[58]

Iran possesses one of the largest CW arsenals, the CIA is quoted that Iran stockpiles several thousand tons of sulphur, mustard, phosgene and cyanide agents (production of 1000 tons annually). It is capable of producing nerve gas as well. German and American intelligence reports in 1995 stated that Iran was building a CW fabrication plant with German and Indian dual-use material. The US Secretary of Defense accused Iran of deploying CW on islands in the Straits of Hormuz, which was denied by Iranian officials. Though obviously not in compliance, the country signed the CWC with reservations. Iran (in a CIA report of 1996) is supposed to have a BW program in the research stage, with some stocks of toxin agents.

At the review conference of the Biological Weapons Convention in 1997, however, Iran proposed to add the word 'use' in the title and in the first article of the convention, which only prohibits the development, production, stockpiling, and acquisition of biological and toxical weapons. Iran contended that the BWC's reference to the 1925 Geneva Protocol precludes only the first-use of BW. Moreover, the convention's commitments would not necessarily preclude the use of such weapons. Iran's proposal was supported by some neutral and non-aligned states. Others pointed to the existing treaty language in the Geneva Protocol and the BWC, which would ban BW use together with the mentioned activities. In the following debate, all states at parties condemned the use of BW in war.[59] Iran's initiative would indicate a shift of the country's WMD policy toward a more norm-oriented policy. In this case, it would constitute a puzzle that no clear signs of renunciation are observable concerning other WMD. It is hard, therefore, to conclude on a general change in Iran's attitude regarding WMD, on which can be inferred from, for example, Algeria's support for the African NWFZ.

Libya is producing mustard gas and other agents in two CW production facilities, which is denied by Tripoli. The country is energetically seeking ballistic missile technology, too.

Syria is also frequently quoted as conducting a secret BW program. Rumours that, in October 1995, 800kg of toxic material was smuggled from Russia to Syria could not be confirmed.

In the 1995 report of the American Arms Control and Disarmament Agency to the US Congress, among others, were listed Iran, Iraq, Egypt, Libya and Syria, though all signatories, as being not in compliance with the BWC. The CWC, open for signature since January 1993 and in force since April 1997, has not been signed by Egypt, Iraq (no need to), Libya and Syria.[60] Egypt has a long history of chemical weapons research and development, being probably the first Middle East country to obtain and use CW. According to US intelligence sources, Syria is reported to be building a new chemical weapons factory near the city of Aleppo.[61]

Beside the alleged deployment of Iranian CW in the Straits of Hormuz, which reflects a willingness to use CW, there are reports, 'unconfirmed by independent experts', about repeated CW use by Bosnian Serbs in 1995 in Yugoslavia.[62] One case made its way into the Western press, when incapacitating gas was used during an attack on Zepa in July 1995. Serbian troops wore protective masks on this occasion. The Federation of American Scientists pointed in April 1999 to the existence of facilities in Yugoslavia designed to do research on and develop chemical toxins. NATO ground troops thus would have faced a chemical threat when entering the country. US officials later confirmed, that Yugoslavia had stockpiled chemical agents usable in warfare. President Clinton threatened a 'swift and overwhelming' response to any chemical attack. There was, however, no direct threat from Belgrade.[63]

Is this the result? WMD are produced, stockpiled, deployed and used in an area, where the deterring effects of NATO non-proliferation campaign could be expected to work. The picture is of course more complicated. Only careful conclusions can be derived, which rest heavily upon the theoretical argument, and need further in-depth analysis in close connection with governments in the countries concerned.

Nuclear weapons proliferation has slowed down. Some possible candidates for proliferation have been either forced to destroy their program, like Iraq, or have dropped the nuclear option. This is a sign, that the non-use of nuclear weapons, the 'nuclear taboo' is gaining ground. This finding is in contradiction to the signal sketched out above, that the use of atomic weapons in certain cases has a legitimate character. The high costs in each case, however, might weigh heavier than the idea of appropriateness. Chemical and biological weapons programs are still pursued by a small number of states that remain unimpressed by the NATO campaign. They show no sign of entering the relevant non-proliferation regimes (or, as in the case of Iran, they do with obvious qualification).

As those states fall into the second category of states with WMD in hand that show no sign of restraint, the only conclusion possible up to this point is, that chemical and biological agents have not lost their image of being, for some states, appropriate instruments in warfare. For a small number of relevant states, the norm prohibiting the use of WMD seems not to be an inducement for renunciation. This does not mean, that these weapons are piled up to once be directed at NATO members or troops in combat. We cannot conclude, that deterrence has failed, but it seems correct, that for several countries, for those at which NATO's campaign was primarily directed, prevention and dissuasion have failed.

For the large number of others, the non-proliferation institutions seem to be the right strategy – and maybe the supplementing effect of the NATO campaign would come as a relief to them. Not a proof, but a hint is the absence of any WMD arms race in the 1990s, India and Pakistan are a sad exception, or of WMD acquisition induced by a program in the neighbourhood (Iraq did so in reaction to the Israeli nuclear weapons).

The candidates for proliferation, probably do not search for B or C weapons out of fear that some opponent has them in the first place. Instead, BCW might be simply seen as useful instruments in international, regional or maybe domestic conflict. They are a means to increase a country's capabilities and enlarge the arsenal of effective military options – remember the signals NATO's campaign contained. B or C weapons maybe not directed against the Western states in any conflict involving NATO troops, but in border disputes, against smaller neighbours, against secessionist groups. This would constitute an adaptation to the counterforce threat.

The negative meaning of B and C weapons has not been 'proliferated' with this strategy: learning does not seem to have taken place. Some negative ethical value of WMD must be known to the decision makers in the proliferating countries, otherwise they would conduct the development more openly or indifferently, but it is not strong enough to succeed over the image of significance and appropriateness these weapons still hold.

This leads back to the known motives for proliferation listed at the beginning. The NATO campaign might eliminate the possibility of using WMD to overcome asymmetry, namely to balance the conventional superiority of Western forces fighting for international law. It would not remove the motive of seeking regional hegemony.

NATO territory and operations probably are secure from B and CW attack. The use of such weapons, however, is as probable today as it was in the past.

NOTES

1. The empirical data here is partly based upon an earlier article, see Henning Riecke, 'Nukleare Nichtverbreitung als Aktionsfeld von NATO und GASP' in Helga Haftendorn and Otto Keck (eds.) *Kooperation jenseits von Hegemonie und Bedrohung. Sicherheitsinstitutionen in den internationalen Beziehungen* (Baden-Baden: Nomos 1997) pp.191–232 (211–18).
2. See David Gompert, Kenneth Watman and Dean Wilkening, 'Nuclear First Use revisited', *Survival* 37/3 (Autumn 1995) pp.27–44.

3. 'NATO's Strategic Concept. Cohesion and Dissent', *Strategic Comments* 5/1 (Jan. 1998).
4. Joachim Krause, *Strukturwandel der Nichtverbreitungspolitik. Die Verbreitung von Massenvernichtungswaffen und die weltpolitische Transformation*, Internationale Politik und Wirtschaft, Bd. 65. Res. Inst. of the German Assoc. for Foreign Policy (Bonn, München: R. Oldenbourg 1998). Focusing on nuclear weapons, see Mitchell Reiss and Robert Litwack (eds.) *Nuclear Proliferation after the Cold War*, Woodrow Wilson special studies (Washington DC 1994) pp.335–50; Gregory J. Rattray, *Explaining Weapons Proliferation: Going Beyond the Secuity Dilemma*, INSS Occasional Paper No. 1, July 1994. Inst. for National Security Studies, US Air Force Academy (Colorado 1994), and Stephen M. Meyer, *The Dynamics of Nuclear Proliferation* (U. of Chicago Press 1984).
5. For basic writing on neoliberal institutionalism, see Robert O. Keohane, *After Hegemony. Co-operation and Discord in World Political Economy* (Princeton UP 1984); idem, 'Neoliberal Institutionalism': A Perspective on World Politics, in idem, *International Institutions and State Power. Essays in International Relations Theory* (Boulder, CO: Westview 1989) pp.1–20. For a thorough discussion see Andreas Hasenclever, Peter Mayer and Volker Rittberger, *Theories of International Regimes*. Cambridge Studies on International Relations, 55 (Cambridge: CUP 1997) pp.23–82 (27–44).
6. Lisa Martin, 'Interest, Power, and Multilateralism', *International Organization* 46/4 (1992), pp.765–92 for the relationship between problems of collective action and institutional functions.
7. This has been done by the US intelligence in aiding the UN Special Commission in Iraq, see Susan Wright, 'Hijacking UNSCOM', *Bulletin of the Atomic Scientist* 55/3 (May/June 1999) pp.23–5.
8. This situation is different from the one conceptualised by hegemonic stability theory, for which a small group capable of upholding the different non-proliferation regimes is needed. For works of reference Charles P. Kindleberger, *The World in Depression, 1929–1939* (Berkeley: U. of California Press 1974); Robert Gilpin, *U.S. Power and the Multinational Corporation* (NY: Basic Books 1975). For a discussion see Hasenclever, Mayer and Rittberger (note 3) pp.86–104; Robert O. Keohane, 'Theory of Hegemonic Stability and Changes in International Economic Regimes, 1967–1977', in Ole Holsti (ed.) *Change in the International System* (Boulder, CO: Westview 1980) pp.131–62.
9. There is the faint possibility, however, that a threshold state is induced to use its weapons in a window of opportunity, that is opened by (a) a prolonged planning phase of NATO or (b) any distraction of the alliance's operational capabilities.
10. Robert O. Keohane, 'International Institutions: Two Approaches', in *International Studies Review* 32 (1988) pp.379–96, who distinguishes rationalist and reflectivist branches of IR theory and asks for an empirical test of the latter.
11. For constructivist thinking on state identity, see Alexander Wendt, 'Collective Identity Formation and the International State', in *American Political Science Review* 88/2 (1994) pp.384–96, for a survey see Steve Smith, 'New Approaches to International Theory', in John Balys and idem (eds.) *The Globalization of World Politics. An Introduction to International Relations* (Oxford: OUP 1997) pp.165–90 (183–7).
12. Jeffrey W. Legro, *Co-operation under Fire. Anglo-German Restraint During World War II* (Ithaca, NY: Cornell UP 1990), a study on restraint in strategic bombing, submarine warfare and CW use in WW II. Legro applies organizational culture theory to account for varying degrees of restraint. This approach would ask for in-depth analysis of bureaucratic decision-making processes in proliferating states and thus cannot be applied here.
13. Wolfgang K. H. Panowsky, 'Dismantling the Concept of "Weapons of Mass Destruction"', in *Arms Control Today* 28/4 (1998) pp.3–8. Panowsky demands not to put the priority for nuclear arms control in question by viewing different sorts of WMD as one type of weapon.
14. William H. Kincade, *Nuclear Proliferation: Diminishing Threat?* INSS Occasional Paper No. 6, Proliferation Series (Aspern, CO: Inst. for National Security Studies, USAF Academy, Dec. 1995) for this aspect of nuclear proliferation.
15. For the development of the norms of non-use of nuclear weapons – emanating from the national discourse in the US toward the rest of the world – and chemical weapons – diffusing from the international level to the national policies – see Richard Price and Nina Tannenwald, 'Norms and Deterrence: The Nuclear and Chemical Weapons Taboos', in Peter

Katzenstein (ed.) *The Culture of National Security. Norms and Identity in World Politics* (NY: Columbia UP 1996) pp.114–52.

16. For this image and a critical discussion, see Krause (note 2) pp.73, fn.20.
17. The section on 'weak cognitivists', in Hasenclever, Mayer and Rittberger (note 3) pp.139–54.
18. This is superbly done by Price and Tannenwald (note 15).
19. Joseph S. Nye Jr, 'Nuclear Learning in US-Soviet Security Regimes', *International Organisation* 41/3 (Summer 1987) pp.371–402 (380).
20. Ernst B. Haas, *When Knowledge is Power* (Berkeley: U. of California Press 1990) pp.23, 33–40.
21. Nye (note 19) p.380.
22. Haas (note 20) pp.20–23, who defines common knowledge as 'any kind of cause and effect linkages about any set of phenomen considered important by society, ...' (p.21) also Lloyd S. Etheridge, *Can Governments Learn? American Foreign Politics and Central American Revolutions* (NY: Pergamon 1985) p.66, who defines learning as improved intelligence and effectiveness.
23. George W. Breslauer and Philip E. Tetlock, 'Introduction', in idem (eds.) *Learning in U.S. and Soviet Foreign Policy* (Boulder: Westview 1991) pp.3–19, who claim that the value of knowledge, in general, contingent to social and historical conditions. Thus, in the complex reality of social life, knowledge consists of beliefs and can refer to values as well (p.7f.).
24. To be sure, effective institutions, beside their functions facilitating co-operation, can also promote learning, see Harald Müller, 'The Internalization of Principles, Norms, and Rules by Governments', in Volker Rittberger (ed.) *Regime Theories and International Relations* (Oxford: Clarendon Press 1993) pp.361–88 (363).
25. For the strategic re-orientation in the US Michael Klare, *Rogue States And Nuclear Outlaws. America's Search for a New Foreign Policy* (NY: Hill & Wang, 1995). Washington directed its military strategy already in the late 1980s against WMD proliferation. See also Michèle A. Flournoy, 'Implications for US Military Strategy' and Philip Zelikow, 'Offensive Military Options', both in Robert D. Blackwill and Albert Carnesale (eds.) *New Nuclear Nations. Consequences for U.S. Policy* (NY: Council on Foreign Relations Press 1993) pp.135–61 and 162–95.
26. It would be myopic to understand Washington's efforts to multilateralise its own counter-proliferation program as if it only wanted to share the burdon of deterring or fighting proliferation. Since some of the missions that would have to be prepared for WMD attack would engage the other members' troops anyhow, and since interoperability is a basic principle for force planning, it is a logical consequence to procure equal equipment for NATO troops.
27. Rome Declaration on Peace and Co-operation, Art. 19, issued by the NAC Meeting in Rome, 7–8 Nov. 1991, *NATO Review* 39/6 (1991) pp.19–21 (21). See also Michael Rühle, 'View from NATO. NATO and the Coming Proliferation Threat', *Comparative Strategy*, 13/3 (1994) pp.313–20.
28. Kommuniqué der Ministertagung des Nordatlantikrates, 17 Dec. 1992, Brussels, in *NATO Brief* 40/6 (1992) pp.28–30 (30); Kommuniqué der Ministertagung des Verteidigungs-planungsausschusses und der NPG in Brussels, 25 and 26 May 1993, in *NATO Brief* 41/4 (1993) pp.27–9 (29); Erklärung der NATO-Verteidigungsminister, Brussels, 29 May 1993, in *NATO Brief* 41/2 (1993) pp.34–5 (34f.); and the Kommuniqué der Ministertagung des NATO-Rates in Athens, 10 June 1993, in *NATO Brief* 41/3 (1993) pp.31–3 (33).
29. Rühle (note 27) and US Information Service. Embassy of the United States of America 'USA bekämpfen Verbreitung von Massenvernichtungswaffen. Ausführungen von Verteidigungs-minister Aspin' in *amerika dienst* 50 (1993). For further comments see Rolf Hallerbach, '"Counter Proliferation". Neue Zauberformel Amerika gegen Terrorwaffen', in *Europäische Sicherheit* 43/3 (1994) pp.139–40. The concept can be considered as reflecting US armed forces' need, in times of budgetary constrains, to gain support for acquiring new equipment and to carry on with old programs. Furthermore, the Clinton adminstration countered conservative criticism against its defence policy. The beginnings of the DCP date back in the Bush administration. Harald Müller and Mitchell Reiss, 'Counterproliferation: Putting New

Wine in Old Bottles', *Washington Quarterly* 18/2 (Summer 1995) pp.143–54 (144).

30. Hallerbach (note 29).

31. For the technological advantages the US might instrumentalise on the battlefield in this regard see Robert H. Chandler, *Counterforce: Locating and Destroying Weapons of Mass Destruction*, INSS Occas. Paper No.21, Proliferation Series (Inst. for National Security Studies, USAF Academy, CO, Aug. 1998).

32. Declaration of the Heads of State and Government participating in the meeting of the North Atlantic Council held at NATO Headquarters, Brussels, on 10–11 Jan. 1994. *NATO Review* 42/1 (Jan. 1994) pp.30–33 (32)..

33. Politischer Rahmen des Bündnisses zum Problem der Verbreitung von Massenvernichtungswaffen. North Atlantic Council, Istanbul, 9 June 1994, in *NATO Brief* 42/3 (1994) pp.28f.

34. Robert Joseph, 'Proliferation, Counter-Proliferation and NATO', in *Survival* 38/1 (Spring 1996) pp.111–30 (116–18).

35. See the German '10 point-initiative' on Nonproliferation policy of Dec. 1993. Point ten clearly states that the use of military force, according to Chapt. VII UN Charter, can merely be regarded as ultima ratio, in *Deutscher Bundestag, Drucksache 12/6985*, pp.85f.

36. Berthold Meyer, Harald Müller and H.-J. Schmidt, *NATO 96: Bündnis im Widerspruch.* Peace Research Institute Frankfurt, PRIF-Report/3 (Frankfurt am Main 1996) p.33; sowie Rühle (note 27) p.314.

37. Gregory Schulte, 'Responding to Proliferation – NATO's Role', in *NATO Review* 43/4 (July/Aug. 1995) pp.15–19; Joseph (note 34).

38. 'NATO's Response To Proliferation of Weapons of Mass Destruction' in *Press Release (95) 124*, 29 Nov. 1995. NATO Integrated Data Service, nataodata@cc1.kuleuven.ac.be, 29 Nov. 1995.

39. Cord Rather, 'Die Ausstattung des Soldaten im Wandel', *Europäische Sicherheit* 47/2 (Feb. 1998) pp.37–9 (p.38) on the new ABC equipment for infantry. The modern ABC protection mask M 65A2, servicable in the next century, will enable the soldier to drink liquids out of a specially designed water-bottle while wearing the mask.

40. Ashton B. Carter and David B. Omand, 'Maßnahmen gegen die Gefahren der Verbreitung von Massenvernichtungswaffen. Anpassung des Bündnisses an das neue Sicherheitsumfeld', in *NATO Brief* 42/5 (1994) pp.10–15 (14f.). Carter was Assistant Secretary in the Pentagon who was in charge for DCI. He and the Brit Omand were the first chairmen of DGP.

41. Kommuniqué der Ministertagung des Nordatlantikrates am 3 June 1996, Berlin, *Bulletin des Presse- und Informationsamtes der Bundesregierung,* No.47 (12 June 1996) pp.505–11 (508).

42. Deliberations of Oberstleutnant Günther F. C. Forsteneichner, Dept. for Public Relations and Information of the Supreme Headquarters Allied Powers Europe (SHAPE), Mons, Belgium. Briefing on 6 Feb. 1997. According to Forsteneichner, there was no consensus to be expected in the alliance for such operations.

43. Joachim Ebersbach and Dieter Naskrunt, 'Erweiterte Luftverteidigung', *Europäische Sicherheit* 47/1 (1998) pp.17–22; David Martin, 'Auf dem Weg zu einem Rahmenkonzept des Bündnisses für eine erweiterte Luftabwehr/taktische Flugkörperabwehr', *NATO Brief* 44/3 (1996) pp.32–5; sowie Rühle (note 27) p.319.

44. Constanze Stelzenmüller, 'Kein Sonderweg. Deutschland will NATO zum Verzicht auf den atomaren Erstschlag überreden', *Die Zeit*, 26 Nov. 1998.

45. William Drozdiak, Urging Shift by NATO, Germany Angers US', *International Herald Tribune*, 23 Nov. 1998.

46. 'US Rejects Any NATO Shift', *International Herald Tribune*, 28–29 Nov. 1998.

47. David S. Yost, *The US and Nuclear Deterrence*, Adelphi Paper 326 (London: OUP for IISS 1999) pp.64–7. By the way, the conservative-liberal government preceding the red-green coalition had shared this conviction. Minister of Defence Volker Rühe has been quoted with a similar argument in 1992, ibid. pp.27; Bruno Tertrais, *Nuclear Weapons in Europe*, Adelphi Paper 327 (London: OUP for IISS 1999) pp.35–44. Yos and Teratrais each offer a survey about the European debate about first-use. Gompert, Watman and Wilkening (note 2), incidentally, propose a first-use doctrine restricted to a first-use against WMD-attack only,

not against conventional attack.

48. The Alliance's Strategic Concept. Approved by the Heads of State and Government participating in the meeting of the North Atlantic Council in Washington DC on 23 and 24 April 1999, *Press Release* NAC-S(99)65, 24 April 1999 (25 June 1999, www.nato.int/docu/pr/1999/p99-065e.htm.

49. The IAEA does already evaluate intelligence information provided by member states, see David A. V. Fischer, 'New Directions and Tools for Strenghtening the IAEA Safeguards', *Nonproliferation Review* 3/2 (1996) pp.69–76 (71); Mark H. Killinger, 'Improving IAEA Safe-guards through Enhanced Information Analysis', *Nonproliferation Review* 3/1 (1995) pp.43–8.

50. An *ad hoc* group of governmental experts called VEREX has been debating possible measures concerning BW verfication in Geneva.

51. 'Die Welt wartet weiter auf Beweise', *Tagesspiegel*, 3 Sept. 1998.

52. This point has also been made by the arms control expert Jack Mendelsohn, stating that NATO's insistence suggest that nuclear weapons have some military roles to play. Remarks at the German American Conference on 'Preventing the Proliferation of WMD: What…Role for Arms Control?' Friedrich-Ebert-Stiftung, Bonn, 28–29 June 1999, Panel on Preventing Nuclear Proliferation: Strengthening the NPT and Implementing the CTBT, p.15.

53. This was part of a disclaimer the US made on the occasion of signing the Protocol containing security guarantees of the African NWFZ, saying, the protocol 'will not limit the operations available to the United States in Response to an attack by an ANWFZ party using weapons of mass destruction', see Rodney W. Jones and Mark MacDonough, *Tracking Nuclear Proliferation. A Guide in Maps and Charts, 1998* (Washington DC: Carnegie Endowment for Int. Peace 1998) p.216.

54. As in the whole study, missiles or other delivery systems are not taken into account here.

55. For the information provided below, see Jones and MacDonough (note 53); Krause (note 4) pp.66–80; *SIPRI Yearbooks 1996 and 1997. World Armaments and Disarmament*, Stockholm International Peace Research Inst. (Oxford: OUP 1996 and 1997), various pp; and various websites, including www.acda.gov, The US Arms Control and Disarmament Agency's homepage, and www.fas.org, of the Federation of American Scientists.

56. *PPNN Newsbrief* No. 16 (Winter 1991/ 92) p.10.

57. *PPNN Newsbrief* No. 21 (2nd Quarter 1993) p.7.

58. Steve Bowman, 'Iraqi Chemical & Biological Weapons (CBW) Capabilities' *CRS Issue Brief*, Congressional Research Service, April 1998 (25 June 1999, www.fas.org/spp/star wars/crs/98042705_npo.html)

59. *SIPRI Yearbook* 1997 (note 55) p.456.

60. Oliver Thränert, 'Das Chemiewaffenverbot ein Jahr nach dem Inkrafttreten', *Europäische Sicherheit* 47/5 (1998) pp.35–8 (38).

61. E.J. Hogendoorn, 'A Chemical Weapons Atlas', *Bulletin of the Atomic Scientists* 53/5 (Sept./Oct. 1997) (25 June 1999, www.bullatomsci.org/issues/1997/so97/so97hogendoorn.html)

62. *SIPRI Yearbook 1996* (note 55) p.662.

63. Julia Malone, 'Group Cites Chemical Weapons Risk In Kosovo', *Coxnews*, 8 April 1999 (25 June 1999, www.coxnews.com/ washington/ kosovo_chemical.htm); 'US: Yugoslavia Has Chemical Agents' (Associated Press, Las Vegas Sun, 15 April 1999 (25 June 1999, www.lasvegassun.com/sunbin/stories/text/1999/apr/15/ 041500873.html); William C. Potter and Jonathan B. Tucker, 'Well-Armed and Very Dangerous. Belgrade: The obstacles to Yugoslavia's acquisition and use of unconventional weapons are not that great', *Los Angeles Times*, 4 April 1999 (25 June 1999, www.latimes.com/home/news/reports/yugo/comment/t000029798.html).

4

Iran and Iraq as Rational Crisis Actors: Dangers and Dynamics of Survivable Nuclear War

CAROLYN C. JAMES

This essay will develop and analyze propositions about the behavior of 'mini-arsenal' nuclear dyads in crisis situations. The specific behavior to be investigated is defined as a strategic interaction between two rivals in a crisis setting who have either a confirmed or highly probable nuclear weapons capacity. The guiding principle of the research is that *the dynamics of nuclear strategy are expected to be different within mini-arsenal, third-, second- and first-level dyads.* (Each of these designations will be explained at a later point.) The specific objective of this study is to present a paradigm of crisis interaction that (a) encompasses these respective types of nuclear states, concentrating on mini-arsenals in this treatise; and (b) indicates whether preferences and predicted behavior adhere to the assumptions of Classical (or Rational) Deterrence Theory.[1]

'Mini-arsenal' is a concept developed to describe more effectively a minimal nuclear capability. A mini-arsenal state is capable of deploying just a handful, two or three at best, crude Hiroshima-style warheads. For example, Israel, Pakistan and India are beyond this category since the arsenals they are believed to possess contain qualitatively and quantitatively much more destructive power. *The most critical distinction of the mini-arsenal is that while potential damage may be extreme, destruction of state or society is not assured.* This perception, which may be held both by the mini-arsenal state leadership and its potential enemies, is expected to result in preferences and behavior that do not match actions of states with more deadly arsenals. After 50 years of nuclear thinking, the possibility of risking a nuclear attack of any kind may seem implausible to many. Yet the possibility does exist, thereby necessitating the task of considering scenarios that may result in a nuclear exchange. It also is recognized that a mini-arsenal condition is not permanent, but can exist for a sufficient length of time to be a valid consideration in crisis situations.

International crisis, the substantive focus of the research, is defined as follows: '(1) a change in the type and/or increase in the intensity of *disruptive*, that is, hostile verbal or physical, *interactions* between two or more states, with a heightened probability of *military hostilities*, that, in turn, (2) destabilizes their relationship and *challenges* the *structure* of an international system – global, dominant or subsystem'.[2] In other words, conflict – either 'verbal or physical' – exists. Mutual cooperation, therefore, does *not* mean the absence of conflict. This definition is sufficient to identify a range of crises that include several long-term rivalries suitable for investigating mini-arsenal dyads. It also includes Intra-War Crises, or sudden shifts in the fortunes of combatants in an ongoing war.[3] Thus the possibility that rivals in a crisis already are at war and may also face the issue of nuclear escalation within that setting is acknowledged.

Thus far, nuclear strategic thought has reflected heavily the superpower competition that existed between the United States and the former Soviet Union. It developed under Cold War conditions, which had a narrowing effect on the direction of theory because the US and USSR both qualified as first-level (also referred to as super-arsenal) states, defined as those capable of implementing a second strike on an effectively global level. For 45 years, nuclear strategic thought revolved primarily around the security needs of the two principal states.[4] Thus it is not surprising that the US/Soviet dyad (and a few others) caused strategic thinking to focus on deterrence.[5] Theorizing converged around the concept of Mutually Assured Destruction (MAD) and the game of Chicken. Underlying all of that analysis is the idea that nuclear weapons exist as bargaining tools because the level of damage they can cause is intolerable. The Cuban Missile Crisis stands as the exemplar of that logic; the superpowers moved to the brink of nuclear war but neither side, in the end, used its missiles and risked unacceptable second strike damage.[6]

This contribution departs from the implicit inference that all 'rational' nuclear states are governed by the same logic.[7] In other words, is it safe to assume that the members of all nuclear crisis dyads either follow the 'rules' of Chicken and MAD, and if not, should be classified as irrational? This project moves away from prevailing trends through specification of a model that allows for alternate preference orderings and a testing program that includes rivalries beyond the US and USSR.

The following section offers a review of Classical Deterrence Theory. The section after that presents a brief review of nuclear proliferation policy for the United States as related to one problematic dyad, Iran and Iraq in the current decade, which will be sufficient to establish the overall project's significance with respect to policy. As will become apparent, US policy continues to be governed by the logic of super-arsenals. In that context, the possibility of a nuclear exchange between Iran and Iraq is viewed as 'irrational', or outside the assumptions of Classical Deterrence Theory. This rivalry, however, contains states that are mini-arsenal capable as defined above. ('Mini' indicates the current or imminent possession of a few primitive or Hiroshima-strength bombs.[8] The states at this level have no greater capability, as opposed to states that simply choose to restrict their arsenals. In addition, this level is not presumed to be permanent, but rather exists for a sufficient length of time to be of concern in interstate crises.) Superarsenal versus mini-arsenal preferences are introduced in the fourth section. The concluding section will summarize the discussion and relate them to policy alternatives.

CLASSICAL DETERRENCE THEORY

The origins of Classical Deterrence[9] Theory trace back to Brodie's assessment in 1946 that, in the nuclear age, even the victors would suffer too extensively to justify any possible gains from all-out war. Just the *possibility* of retaliation would deter an aggressor from risking a nuclear counterattack.[10] Brodie wrote of scenarios in which New York City could be destroyed quickly by ten accurately targeted, Nagasaki-type bombs.[11] The nuclear states he depicted would be capable of building arsenals large enough to ensure a second strike that could guarantee state-wide, if not global, annihilation. Many theorists cite this destructive power, coupled with a bipolar systemic structure, as the primary cause of Cold War stability.[12]

Zagare reminds us that Classical Deterrence Theorists can be classified into two basic groups: Structural (or Neorealist) Deterrence Theorists and Decision-Theoretic Deterrence Theorists.[13] The former identify the distribution of power as the best explanatory variable in the causal relationship between system structure and stability.[14] Zagare also discusses the assumptions and implications of Structural Deterrence Theory.[15] He indicates that deterrence ultimately depends on costs, so specific numbers of warheads and missiles are critical. The difference between 'attacking' and 'deterring' rests on whether or not a first, or preemptive strike, will result in unacceptable damage from a second strike. A balance with high potential costs encourages stability, balance with low potential costs can be unstable, and imbalance alone is unstable, but particularly so when costs are low and preemption is attractive.

A situation in which potential costs are perceived to be low by both members of a conflictual dyad have been referred to as a 'region of initiation'.[16] This can be interpreted as the onset of an area of possible conflict that has not achieved stable mutual deterrence. Viewed in comparison to nuclear proliferation, the earliest stages of nuclear weapons possession place states in this same 'region of initiation'. The state technically possesses a nuclear arsenal, but of the most minimal destructive power. This is the zone in which mini-arsenal capable states are trapped. While many states, if they choose, can develop a nuclear weapons capability whose growth is inhibited merely by time, a mini-arsenal capable state is confined to this level by limited resources (rather than technological know-how), a condition often exacerbated by various measures under the Nuclear Nonproliferation Regime (NPR).[17]

Zagare draws five conclusions from the Structural Deterrence school: quantitative arms races increase potential costs and reduce the likelihood of conflict, qualitative arms races could give one side a destabilizing first-strike advantage, defensive systems are destabilizing, war is most likely to be accidental, and selective proliferation can be stabilizing to the system.[18] He points out that Structural Deterrence Theorists usually qualify the last point to exclude 'crazy states' and 'irrational leaders'.[19] A rational leader is a self-interested power maximizer. Suppose this rational leader exists in a mini-arsenal dyad, recalling that potential damage is limited and perceived to be survivable. Consider as well the possibility that the ultimate cost for decision-makers could be loss of personal power rather than casualties. In this case, the point of deterrence may be loss of power rather than loss of a state to rule. The results of a 'rational' cost/benefit analysis may not match that of a leader facing more formidable nuclear retaliation.

Decision-Theoretic Deterrence Theorists accept the conclusions drawn by Structural Deterrence and build on them to provide an analysis of decision behavior. In other words, they begin with the assumption that a nuclear war is too costly to be fought. Nuclear crises are games depicted as 'Chicken', or the 'contest for exhibiting and measuring power'.[20] Ellsberg is representative of this school.[21] He describes 'critical risk', or the maximum point of acceptable punishment before a decision-maker is deterred. In a crisis the state with the highest critical risk would 'win'. According to Zagare, this is the 'conventional wisdom' among Classical Deterrence

Theorists, many of whom base policy prescriptions on these assumptions.[22] For example, the best way to approach crisis management would be to lower an opponent's critical risk and raise your own relative to the opponent. Another approach would be to make an opponent believe you cannot make concessions.[23] This leads to metaphors such as Kahn's ripping the steering wheel off in a game of Chicken[24] or the strategy of pretending to be irrational.[25]

At an extreme, Decision-Theoretic Deterrence Theorists claim that the mere existence of nuclear weapons is sufficient to deter.[26] In this scenario, the weapons 'create their own logic'.[27] Therefore, anyone who does not follow that logic is 'irrational'. In terms of policy recommendations, this paints a gloomy picture: How can a state effectively deal with an irrational actor? Is there any hope of preventing proliferated states from engaging in a nuclear exchange if their leaders do not accept this kind of nuclear logic? It is helpful to return to the Chicken metaphor. Instead of two automobiles racing headlong toward one another at high speed, suppose our antagonists are on bicycles. The riders are not the decision-makers, but their states and societies. A crash would certainly cause injury, perhaps even death. But the most likely result would be a survivable injury. The sanity of this scenario may still be questioned, but cannot be assessed until the details of a specific crisis are known. The need, then, is for a paradigm that accommodates a *variety* of decision-makers and scenarios. The argument here is that it already exists. The tendency among Structural Deterrence Theorists is to assume large arsenals and among Decision-Theoretic Deterrence Theorists to assume an independent logic to the strategy surrounding nuclear weapons. Yet, if the essence of Classical Deterrence Theory, a rational cost/benefit analysis, is appropriately applied to *rational* mini-arsenal states, the theory may well retain its explanatory power and resultant policy applications.

MINI-ARSENAL DYADS: IRAN AND IRAQ

The core of international efforts to curb the horizontal spread of nuclear weapons is the Nuclear Proliferation Regime (NPR). The NPR has many parallels to Cold War, super-arsenal challenges. The development of the NPR has been shaped significantly by the US and USSR's security policies and is not necessarily suited toward preventing proliferation and nuclear weapons use in mini-arsenal capable states. This can be seen in two of NPR's basic assumptions which mirror much of Classical Deterrence Theory to date. First is the assumption that proliferation creates greater system-level instability.[28] Second, and especially pertinent to this work, is the belief that only irrational actors would use nuclear bombs as weapons of war (or at least rational actors committing an irrational act). Former Secretary of Defense Les Aspin used terms such as 'terrorists and rogues' to describe these individuals.[29] This kind of generalization is questionable. Rational actors not only commit acts of war, they also are capable of making the decision to acquire nuclear weapons, use the weapons against an enemy state or possibly even risk nuclear retaliation based on a rational, cost/benefit calculation. These conditions are more likely to exist within a mini-arsenal dyad.[30]

The US' contribution to the NPR has been built on the assumptions of Classical Deterrence Theory as it applies to super-arsenals. Former Secretary of Defense Robert S. McNamara's position reflects that of most nuclear strategists:

> Having spent seven years as Secretary of Defense dealing with the problems unleashed by the initial nuclear reaction 40 years ago, I do not believe we can avoid serious and unacceptable risk of nuclear war until we recognize – and until we base all our military plans, defense budgets, weapons deployments, and arms negotiations on the recognition – that *nuclear weapons serve no military purpose whatsoever. They are totally useless – except only to deter one's opponent from using them.*[31] (emphasis in original)

How this attitude has played out in reference to recent US policy toward Iran and Iraq is highly instructive. US and UN relations with Iraq continue to be highly publicized. Iran has been less prominent in the news. Iran has renewed proliferation efforts begun under the Shah. There is little concrete proof available since the Iranian Revolution as to Iran's intentions, but they can be inferred. Iran is energy-rich. It is very expensive to create a nuclear energy program. The cost of using its existing electrical power based on natural gas would be less than 10 per cent of nuclear generated power, yet Iran wants as much as 20 per cent of its energy to come from nuclear power plants. The desire to create nuclear power facilities simply does not make financial sense. The nature of this state's nuclear purchases also has raised suspicion. The evidence indicates that Iran's true intent is to gain the ability to build its own nuclear warheads.[32]

Iran and Iraq are also traditional enemies. Repeatedly in recorded history, the Shatt al'Arab waterway has been the locus of contention. Many of the struggles have had causes rooted in demographic and cultural differences. Iran is the home of the Persian ethnic group. The Persians speak

Farsi and are predominantly Shi'a, a sect of Islam composing about 10 per cent of the world's Muslim population. In Iraq, Arab Sunnis comprise only 20 per cent of the general population, but in modern times have represented the most powerful political and military leaders. Over 60 per cent of the population is Arab Shi'a. The Shi'a dominated government of the Islamic Republic of Iran is seen as a political, military, and religious threat to the Iraqi regime.

Future armed conflict between Iran and Iraq is a real danger. Both Iran and Iraq were expected to be capable of assembling one to three fission weapons by the late 1990s or early in this century.[33] This process may only have been slowed or delayed by sanctions. Estimates such as these can be dangerously optimistic. In May 1998 experts predicted Iran would obtain medium-range missile capability in one to two years, yet successful testing took place as early as July. The 800-plus mile range is capable of striking Israel, Russia, Saudi Arabia and Turkey.[34]

Iran and Iraq, and the political entities that preceded these modern states, have been embroiled in a protracted conflict. Protracted conflicts are defined as 'hostile interactions which extend over long periods of time with sporadic outbreaks of open warfare fluctuating in frequency and intensity'.[35] Hatred can be ethnically based and permeate the entire society of a state. When conflict flares, stakes are high. When conflict ends, there is no final resolution to the sources of animosity.

Protracted conflicts are not peculiar to the Middle East. The Arab–Israeli and Arab–Persian hostilities do not find their commonalties in the Arab peoples, the Fertile Crescent or the Northern Tier. Protracted conflicts can occur anywhere.[36] The intensity of antagonism may make the acquisition of nuclear weapons more attractive. Introducing mini-arsenals that cannot guarantee nuclear escalation and unacceptable damage into protracted conflicts may increase the possibility of an event that has never occurred – a nuclear exchange.[37]

Prior to the 1980s, the United States tried to neutralize the Northern Tier by maintaining a regional balance of power. Balance had been pursued by supporting one state against the other. When relations were friendly with Shah Reza Pahlavi, Iran received assistance from the US in countering a more hostile Iraq. After the Iranian Revolution, the US perceived Iraq as critical to its national security interests in the region and subsequently made it the recipient of increased American military aid. The armaments previously given to Iran by the US were subsequently used against Iraq. After Iraq invaded Kuwait, the United States found itself in direct confrontation with a country it had helped to gain military power.

On 23 October 1992, President Bush signed into law the Iran-Iraq Non-Proliferation Act. The Act stated that the US would increase efforts to prevent either state from obtaining any technology or machinery that could be used to acquire weapons of mass destruction. Sanctions could be imposed upon individuals or states believed to be suppliers to Iran or Iraq, the two most prominent 'rogue' states in Washington's eyes.[38]

Soon thereafter, the Clinton administration sought a more effective policy through 'dual containment'.[39] Announced on 13 May 1993, dual containment assumes that both states have policies which are hostile to US interests. This includes the acquisition of nuclear weapons. Theoretically, dual containment delays proliferation until friendlier regimes come to power in Iran and Iraq.[40] The downfall of Saddam Hussein, for example, clearly remains of interest to the Clinton administration.[41] It has gone as far as to meet with the outlawed Iraqi National Congress, which strives to remove and replace Hussein.

The US has been careful, however, not to speak as harshly against Iranian leadership, fearing that it would be accused of objecting to the Islamic nature of the government.[42] Instead, criticism focuses on Iranian policies hostile to the US and its allies. Dual containment attempts to go further than the Iran-Iraq Non-Proliferation Act. Theoretically, by strangling loans, investments and arms sales overall, neither state should have the ability to proliferate. This policy has been augmented by the 1996 Iran-Libya Sanctions Act, which penalizes foreign companies investing $20 million or more in either state's energy industry.

According to Anthony Lake, dual containment does not reject balance of power considerations altogether. The balance, however, no longer would pivot around the Northern Tier. Lake asserts that isolation and balance continue to be easier to accomplish since the mid-1990s than during previous administrations. For instance, the US no longer needs to worry about the former Soviet Union allying itself with either Iran or Iraq. The need to maintain a superpower balance of influence in the region is removed. The equilibrium between Iran and Iraq also is easier to achieve since both states have restricted ability to increase military power. In addition, US relations with the Gulf Cooperation Council (GCC) improved as a result of the Iraqi invasion of Kuwait. In the aftermath the US has been able to elicit more cooperation from the GCC in strengthening regional stability. The ongoing peace process with Israel and its neighbors also has reduced tensions in the Middle East, even in spite of the recent setbacks. Lake's optimistic views, however, are not universally held.

The Clinton administration came to office claiming that prior policies toward Iran and Iraq overlooked a critical component. In the Iranian case, the Reagan and Bush administrations actively tried to keep the lines of communication open with Tehran. The purpose was to search for more moderate elements that might be less hostile towards the US.[43] The current administration's prevailing attitude during the early years was that an open dialogue with the Iranians would be unlikely to pay dividends. However, if the situation in Tehran changed, closing communication links probably would have impeded opportunities for *rapprochement*. Perhaps this fear was a motive behind what Lake called an 'authoritarian dialogue', or an exchange that addressed US grievances, and possibly exerted some pressure, against Iran.[44] With the overwhelming electoral victory in 1997 for President Muhammed Khatami, it appeared more moderate voices would be heard. This has been confirmed, in part, by the reformist victories in the February 2000 *Majlis* election. Secretary of State Madeleine Albright has made overtures in this direction, but continues to recognize and discourage Iranian efforts to acquire long range missiles and nuclear weapons.[45]

Dual containment focuses on a comprehensive and simultaneous isolation of both states, and continues to be US policy for weapons of mass destruction in spite of the move away from rhetoric of duality.[46] While logic would seem to dictate that it is in the US's best interest to minimize any potential nuclear threat against its troops or allies in the Gulf region, the policy contains an inherent paradox. By reducing the threat to third parties, a policy of dual containment actually may be pushing Iran and Iraq toward a more dangerous mini-arsenal potential. Their ability to proliferate has slowed, but the desire has persisted.[47] Policies aimed at eliminating a nuclear force capacity may insure that the threat of nuclear use is maintained at a potentially more volatile mini-arsenal level. This is dangerous within any dyad and particularly so for this one.[48] Dyadic stability, therefore, would appear to be even more critical to maintaining peace in the region.

Dual containment proves to have other inherent weaknesses. Most notably, it can be effective only if all states are committed to isolating Iran and Iraq. It needs to become an effective part of the multilateral NPR. But this is not the case. With the exception of Israel, Middle Eastern states are building diplomatic and economic ties with Iran. Recent high level exchanges have occurred with both Saudi Arabia and Egypt. This is in drastic contrast to less recent years when Egypt experienced terrorist attacks against the government and tourist industry that it blamed on Iranian-supported Islamic fundamentalist extremists. Saudi Arabia's anti-government Shia's were accused of being supported by Iran. There also have been disturbances during the annual pilgrimages to Mecca.

Furthermore, support for US policy from outside the Middle East has been shaky. For instance, in 1987, Iran signed a nuclear cooperation agreement with Pakistan and a similar agreement with China in 1990. It also is suspected that thousands of pounds of uranium dioxide were obtained by Iran from Argentina through Algeria in the mid-1980s. Iraqi examples include the purchase in 1980 and 1981 of natural uranium, unsuitable for reactor fuel, from Brazil, Portugal and Niger.[49] Russia currently has been found in violation of exporting missile technology to both states.[50]

The fact that Soviet client states no longer can exist in the Middle East does not mean that the region is any safer. Instead of being concerned about a balance of power, the new danger is 'loose nukes'. They could be acquired by states such as Iran and Iraq that have tremendous oil revenues to spend. The problem already has been in the headlines. From 1993 through 1995 over 130 confirmed cases of nuclear-related smuggling were reported by the International Atomic Energy Agency.[51] The potential supply is enormous. By the year 2003, it is estimated that (worldwide) 1530 metric tons of weapons grade plutonium and uranium will be recovered from spent fuel and dismantled weapons, enough to build 105,000 primitive bombs.[52]

Iran and Iraq's weakened conventional military strength does not help the situation. Nuclear weapons have long been perceived as cheaper than conventional forces. Containing Iran and Iraq will impede their ability to rebuild their militaries. The US unintentionally may be encouraging them to choose nuclear proliferation if it seems easier and cheaper. As for the relaxed relations between Israel and the Arab states, the Iran–Iraq grievances are not based upon anti-Israeli sentiment. Their relations have not been impacted inherently by the peace process.[53] The advantage of improved relations with the GCC also may not do much toward counterbalancing proliferation problems.

Iraq's sanctions, supported by military threats from the US and, to a lesser extent Britain, receive strong multilateral support. They are given nominal official approval due to UN Resolution 687, which ended the 'Desert Storm' hostilities. The day inevitably will come when sanctions are lifted.[54] As for Iran, the US seems to be attempting an unfeasible unilateral isolation. In September, 1993, the House Foreign Affairs Subcommittee on International Security, International Organizations and Human Rights completed a study that showed over 230 firms were selling technology and goods to Iran that could be used to create weapons of mass destruction, including nuclear weapons. Only about 50 of these companies were from the US.[55] As long as the US does not have universal support, containment of Iran is essentially a 'non'-policy.

In addition, the Clinton administration recently waived sanctions against three foreign firms in violation of the Iran-Libya Sanctions Act. As for Iraq, compliance with UN sanctions is more effective but the impact is less than anticipated. At this time of writing, Saddam Hussein is still firmly in power. Once the sanctions are lifted, Iraq may be just a few years away from assembling a nuclear warhead, especially since many nuclear weapons components remain at large.[56] Iran already may be at that point.[57]

Dual containment does not address a primary danger. Unless nonproliferation can be guaranteed, which it cannot, the policy may promote a more unstable mini-arsenal dyad, which could spiral out of control under crisis conditions. Dual containment is not sufficient to prevent proliferation by Iran and Iraq. Counterproliferation recognizes that nonproliferation has failed to halt the spread of nuclear technology and equipment. Counterproliferation intends to augment nonproliferation by adding protection from nuclear armed adversaries to the NPR's traditional policies of prevention. Neither dual containment nor counterproliferation have been well-received among US allies and therefore these policies do not have the strength of a multilateral approach. If proliferation cannot be eliminated, mini-arsenal potentials are possible. When mini-arsenal levels of nuclear forces exist, so do mini-arsenal dynamics. Unacceptable damage is not assured and deterrence is not robust.[58]

If containment of Iran and Iraq fails, the question of offensive versus deterrence based use of nuclear weapons again moves to the forefront of the debate. In terms of sheer numbers, Iran and Iraqs' ongoing mini-arsenal capability would not be under the influence of what Bundy calls 'existential' deterrence. Existential deterrence implies that the mere existence of an adversary's super-arsenal is the most influential factor in nuclear decision-making – more than the treaties, political policy or military strategies.

> As long as each side has large numbers of thermonuclear weapons that *could* be used against an opponent, even after the strongest possible preemptive attack, existential deterrence is strong and it rests on uncertainty about what could happen.[59] (emphasis in original)

Mini-arsenal states do not have 'large numbers of thermonuclear weapons'. Between mini-arsenal states, existential deterrence, or nuclear deterrence of any kind, might not exist. Nuclear policies and strategies, therefore, become more decisive when considering the use of nuclear weapons in war.

Dual containment does not remove the underlying motivation for mini-arsenal proliferation in Iran and Iraq. If that motivation is not to create a deterrent stance, its true nature needs to be determined. As already noted, containment also inhibits Iran and Iraq's ability to rebuild their conventional military strengths. Obstructed in both areas, nuclear weapons could appear easier and cheaper to acquire than tanks and bombers. In reality the NPR may be placing the leadership in Baghdad and Tehran in a situation where acquisition and subsequent use of nuclear weapons are more likely. If their domestic situations were to decay, leaders might be more willing to take the greater risk of using nuclear weapons offensively. Nonproliferation, containment and counterproliferation policies could actually be making desperate regimes even more desperate and 'irrational'.

Efforts to contain or seal off Iran and Iraq from the rest of world will only delay proliferation. Waiting for a friendlier regime to come to power is too risky. Another war in the Persian Gulf, if raised to nuclear levels, would be devastating to the entire world, particularly if the flow of oil is disrupted for any significant period of time. If the goal of the United States and other members of the NPR is to prevent further proliferation, Iran and Iraq must be assessed on their own terms and according to their unique situations; this is essential to nonproliferation choices. It can never be assumed that a state's motivation to proliferate is based on an intent to create a relationship of deterrence with a potential enemy. Limited nuclear war may appear possible due to limited nuclear capabilities. These motivations may not only be offensive in nature, they also may be more compelling to decision-makers. Even if deterrence is the primary goal, the constraints created by a mini-arsenal capability may weaken the state's deterrent stance. Broader scenarios need to be examined when proliferation and nuclear weapons deployment are considered within a potential mini-arsenal dyad.

Perhaps the most serious problems related to policies such as dual containment and counterproliferation derive from their fundamental misunderstanding of the various possible alternative logics within mini-arsenals dyads. States could end up in the mini-arsenal category as a result of sanctions and other pressures exerted by the US and, to a lesser degree, other states. However, what if analysis suggests that mini-arsenal states may be inherently unstable and possess propensity toward the use of nuclear weapons? Ironically, sanctions might serve to lengthen the time that states spend at the potentially volatile mini-arsenal level. Proliferation 'optimists' could argue that it might be better to lighten the pressure on them and permit movement into a more stable, third-level status, defined as the ability to destroy the state but not the society of the rival.[60] At the very least it is worth learning whether crises, either in theory or reality, are more likely to be resolved with a minimum of destruction when rivals possess something other than mini-arsenal endowments.

ALTERNATE MINI-ARSENAL PREFERENCES

The essential question to pose is: Would every nuclear-capable crisis dyad necessarily behave as if its members were racing toward each other in a game of Chicken? With respect to policy, this analysis goes beyond the bulk of prior analysis by discarding the implicit assumption that the logic of superpower rivalry and super-arsenals will be present in other nuclear-capable dyads as well. Obviously this cannot be reduced to an all-or-nothing question about the use of nuclear weapons; it is known that the last instance of that remains Nagasaki. The relative dangers posed by nuclear dyads of various kinds, and how best to cope with them, must be assessed by careful consideration of each state's nuclear capability and crisis preferences. In other words, does the US in particular need to think about a wider range of approaches to coping with the results of proliferation, that is, dyads with varying levels of nuclear strike capacity? Or, instead, are these dyads, regardless of the exact level of capability they possess, still acting as would be expected by the vision of crisis generated by 45 years of superpower nuclear rivalry?

While it has been assumed that nuclear dynamics between smaller powers will manifest the same underlying assumptions, theory and research rather than faith would seem more appropriate as a basis for beliefs when the consequences of error may be serious. Consider the example of the shock among policy community analysts over the May 1998 Indian and Pakistani nuclear testing.[61] It almost goes without saying that the Indo-Pakistani rivalry became more complicated and potentially dangerous as a result of these events. This is particularly true if India has crossed over into thermonuclear capability. This would raise India to a second-tier state, or possessing the ability to practice MAD at a dyadic rather than global level. Relations with China could become more intricate and the ongoing sparks of crisis with Pakistan may become more urgent as they occur. Standard approaches based on the experiences of the superpowers with super-arsenals are unlikely to generate useful theory and policy for a rapidly changing situation that involves other kinds of arsenals.[62]

When nuclear weapons enter the equation, standard treatises concentrate almost exclusively on one set of preferences, referring to those of Chicken or first-level, super-arsenal adversaries.[63] If the possibility of a nuclear exchange is contemplated, most scholars consider a single set of state preferences that fit with Cold War, super-arsenal expectations. Stated as a set of four preferences, from best to worst, these Cold War assumptions about nuclear use are:

1 – (best outcome) – mutual nuclear restraint[64]

2 – (second best outcome) – unilateral use without nuclear retaliation from the enemy

3 – (second worst outcome) – unilateral use by the enemy without nuclear response

4 – (worst outcome) – mutual nuclear use

At the theoretical level, the point of departure for this analysis is an objection to the assumption that all nuclear rivalries, when manifested in crisis interactions, necessarily follow this logic.

Iran and Iraq as a conflictual nuclear dyad suggest other dynamics and preferences. The following is a proposed set of preferences to be considered for this particular case:

1 – (best outcome) – unilateral use without nuclear retaliation from the enemy

2 – (second best outcome) – mutual nuclear use

3 – (second worst outcome) – mutual nuclear restraint

4 – (worst outcome) – unilateral use by the enemy without nuclear response

Area experts and policy advisors may well disagree with this assessment, but it stands as an example of alternate ways to consider behavior during a crisis within a mini-arsenal dyad. Recall that a mini-arsenal refers to a state's nuclear force capability. Assured destruction of either society or state is not guaranteed. In fact, crude delivery of two or three Hiroshima-strength bombs are the highest risk perceived by state leadership.

The assumption is that a crisis exists, either prior to the onset of use of force or as an intra-war crisis. In other words, neither peace nor a diplomatic resolution is at hand. The proposed worst-cast scenario is defeat since nuclear annihilation is not considered feasible. In order to better understand the four preferences, consider each of the four possible outcomes individually.

Mutual Use (second best outcome) – This is by far the most controversial conclusion to reach. It helps to approach this possibility from the experience of these two Northern Tier states. A conflictual situation, with use of force either threatened or commenced, already exists. If neither side uses its nuclear weapons, the result, if conflict occurs, is restricted to conventional warfare.[65] Iran and Iraq fought an eight-year war in the 1980s that quickly became a long, bloody war of attrition. Over one million people were killed and the cost rose to the hundreds of billions of dollars. The level of barbarity was exemplified by Iranian use of the 'human wave' against fortified positions and intensive Iraqi bombings of Iranian population centers.[66] Chemical weapons were used on both sides, plus Iraq used chemical weapons against its own Kurdish civilians.[67] It still can be assumed that neither state has renewed military power sufficient to decisively win a conventional war. The prospect, therefore, is another conflict extracting terrible demands on both societies without eliminating the protracted nature of Iranian–Iraqi animosity. Risking a nuclear exchange could shorten subsequent conventional conflict or even tip the balance of one side toward a decisive resolution of the protracted conflict. The type of regional or global devastation envisioned by a superarsenal exchange, such as state-wide radiation poisoning, is not possible. Victory, of course, is best, but a mini-arsenal exchange is preferred to stalemate or defeat.

Unilateral Use Without Nuclear Retaliation From the Enemy (best outcome) – If only one state engages in a nuclear attack, it is technically feasible (although not assured) that the other state in this scenario either may have its second strike capability in jeopardy or completely neutralized. Recall that neither side perceives a mini-arsenal attack as capable of destroying state or society. Gaining whatever military advantages that might accrue is worth suffering a terrible, but survivable second strike. Military resources can be protected in this scenario. Lessons from Pearl Harbor warn against concentrating strategic resources, including manpower, in any given location. Force structures, in anticipation of a limited nuclear attack, can be dispersed. The attractiveness of preemption is strong if the second strike is not only survivable, but might be reduced or eliminated.[68] Or, if the prospect of defeat is certain, the recipient of a first strike may choose not engage in a nuclear retaliation if no strategic advantage can be gained. A more desirable defeat may even be bargained *vis-à-vis* the threat of a second strike or international condemnation of the aggressor state. The important point is that, if each side believes a unilateral attack is strategically critical, it could easily be treated as a choice between absolute victory versus loss. The attacker would receive its best payoff and the victim nation its worst.

Mutual Nuclear Restraint (second worst outcome) – If a conflict is kept at the conventional level, neither Iran nor Iraq has an advantage significant enough to achieve decisive victory. In fact, the prospect of another war of attrition may not be escaped. The toll to human life and the societies of these two states not only would be devastating, but could reach a scope beyond the damage suffered in two or three primitive nuclear strikes. The blunt force of these weapons may be perceived as less costly than the potential universal drain on state resources, human and material alike. Only defeat is worse.

Unilateral Use by the Enemy Without Nuclear Response (worst outcome) – In this case, the enemy has exacted a nuclear strike and achieved a situation in which response is either physically or politically impossible. If the ability to retaliate no longer exists, so may a decisive disadvantage on the military side. Defeat may be impossible to avoid, leaving the best course of action to negotiate an acceptable end to hostilities as soon as possible. For the leadership of these two states, Iraq in particular, this easily could be viewed as the worst case scenario.

The assumption remains that these preferences can be reached based upon a rational, cost/benefit analysis. The possibility of another million-casualty conflict with no stable resolution compared to a potentially less deadly and more decisive nuclear attack is clearly a 'lesser-of-two-evils' choice, but decision-makers often are forced to make these determinations.

CONCLUSION

The preceding mini-arsenal preferences suggest a frightening propensity toward a nuclear exchange. At first glance this kind of scenario appears quite pessimistic, particularly if the actors are depicted as 'crazy', 'pariah', 'rogue' or 'backlash' states. According to Herring's typology, the US would seem to reflect the 'conservative' perspective of the label 'rogue state'.[69] Potential threats to the US, while an appropriate focus of any administration's concerns, create a biased and often negative view of behavior in other states. It obviously is critical to recognize possible instances of nuclear use, particularly against targets of perceived national security interests. It is counterproductive, however, to allow normative labels to restrict policy options.

This need not to be the case. Policies can be tailored to alter the preferences of rational actors, even if the value systems attributed to these antagonists might appear reprehensible. It is worth pursuing more creative policies than those in force, such as dual containment and counterproliferation, which would seem to have little or no chance to change the preferences just described.

Consider the tenets of Classical Deterrence Theory. The alternative mini-arsenal preferences of Iran and Iraq put forward in this study would seem to abide by the Structural Deterrence Theorists' emphasis on the relationship between distribution of power and stability. In this case, a commonly weakened conventional military capability held static by sanctions and embargoes have a direct impact on considerations of nuclear use. Specifically, a military balance with low potential costs appear to be de-stabilizing and may result in escalation to nuclear levels. Existence in this 'region of initiation' is being maintained and reinforced by containment policies. Zagare's conclusions from Structural Deterrence Theory, viewed in terms of a mini-arsenal dyad, do not appear to describe the Iran/Iraq dyad effectively, since they refer to arms racing and sophisticated defense systems that do not exist in this case. Yet they are quite well-suited to serve as prescriptions. These judgments suggest a path toward greater stability, if indeed, proliferation cannot be halted. They are not without controversy, however, since quantitative improvements and selective proliferation are to most decision-makers a policy of last resort. Other options must be considered.

Ironically, Decision-Theoretic Deterrence Theory adds to an understanding of mini-arsenal dynamics by its purer reflection of super-arsenal assumptions, in particular the premise that nuclear use will not occur since the costs are prohibitively high. In a zero-sum situation, this statement would appear to have sound logic. However, mini-arsenals may view a potential exchange differently, in that one side may gain an advantage over the other. 'Critical risk' may not be attainable, since the perception of potential costs may be tolerable, even preferable to a conventional conflict. Policy prescriptions such as feigning an inability to make concessions or irrationality would not strengthen a goal of stable deterrence. Rather, it could attract preemption if a nuclear exchange becomes increasingly likely.

Is it possible, therefore, to alter a given set of preferences in order to lower the danger of nuclear use in a crisis? What lessons are to gained by applying Classical Deterrence Theory and policy recommendations that flow from its utilization? NPR operates under the premise that by substituting the perceived need to proliferate, states will not suffer the international condemnation and national risk by doing so. Perhaps preventing proliferated states from initiating nuclear use can be approached in the same manner, providing substitutes for perceived advantages associated with first use. In other words, the instability that is inherent in mini-arsenal dynamics could be controlled or removed.

One possibility would be to allow Iran and Iraq to fulfill their security needs at the conventional level. Theoretically, if either believes it can meet national objectives without first-use, there would be little logic in risking a second strike. This would not necessarily deter war, rather escalation to nuclear use. As mentioned above, another debatable option some scholars advocate is a safe, assisted increase in nuclear capability to obtain a level of destructive potential required to reach unacceptable damage and stable deterrence.

Regional answers may appear more reasonable. Mimicking South America, the major powers in the Middle East could forswear nuclear arsenal development programs. This, of course, centers around Israel, since it is a known, although not declared, nuclear state. Credible security umbrellas over regional actors could provide sufficient substitutions for security needs. Interallied control, such as NATO implements in keeping Turkey and Greece at bay, could also serve to increase costs of certain kinds of aggressive military action between states without forcing disarmament.

Alternative energy options, as opposed to sanctions, may help with the basic problem entailed by dual-use technologies: the ability to convert nuclear energy programs to weapons capability. In other words, it may be better to seek *indirect* control over the growth of arsenals. The technology already exists to build nuclear energy reactors that do not produce weapons-grade fissile material as a byproduct. Under-utilized sources of energy could be developed further. For example, Iran has considerable natural gas resources and Iraq a greater potential for hydroelectric power than it currently operates.

The final goal of any of these policy prescriptions is to place Iranian and Iraqi state leadership in a strategic situation that reorders their preferences from the possibility that a nuclear exchange would be preferred to purely conventional war, toward preferences that promote mutual non-use in a crisis. Classical, or 'Rational', Deterrence Theory can still be instructive in reaching this end. Deterrence strategies based on distribution of power and potential costs remain a consideration as the basis for preventing war, including nuclear war. Viewed as rational actors, and with recognition of the impact of various nuclear capabilities (including the most limited), states such as Iran and Iraq can be targeted with more effective policies. In sum, the goal is not to isolate them as irrational pariahs, but rather to achieve movement toward functional incorporation into the international system.

NOTES

The author wishes to thank the following individuals for their valuable commentaries on various stages of this project: Michael Brecher, Frank Harvey, Efraim Inbar, Arie Kacowicz, Benjamin Miller, Galia Press-Barnathan, Barry Rubin, Paul Senese, and Jonathan Wilkenfeld. I also appreciate the many helpful exchanges, both during and after a series of panels at the International Studies Association meeting in Vienna, 1998, with the editor and the other contributors to this volume.

1. A game-theoretic version of this project has been developed to assess the range of possible

behavior among rivalries that include first-, second-, third-level and mini-arsenal states (Carolyn C. James, 'Nuclear Arsenal Games: Coping With Proliferation in a World of Changing Rivalries', paper presented to the International Studies Association Annual Conference, Los Angeles, CA, 15–18 March 2000. 'NAG', or Nuclear Arsenal Games, are based on Brams' Theory of Moves (Steven J. Brams, *Theory of Moves* [Cambridge: Cambridge UP 1994]).

2. Michael Brecher and Jonathan Wilkenfeld. *A Study of Crisis* (Ann Arbor: U. of Michigan Press 1997) pp.4–5.

3. Ibid.

4. See Bernard Brodie, *From Crossbow to H-Bomb* (Bloomington: Indiana UP 1973); Robert Jervis, *Perception and Misperception in International Politics* (Princeton UP 1976); Klaus Knorr, *On the Use of Military Power in the Nuclear Age* (Princeton UP 1966); Thomas C. Schelling, *Arms and Influence* (New Haven, CT: Yale UP 1966); and Albert Wohlstetter, 'The Delicate Balance of Terror', *Foreign Affairs* 37 (1959).

5. See Bernard Brodie, *The Absolute Weapon: Atomic Power and World Order* (NY: Harcourt Brace 1946), *Strategy in the Missile Age* (Princeton UP 1965), *War and Politics* (NY: Macmillan 1973); Stephen J. Cimbala, *Nuclear Strategizing: Deterrence and Reality* (NY: Praeger 1988); Alexander L. George and Richard Smoke, *Deterrence in American Foreign Policy: Theory and Practice* (NY: Columbia UP 1974); Herman Kahn, *On Thermonuclear War* (Princeton UP 1961); and Robert Powell, *Nuclear Deterrence Theory: The Search for Credibility* (NY: Cambridge UP 1990).

6. Acceptable versus unacceptable damage are purely subjective terms. It is not the intent of this essay to provide either a universal or case-specific formula to determine these levels. There are many examples, however, of states and societies surviving extreme damage (even if the war was lost). For example, the atomic bombings of Hiroshima and Nagasaki did not approach the destruction of Japanese leadership or society. There also has existed a tendency to overestimate the extent of damage in certain situations; projections by the British in 1945 indicated it would take 30 years to remove the rubble from Berlin (Richard J. Barnet, *The Alliance–America, Europe, Japan: Makers of the Postwar World* [NY: Simon and Schuster 1983] p.19). For other examples of damage assessment, see Edwin Hartrich, *The Fourth and Richest Reich* (NY: MacMillan 1980) pp.32–6, for Germany in 1945; *The Committee for the Compilation of Materials on Damage Caused by the Atomic Bombs in Hiroshima and Nagasaki* (NY: Basic Books 1981); and Thomas A. Keaney and Eliot A. Cohen, *Gulf War Air Power Survey Summary Report* (Maxwell AFB, AL: Air University US Air Force 1992) pp.55–119, for an assessment of the 1991 Gulf War damage to Iraq.

7. 'Rational' is defined according to Morgan's discussion of deterrence under rational decision-making. 'What is '"rational" action varies with one's goals and resources; what does not vary is the process itself: specifying and ordering objectives, defining the particular situation, gathering relevant information on alternatives, and choosing the alternative that maximizes one's welfare' (Patrick M. Morgan, *Deterrence: A Conceptual Analysis* [Beverley Hills, CA: Sage 1983] p.84).

8. Before the 1991 Gulf War, it was known that Iraq had been trying to assemble one crude warhead using enriched uranium derived from energy reactors. While the expertise existed, other impediments (such as those imposed by the international effort to stop the spread of nuclear weapons) forced Iraq to proliferate at this minimal level (Judith Miller and James Risen, *New York Times* [16 Aug. 1998]).

9. I will be referring only to nuclear, rather than conventional, deterrence. I also do not cover similar phenomena associated with biological and chemical weapons of mass destruction.

10. Brodie (note 6) p.74.

11. Ibid. p.26.

12. See John Lewis Gaddis, *The Long Peace: Inquiries into the History of the Cold War* (NY: Oxford UP 1987) and Kenneth N Waltz, 'The Emerging Structure of International Politics', *International Security* 18/1 (Fall 1993) pp.44–79.

13. Frank Zagare, 'Classical Deterrence Theory: A Critical Assessment', *International Interactions* 21/4 (1996).

14. See Michael D. Intriligator and Dagobert L. Brito, 'The Stability of Mutual Deterrence' in

Jacek Kugler and Frank C. Zagare (eds.) *Exploring the Stability of Deterrence* (Denver: Lynne Reinner 1987); Morton Kaplan, *System and Process in International Politics* (NY: John Wiley 1957); John J. Mearsheimer, 'Back to the Future: Instability in Europe After the Cold War', *International Security* 15/1 (Summer 1990) pp. 5–56; and Kenneth N. Waltz, *Theory of International Politics* (Reading, MA: Addison-Wesley 1979). More specifically, a bipolar system is often regarded as more stable than a multipolar system, nuclear weapons (when properly managed) increase stability, and the weapons provide a defensive rather than an offensive advantage (Zagare, note 13, p.368). Other views see multipolarity as more stable. The classic exposition for this is Karl W. Deutsch and J. David Singer, 'Multipolar Systems and International Stability', *World Politics* 16 (1964), pp.390–406.

15. Zagare bases this discussion on Intriligator and Brito's formal model of a missile war (Michael D. Intriligator and Dagobert L. Brito, 'Can Arms Races Lead to the Outbreak of War?' *Journal of Conflict Resolution* 28 [1984] pp.63–84 and Intriligator and Brito, note 14.

16. I offer a summary of Intriligator and Brito's diagramatic exposition in mutual deterrence in laymen's terms.

17. Another interpretation could be that states with the ability to build more threatening arsenals pass through this dangerous state as their programs produce the very first weapons. Nuclear opponents have not reached a mutually secure second strike capability, and may engage in nuclear strategic thought that tends toward 'conventionalization' (James J. Wirtz, 'Beyond Bipolarity: Prospects for Nuclear Stability after the Cold War', in T.V. Paul, Richard J. Harknett and idem (eds.) *The Absolute Weapon Revisited: Nuclear Arms and the Emerging International Order* [Ann Arbor: U. of Michigan Press 1998]). While not a subject here, this narrow window of time could be highly unstable and would appear to warrant further investigation.

18. For additional discussions about selective proliferation enhancing systemic stability, see Bruce Bueno de Mesquita and William H. Riker, 'An Assessment of the Merits of Selective Nuclear Proliferation', *Journal of Conflict Resolution* 26/2 (June 1982); Peter Feaver and Emerson M. S. Niou 'Managing Nuclear Proliferation: Condemn, Strike, or Assist', *International Studies Quarterly* 40 (June 1996), pp.209–33; Steven J. Rosen, 'A Stable System of Mutual Nuclear Deterrence in the Middle East', *American Political Science Review* 71/4 (Dec. 1977); and Kenneth N. Waltz, *The Spread of Nuclear Weapons: More May Be Better*, Adelphi Paper 71 (London: IISS 1981). A recent update of the Waltz argument, along with representation of an opposing view based on organizational theory, see Scott D. Sagan and Kenneth N. Waltz, *The Spread of Nuclear Weapons: A Debate* (NY: Norton 1995).

19. Zagare (note 13) p.383, fn. 10.

20. Kenneth N. Waltz, 'The Stability of the Bipolar World', *Daedalus* 93 (1964) p.884.

21. Daniel Ellsberg, 'The Theory and Practice of Blackmail', in Oran R. Young (ed.), *Bargaining: Formal Theories of Negotiation* (Urbana: U. of Illinois Press 1975).

22. Zagare (note 13) p.376.

23. Glenn Snyder, 'Crisis Bargaining', in Charles F. Hermann (ed.) *International Crises: Insights from Behavioral Research* (NY: Free Press 1972).

24. Herman Kahn, *Thinking About the Unthinkable* (NY: Horizon Press 1962) p.11.

25. Ellsberg (note 21) p.360; and Robert Jervis, 'Bargaining and Bargainings Tactics', in J. Roland Pennock and John W. Chapman (eds.) *Coercion* (Chicago: Aldine 1972) p.285.

26. McGeorge Bundy, 'The Bishops and the Bomb', *The New York Review of Books* 30/10 (16 June 1983); Robert Jervis, *The Illogic of American Nuclear Strategy* (NY: Cornell UP); and Kenneth (note 12) pp.53–4.

27. Zagare, note 13, p. 379.

28. See note 18.

29. MacNeal/Lehrer News Hour, 7 Dec. 1993.

30. For a discussion of the concept 'rogue state' as it applies to preventing nuclear use, see Eric Herring, 'Rogue Rage: Can We Prevent Mass Destruction?' in this issue.

31. Robert S. McNamara, 'The Military Role of Nuclear Weapons: Perceptions and Misperceptions', *Foreign Affairs* 62/1 (Fall 1983) p.79. These sentiments were reinforced by McNamara in a 23 Feb. 1993 editorial to the *New York Times* entitled 'Nobody Needs Nukes', p.A21.

32. Shahram Chubin, *Iran's National Security Policy: Capabilities, Intentions & Impact*

(Washington DC: Carnegie Endowment for International Peace 1994) pp.50–5; Patrick Clawson, *Iran's Challenge to the West: How, When and Why* (Washington DC: The Washington Inst. for Near East Policy 1993) pp.59–66; and Anthony H. Cordesman, *Iran and Iraq: The Threat From the Northern Gulf* (Boulder: Westview 1994) pp.105–7.

33. Lewis A. Dunn, 'New Nuclear Threats to US Security', in Robert D. Blackwill and Albert Carnesale (eds.) *New Nuclear Nations: Consequences for US Policy* (NY: Council on Foreign Relations Press 1993) p.37.

34. 'H.R. 2709 – Iran Missile Proliferation Sanctions Act of 1997', Legislative Notice No. 68, 20 May 1998, US Senate Republican Committee; Tim Weiner, 'Iran Said to Test Missile Able to Hit Israel and Saudis', *New York Times* (23 July 1998).

35. Edward E. Azar, Paul Jureidini and Ronald McLaurin, 'Protracted Social Conflict: Theory and Practice in the Middle East', *Journal of Conflict Resolution* 32/3 (Sept.1988).

36. Michael Brecher and Patrick James, 'Patterns of Crisis Management', *Journal of Conflict Resolution* 32/3 (Sept. 1988).

37. Mueller notes that the absence of escalation could be one factor that may make nuclear weapons appear usable, citing credibility of a nuclear response to a conventional attack as a weakness; see John Mueller, 'The Escalating Irrelevance of Nuclear Weapons', in Paul (note 17) pp.81–2. Overall, however, his argument is against the likelihood of rampant proliferation as nuclear weapons become increasingly 'irrelevant' to preventing international wars. See also Eric Herring, *Danger and Opportunity: Explaining International Crisis Outcomes* (Manchester UP 1995) on the link between escalation and the political value of nuclear weapons, which places emphasis on fear of annihilation rather than military advantage.

38. Zachary S. Davis and Warren H. Donnelly, 'Iraq and Nuclear Weapons: Continuing Issues', CRS Issue Brief IB92107, updated 28 Jan. 1994.

39. Martin Indyk, Speech to the Washington Institute for Near East Policy, 18 May 1993, as reported in *Middle East International* 452, 11 June 1993.

40. Jeffrey R. Smith and Daniel Williams, 'White House to Step Up Plans to Isolate Iran, Iraq', *The Washington Post*, 23 May 1993.

41. Stephen Zunes, 'The Bankruptcy of U.S. Iraq Policy', *Middle East Policy* 6 (1998).

42. Charles Kurzman, 'Soft on Satan: Challenges for Iranian-U.S. Relations', *Middle East Policy* 6/1 (June 1998).

43. George Lenczowski, 'Iran: The Great Debate', *Middle East Policy* 3/2 (Sept. 1994) p.53.

44. Anthony Lake, 'Confronting Backlash States', *Foreign Affairs* 73/2 (March/April 1994) p.50.

45. Madeleine Albright, Remarks at the Asia Society Dinner, 17 June 1998, as released by the Office of the Spokesman, Dept. of State, 18 June 1998.

46. James P. Rubin, US Dept. of State Daily Press Briefing, 18 June 1998.

47. William Cohen, 'Threat Posed to America by WMD', Dept. of Defense News Briefing, 17 March 1998; Rubin (note 46); and US Government White Paper, 'Iraq Weapons of Mass Destruction Programs', 13 Feb. 1998.

48. A policy of assisted proliferation mentioned above may indeed result in robust mutual deterrence between Iran and Iraq, yet defeat attempts to protect other potential adversaries. In other words, what is best for stability within one dyad may well undermine other sets of conflictual actors. This dilemma would complicate any potential scenarios that do not exist according to the assumptions of existential deterrence.

49. Cordesman (note 32).

50. Anthony H. Cordesman and Ahmed S. Hashim, *Iraq: Sanctions and Beyond* (Boulder, CO: Westview 1997) and Stuart E. Eizenstat, Testimony Before the House International Relations Committee, 3 June 1998.

51. Rensselaer Lee, 'Smuggling Update', *Bulletin of the Atomic Scientists* 53/3 (May/June 1997).

52. Brian G. Chow and Kenneth A. Soloman, *Limiting the Spread of Weapons-Usable Fissile Weapons* (Santa Monica, CA: Rand 1994).

53. Lewis A. Dunn, 'Rethinking the Nuclear Equation: The United States and the New Nuclear Powers', *Washington Quarterly* 17/1 (Winter 1994) p.20.

54. The resignation of UN Assistant Secretary General Denis Halliday, former UN coordinator in Iraq, over the sanctions issue supports rising criticism among political actors and

academics alike that the sanctions were created in a way that would promote the downfall of Saddam Hussein's power more than they would alter policies by the existing Iraqi regime. Halliday believes now that the sanctions will not result in disarmament. Rather, they are responsible for malnutrition among $1/3$ of Iraqi children under the age of 5 and in the deaths of 6,000–7,000 children per month (Phyllis Bennis, 'The US and Iraq: towards confrontation?', *Middle East International* 587, 13 Nov. 1998, pp.4–5; Ian Williams, '"Why I resigned"– an interview with Denis Halliday', *Middle East International* 587, 13 Nov. 1998, pp.6–7.

55. Kenneth R. Timmerman, 'Cavaet Venditor', *New York Times*, 25 Oct. 1993.

56. Cordesman and Hashim (note 50).

57. In 1997 Cordesman wrote that Iran would most likely be able to develop a nuclear warhead using the same triggering system that used in 'Little Boy', the bomb dropped on Hiroshima. The estimation at that time stated if Iran was able to purchase the fissile material from abroad, with that kind of a gun or simple implosion method, it could develop a nuclear weapon in 9 to 48 months. Anthony H. Cordesman, *US Forces in the Middle East: Resources and Capabilities* (Boulder, CO: Westview 1997) p.94.

58. There is debate within the literature on deterrence whether or not MAD is truly robust or if it has an element of permanence. For example, Harvey and James argue that, based on a review of existing studies, crises in nuclear versus non-nuclear dyads do not appear to be resolved differently (Frank P. Harvey and Patrick James, 'Nuclear Deterrence Theory: The Record of Aggregate Testing and an Alternative Research Agenda', *Conflict Management and Peace Science* 12/1 (1992) pp.17–45).

59. Bundy (note 26) p.4. The argument that damage from a limited nuclear attack may be considered acceptable if the enemy could be defeated is supported in Lawrence Freedman, 'I Exist; Therefore I Deter', *International Security* 13/1 (Summer 1988) p.183.

60. Scott D. Sagan, 'More Will Be Worse', in idem and Kenneth N. Waltz (ed.) *The Spread of Nuclear Weapons* (note 18) p.48.

61. David Albright, 'The Shots Heard "Round the World"', *Bulletin of the Atomic Scientists* 54/4 (July/Aug. 1998).

62. Innovative policies for management of nuclear rivalries also might be relevant to other weapons of mass destruction, ranging from chemical to germ warfare. In addition, mixed WMD capabilities, such as a nuclear capable state facing crisis with a chemical capable states, also may exhibit behavior inconsistent with Cold War, superpower deterrence.

63. Unilateral use, without second strike, has been questioned on both moral and strategic terms. However, Cold War MAD was based on the credibility of nuclear use which, according to Zagare, is an inherent flaw in Classical Deterrence Theory, Zagare (note 13) p.13.

64. For heuristic purposes, these preferences are stated only as 'use' versus 'non-use'. In any crisis situation, of course, state actions are nuanced with multiple options. However, this is appropriate since nuclear use does carry the connotation of 'all or nothing', i.e. stepping over a 'line in the sand'.

65. Recall that the only weapon of mass destruction discussed here is nuclear.

66. Iran also bombed Iraqi cities, but its missile capability was limited and failed to match the devastation inflicted by the Iraqis.

67. Iranian use of chemical weapons against Iraqi troops is not as well publicized, perhaps due to the fact that the use was limited and ineffectual as Iranian chemical capability was quite primitive compared to Iraq's chemical arsenal and delivery capability (Anthony H. Cordesman and Abraham R. Wagner, *The Lessons of Modern War, Volume II: The Iran-Iraq War* [Boulder: Westview Press 1990] pp.517–18; Office of the Secretary of Defense, *Proliferation: Threat and Response* [Washington DC: Dept. of Defense April 1996] p.15). It is interesting to note, however, that they did cross the infamous WMD 'line' which violates international norms and should have produced extreme condemnation. The lesson may not be lost on these two antagonists in future conflicts, since the outside world does not appear to dole out consistent levels of punishment for WMD violations.

68. Morgan states that the only time striking first is not rational, even with nuclear weapons, is when the costs for both sides are extreme to the point of 'virtually total destruction' (Morgan, p.94).

69. Herring (note 30).

5

Beliefs, Culture, Proliferation and use of Nuclear Weapons

BEATRICE HEUSER

Man's deadliest weapon is *language*. He is as susceptible to being hypnotised by slogans as he is to infectious diseases. And when there is an epidemic, the group-mind takes over. It obeys its own rules, which are different from the rules of conduct of individuals. When a person identifies himself with a group, his reasoning faculties are diminished and his passions enhanced by a kind of emotive resonance... The individual is not a killer, but the group is, and by identifying with it, the individual is transformed into a killer.

(Arthur Koestler)[1]

Before tackling the subject of this essay, there is need for an introductory remark: in the following, we will be focusing to a large extent on nuclear weapons, but these must not be seen entirely in isolation from other weapons of mass destruction. The reason for this is twofold. First, nuclear weapons were invented in an age of scientific plenty, by which I mean an age in which well-subsidised scientific research has been conducted in many different directions to produce a weapon more powerful than anything known before. Research pursued several different avenues. Chemical weapons already existed and could be made more easily manageable; research into biological weapons was conducted simultaneously. Since the invention of uranium or plutonium fission bombs, hydrogen fusion bombs were developed, and several other mixed systems including enhanced radiation weapons with minimal long-term radiation and pollution effects ('fall-out'). Fuel-air explosives, which are usually classified as 'conventional weapons', have been developed more recently and have effects similar to those of low-yield ('tactical') nuclear weapons. A range of weapons thus exists which could be used to inflict very large numbers of deaths, on the scale at which the bombs dropped on Hiroshima and Nagasaki did.

The second reason for linking these weapons is that in giving up biological and chemical weapons, nuclear powers such as Britain, France and the US and the non-nuclear allies depending on them are tempted to link the threat of nuclear retaliation to any chemical or biological weapons use by an adversary. Although there is growing consensus that chemical weapons should be regarded as coming in a category different from that of biological and nuclear weapons, the latter two have much in common, where lethality of effect is concerned. For this reason there has been speculation, in the context of the shift of US nuclear strategy in late 1997, as to whether it meant a retreat from the so-called 'negative security assurances' which the nuclear powers gave to non-nuclear powers in the late 1980s, that is, the assurance not to use nuclear weapons against them.[2]

There is one non-technological difference between nuclear and any other weapons of mass destruction (WMD): nuclear weapons have acquired a mythical dimension which chemical weapons only had temporarily (mainly during World War I) and which is not associated with biological weapons. To some, nuclear weapons are status symbols; to some, they are the ultimate guarantee that a traumatising historical experience they have had will not repeat itself; to some, they serve important domestic purposes; to some, they are the magic that keeps wars at bay; to some, they symbolise, or indeed incarnate, ultimate evil. In the 1950s and early 1960s, nuclear weapons were symbols of modernity, and successful nuclear tests were celebrated with naïveté, champagne and celebration cakes much like successful space-rocket launches even more recently than that. Nuclear weapons have a certain *cachet* which other WMD lack; they are political as well as military instruments, and can be made to convey a series of political signals, from *noli me tangere* to a claim to superpower status which no other existing weapons system presently confers.

On a different level, the question remains whether massive fatalities inflicted by using nuclear or biological weapons are ultimately different from fatalities inflicted in more conventional ways. It is worth recalling in this context that the 'conventional' 1945 bombing of Tokyo and Dresden inflicted casualties (88,000 and 34,000 respectively) in the same range of figures as the atom bomb of Hiroshima and Nagasaki (90,000 and 40,000 respectively).[3] More importantly, perhaps, systematic murder conducted by the National Socialists and their 'willing executioners' (Daniel Goldhagen) in Germany, Austria and all their occupied territories caused hundreds of times more deaths to children and non-combatant adults than did the two atomic bombs. Most recently, we have witnessed the killings of large numbers of Hutus and Tutsis in Rwanda through machetes alone, and it is worth keeping in mind that a group determined to carry out mass homicide, particularly where the victims are undefended, is usually capable of carrying out their scheme with horrendous consequences, whatever the technology available.

Having introduced this initial *caveat* against any exclusive focus on nuclear weapons, our purpose is to examine the links between beliefs and the development or procurement, and consequent possible employment, of any particular instrument or means designed to kill very large numbers of people indiscriminately. Before concentrating all analytical efforts on how to prevent the use of WMD in any future conflict, it is worth focusing policy on measures to prevent the proliferation of such weapons. Such measures are unlikely to succeed, if they are exclusively of a merely coercive nature: there are motivations for procuring nuclear weapons which are worth exploring at least in order to ascertain whether other answers can be found to satisfy certain needs and aspirations, or whether the acquisition of WMD is likely to be the only path a particular state (or indeed non-state actor) is determined to follow. While the latter might be the case, even there a close understanding of the motivations which lead to the determination to acquire WMD can give a strong indication as to whether such an acquisition is made precisely with the aim *never* to have to use them, or whether they are acquired with a possible intention of using them to offset enemy forces of another sort.

In other words, we can gauge whether the acquisition is made purely with deterrent intentions in mind, or with a high degree of preparedness to use them in a conflict. The motivations of a state or other actor in procuring WMD, its underlying beliefs about the world, about itself and its perceived adversary or adversaries and their likely (re)actions are crucial elements in any analysis of the immediate or more long-term danger presented by proliferation.[4]

A further explanatory note needs to be added here, and it again concerns terminology. The term 'beliefs' is used here, which some would argue is excessively vague. Yet, as we shall see, one rarely encounters decision-makers who act on the basis of completely coherent ideologies or belief-systems (Pope Urban II who proclaimed the First Crusade, Trotsky and Hitler are probably exceptions). A more useful concept is that of belief-clusters: an assortment of beliefs, which individually may have their roots in several half-digested ideologies, traditions, folklore, parental *dicta*, bits read here and there, and superficially persuasive soundbites generated by propaganda. Taken together, such belief-clusters are rarely logically coherent, nor are they universally shared by the members of a group, let alone country. However, in many contexts a culture can clearly be identified by a belief-cluster common to most of its members, which *overall* distinguish them from other groups. It is important to understand, however, that these distinctions can be small, and may yet make two distinct groups relatively similar compared with a third group, and does not stand in the way of individual members of any group having a great deal in common with majority beliefs of another group.

Here, the term 'culture' will be taken to refer to a group which has common beliefs, which, for the purpose of any argument, can be seen as sharing a distinctive cluster of beliefs. Such cultures can be overlapping circles, or smaller circles within different circles. On one level, cultures can be largely co-terminous with modern nations (so we can talk about French culture and beliefs, or British culture and beliefs). But inevitably, even within that nation, elements of the predominating culture will have their critics, so that a culture can be seen as containing within itself several cultures. It can also itself be a part of a larger culture. To give a concrete example, the British 'disarmers', that is, the anti-nuclear campaigners, tended to have a stronger Puritan heritage than the more pro-nuclear cultures within Britain, and had much in common with anti-nuclear movements in West Germany, the Netherlands and Scandinavia. Their belief-clusters were thus at once sub-national and supra-national, and cannot be usefully described by a term ('strategic culture') which takes as its defining starting point a 'nation'.[5] We will look at some examples in the following.

CAUSES OF WARS AND BELIEFS

It is worth beginning with a discussion of causes of wars generally, as relevant to our subject. In looking at the likelihood that we can prevent, or the likelihood that we will be forced to witness further use of WMD, we have to be clear, first, what factors cause wars, and which of these, if any, are invalidated by the dimensions of destruction made possible by WMD. There is not the time or space here to dwell on different theories about the causes of wars, but it is worth echoing a postulate heard increasingly often: namely, not to seek monocausal, monistic explanations.

Let us recall briefly two analytical approaches that seek to integrate different levels of analysis. In his great classic of 1959, Kenneth Waltz proposed a threefold approach of studying causes of wars that lie within human nature, those that lie within societies, and those that lie within state systems.[6] Karl Deutsch and Dieter Senghaas a dozen years later proposed a more refined structure that dealt with 'interests' on five levels:

- the interests of individuals and very small groups of key decision-makers;

- the interests of sub-systems within states, such as political parties, classes, interest groups;

- the interests of individual states;

- relations and interests within regional systems;

- relations and the distribution of power and interests in the inter-state system as a whole.[7]

While these authors have refined their argument to take account of multiple factors shaping 'interests', such as economic issues, political pressures, etc., there is still a great tendency in studying war and peace to deal with 'interests', as though one was dealing with the reactions of share-holders rather than with the enormously complex interplay of ideas, facts, needs and pressures that come together in the minds of decision-makers when deciding on a policy, a strategy, and a military posture to go along with these. Even share-holders, who arguably only have a finite set of considerations influencing their behaviour in the market, are difficult to predict collectively. In dealing with war and peace, defence and aggression, decision-making is likely to be subject to far more different factors interacting, and is likely to be even less predictable on purely statistical or games theoretical grounds. Among all the factors at play, this study concentrates on the most elusive ones: the beliefs particular to individual actors, or select groups of actors or policy-makers.

Hitler, for one, believed that it was in the interest of his race (he, for his part, did not think in the narrow terms of nation-states) that it should exile and kill people whom he defined as Jewish (whether or not they saw themselves as such), that Slavs should be turned into a sort of slave-people for the 'Aryans', and that he should finally declare war on the US. His writings show that he was quite convinced that the Germanic or Aryan race was short of living space, with a population density of the time which was significantly lower than it is in Germany and Austria today.[8] With the benefit of hindsight, we can say that Hitler was wrong in thinking that Germany and Austria were too densely populated, but he was not even the only one holding this view, which was widespread among his supporters. Even his rivals on the racist Right, such as General Ludendorff, held beliefs virtually indistinguishable from those of Hitler on this subject.[9]

Similarly, the Japanese government ministers (mainly on the military side) who opposed Japanese surrender until swept aside by the emperor's decision of 15 August 1945 held that surrender would be worse for Japan than to continue to fight. The determination of Japanese soldiers to die rather than to be taken captive, or the mass-suicides among the inhabitants of Okinawa show that this belief was quite widely shared. Even without the benefit of hindsight, Westerners could have told them that the Americans were unlikely to treat their prisoners badly, let alone the civilian populations, and yet it was the opposite that was believed very firmly and widely in Japan.[10] The Germans, the Austrians and the Japanese fought World War II, and in the case of the former, carried out the genocide of Jews and gypsies based on these assumptions which we do not share: these beliefs were crucial to the cause and their conduct of World War II.

At this point in the argument, somebody will usually nod and say that in dealing with Hitler, or perhaps even the Japanese regime of World War II, one was obviously dealing with madmen. This in no respect seems a helpful approach, not least because it amounts to an admission of total analytical bankruptcy. The logical fault lies in assuming madness, and equating it with a lack of logic and predictability, rather than in the attempt to find method in this madness, or rather, to assume a fairly logically coherent behaviour based on certain beliefs which we may not share. Thus the belief itself needs not be scientifically provable or empirically derived, but the logic that is applied in building on it and deducing postulates for action on its basis may still be – and, I would argue, mostly are – quite reasonable.

Cultures that are based on the belief in an eternal afterlife in which rewards and punishments will be meted out depending on behaviour in this world have a different attitude to life and death than most agnostic cultures. Cultures that put the collective good far above the happiness and life of individuals differ from the highly individualistic societies of Europe, North America, Australia and New Zealand, where casualties in war are accepted less willingly. Public executions still take place in China and in many Islamic countries, while even the death penalty carried out far from the public eye is regarded as unacceptable in most European countries. Attitudes to suffering and pain differ strongly, as do attitudes to their prevention, and underlying motives can be manifold.

To give examples of attitudes to life and death, the German National Socialists as much as the Vichy régime regarded abortion as a crime meriting capital punishment, and their ferocious opposition to contraception (with the aim both in Germany and France of increasing their the own population, seen as engaged in a competition for more sons to be born and later to be turned into soldiers) is paralleled only by the tenacity of opposition to contraception in the Roman Catholic Church (and countries where it has a strong standing, such as Ireland and Poland). Mother Teresa explained many times that it was categorically preferable morally that undernourished and diseased children should be born into this world to die young and after great suffering than that their conception should be prevented in the first place.

Turning more specifically to attitudes to casualties in war, the Iranian government during the Iran–Iraq War, recruiting young boys for military service, thrust golden keys into their hands as symbols of their assumption into heaven should they fall in the war. The 'cherry blossoms', as the young *kamikaze* fighters of Japan were called, were prepared to go into *certain* death for the sake of their emperor, in a cause about which the Japanese population as a whole thought little.[11] Fatalities in World War I were proportionally much greater than during the Vietnam War, and yet in the cultural climate of the early twentieth century, there were more volunteers on the Western side in the former than in the latter. Differing beliefs are thus clearly factors of very considerable importance in dealing with war.

Culture and the Conduct of Wars

Short of falling into the trap of developing a new monocausal approach, a different, or perhaps complementary analytical approach is sought here. It is the focus on the conduct of war (and its preparation) in relation to culture. For this, we can go as far back as to Carl von Clausewitz, who towards the end of his life – the post-Napoleonic peace was being disturbed by local insurrections, particularly in Poland, against Prussian and Russian occupiers – reflected on the past and future nature of wars.

> We must … take into account, above all, that the judgement about an imminent war, about the aim it may have, about the means which are needed, can only arise from a comprehensive overview of all factors and the relations between them, … and will be determined by the mental disposition and characteristics of the princes, statesmen and military leaders …

> Half-educated Tartars, the republics of Antiquity, feudal lords and medieval trading cities, kings of the eighteenth century, and finally princes and peoples of the nineteenth century all conduct war in their

own way, conduct it differently, … with a different aim.[12]

Clausewitz was fascinated by the difference that this mental disposition made in the way in which different princes and peoples conducted their wars, and it was with this in mind that he conceived of the idea that war itself is dominated by the greater policy, indeed by the political thinking of those conducting war, by their beliefs. His fascination was shared by other thinkers who sought to understand why different groups prepared for, and fought wars so differently. In his reflection on Clausewitz, Lenin wrote:

> War is the continuation of policy by other means. Every war is inseparable from the political order from which it has sprung. The policy which a given state, a given class within that state, pursued for a long time before that war is inevitably continued in that same class during the war, the form of action alone being changed.[13]

Building on them, we can modify the above analytical approaches to the study of war, its causes, the preparation for it, and its conduct, by introducing the element of beliefs into it: what do the protagonists believe about themselves, about their potential or actual enemies, and about potential allies? What are their war aims? How do they expect to conduct the military campaign, and what sacrifices are they willing to make in the pursuit of their aims? How do they envisage a future war? For it is fair to assume that in most wars the defeated party, particularly if it initiated the war, anticipated the outcome differently, or else would have avoided hostilities in the first place, and even the victorious powers are often mistaken in their prediction of a future war, as the Allied Powers in World War I realised when their soldiers were not 'home by Christmas' 1914. Such miscalculations in themselves, however, contribute to unleashing wars which demand sacrifices on an unexpected level – which applies to World War I, in which chemical weapons were used, and for World War II with its cataclysmic nuclear finale.

All these factors are of outstanding importance in any reflection on the future of WMD. Recently, the nuclear tests by India and, as a not unexpected newcomer, Pakistan have reminded us that nuclear proliferation has not come to an end. Yet the step from the acquisition of nuclear weapons to their use in war has so far only been taken by one power, and even this power did not start a war or indeed enter it with the intention of using nuclear weapons against its aggressor. We will therefore in the following have to remain wary of the assumption that the limited intentions of a protagonist in times of (tense) peace or even at the start of a conflict will outlast the experience of war, daily reports of casualties, the return of body-bags, and a state of desperation among even the most humanitarian minded decision-makers.

BELIEFS AND NUCLEAR POSTURES: EXAMPLES

To illustrate the hypothesis presented here, that beliefs play a crucial role in decisions to acquire nuclear weapons, and in the adoption of the doctrine according to which they might be used, some will be presented briefly in the following. This gives a taste of the beliefs on the basis of which other countries have, in the past, decided to acquire nuclear weapons, or have decided not to proceed along this line. I shall draw on my own in-depth studies of the cases of Britain, France and the Federal Republic of Germany (FRG), and more briefly on further case-studies conducted by other scholars.[14]

When it comes to technical details, defence elites in the three large West European powers had similar views during the Cold War both of the nature and intensity of the Soviet threat and the policies of their major protector, the USA. The first was assessed by the governments of all three countries to be a vital challenge to their own cultural and political survival, but from the late 1950s onwards, government defence analysts also thought it unlikely that the Soviet Union would consciously bring on a nuclear war in Europe. They continued to fear that the USSR might be led into adventurist behaviour by the perception in Moscow that the West was unwilling to defend itself using *nuclear* weapons. In order to quash that possible perception among the Soviet leadership, they all wanted NATO to put strong emphasis on nuclear weapons, arguing that the threat to resort to them even in response to a conventional attack, was needed as a security guarantee for the Alliance. Also from the second half of the 1950s onwards, in the light of the experience of American behaviour in the Suez crisis and in response to the flight of the Sputnik, all three countries' governments (and also Italy's) began to worry about the reliability of America's nuclear commitment.

Yet they drew different conclusions from this: Britain used its own nuclear arsenal to establish a privileged co-operative relationship with the US, to bind America more closely into Europe, while safeguarding maximum independence 'on the cheap' (with US technological aid).

France drew the conclusion that she could only trust herself, and after some experiments in European integration and in constituting a European nuclear force, she developed her own nuclear arsenal, jealously guarding its independence, doing more than any other European country to put the cohesion of the Atlantic Alliance at risk.

The FRG's government decided, like Britain, but without acquiring nuclear weapons of its own, to do everything to bind America to Europe, while repeatedly riding out storms of internal opposition against any association with nuclear weapons. Despite the similarity of analysis in the defence ministries of these three governments, there were thus different forces at work in their governments' decision-making processes.

Britain

An in-depth analysis of the writings of Britons, Frenchmen and Germans about nuclear weapons reveals very distinct beliefs held in each country. Britons in general clung to the idea that their country somehow had to play a special role in world affairs, that of a noble knight who comes to the defence of the weak and stands up for what was right. Whether they support nuclear weapons or not, Britons see their country as a great power, and most see it as predestined to play a martial role; few Britons dislike the military or regard it as in any way threatening within their society. This is rarely articulated – Britons shy away from articulating their sentiments – but classically expressed by Sir Michael Quinlan, one of the key shapers of British government policy on nuclear weapons: why did Britain, he asked, with a 'broadly similar size, population and wealth', have almost twice as large a defence budget as Italy? To him, the reason for this was 'our national judgement – ultimately largely a gut political judgement – of what sort of role we wish to play in the world, and what influence we seek to command; what sort of people, to adapt a wartime song, do we think we are?'[15]

Consequently, however much it was also rationalised in terms of the need for a deterrent force, British politicians almost instinctively opted for a nuclear role for Britain. Unlike France, the majority of Britons equally instinctively saw Britain as a country that had to contribute to the security of others, that had to play its part in the NATO team, that could not let down allies. The strong cultural proclivity to see the world in terms of team sports, but also in terms of economic bargains and fair dealing pervaded British attitudes to the greatest team fielded, NATO, and shaped Britain's role within it as that of the honest broker, putting alliance interests above narrow 'national' interests, acting for the greater good of all. All these points are faithfully reflected in Britain's nuclear posture. British nuclear weapons are assigned to NATO and integrated in alliance nuclear contingency plans, and would have been used early on, even if Britain itself had not yet been invaded or otherwise attacked by Warsaw Pact forces. British nuclear weapons thus benefited the alliance as a whole, and Britain plays a particularly prominent role in the alliance, with a (proportionally) particularly large number of officials among the international staff.

There is an important dissenting minority culture in Britain on the issue of nuclear weapons, but only a very small minority indeed could see Britain relinquishing its military leadership and concentrate on other activities (e.g. pure commerce, or pure diplomacy without military might to give it extra clout). Moreover, anti-Americanism, which reached substantial proportions in several European countries, is relatively insignificant in Britain: there is a distinct heritage still of a somewhat racist belief in Anglo-Saxondom, in which America is seen merely to play a very important part, almost like the main heir to her responsibilities among the many colonial children of ageing but wise Britannia. Many Britons feel very much at home with American popular culture, American openness to discussion (in the language common to both), and instinctively see (particularly WASPish Americans) as part of a greater 'us'. 'We', 'our defence', thus easily includes American arsenals and NATO in general in British parlance.

Notwithstanding the experience of World War II, which contradicted the previous hope that Britain's bomber force by existing alone might deter Germany from any strategic bombing raids on Britain, British strategists continued to believe in a posture of deterrence. They were thus the first to focus on the deterrent potential of nuclear arsenals, which they strongly felt Britain needed, too. While in the late 1950s and early 1960s, and again in the early 1980s, a good number of Britons had less faith in the safety of this deterrence posture than their governments, the British faith in common sense in general, shared, it is believed, across nations, races, political boundaries, predominated, and generations of civil servants and politicians persuaded themselves that deterrence would not break down because the Russians ultimately must fear any nuclear war as much as the British did. The complex doctrine which NATO adopted under British influence, which assigned to tactical nuclear weapons the role of signalling to the enemy that he had 'miscalculated', if he attacked, hinged on the British conviction that the enemy would, in fairly cold blood, react to strictly limited nuclear use by making a merchant's calculations of costs and benefits. He would accept an armistice, and, persuaded, not outraged, by the nuclear explosions, would come to the negotiating table in the hope of negotiating a mutually satisfactory compromise solution (in the style of decision-making among the British government ministries).

A strong Puritan strand characterises culture in Britain and has ensured that not all Britons have always felt morally righteous about the ownership of nuclear weapons. In times of particular East–West tension, when the chances of pre-emptive Soviet nuclear strikes against nuclear bases in Britain seemed particularly high, an important minority felt that it was distinctly unwise, never mind immoral, to have such bases on British soil. They might provoke a Soviet attack in a race to get one's retaliation in first. Yet throughout most of the Cold War, a general faith in the exceptional common sense of British governments, as opposed to the folly of foreigners, has led a majority to hold that as long as any nuclear powers exist, Britain should be among them, not least so that her wise counsel can be heard.[16]

While there was an element of belief in the importance of deterrence in the British decision to acquire nuclear weapons, and in the importance of controlling an independent nuclear force, there is also a large status factor. With the end of the Cold War and the waning of a direct military threat against Western Europe (and Britain), there is the perception that the new currency of great power status lies less in nuclear weapons than in the projection of conventional forces. The 1990s, from *Options for Change* of 1990 to the 1998 defence review, have seen a shift in British priorities from one to the other. Accompanying it, there has been a pruning to the barest minimum of British nuclear forces.[17]

Could nuclear proliferation to Britain, in the sense of the acquisition of an independent nuclear force, have been avoided? To my mind, it is imaginable, if the USA had allowed Britain to continue the same degree of close co-operation that Britain had had with the Manhattan Project until the passing of the McMahon Act of 1946. Britain might have been content to continue a working arrangement whereby British bombers would have had access to US nuclear weapons in case of war, just as the US conceded for interested NATO-members from the late 1950s (precisely to avoid further proliferation), but by then the British horse had bolted. Special status in Washington, special access to US decision-making, a chance to play the role of the respected elder statesman in the North Atlantic Alliance, and unrestricted access to nuclear weapons if war had actually broken out, this is really what Britain wanted. It is imaginable that the US could have fulfilled these requests without Britain acquiring an independent nuclear force.[18]

France

There was a similar instinctive feeling among members of the predominating elite in France since the mid-1950s that their state needed nuclear weapons, if these were the currency of greatness in the modern world. To some extent, nuclear weapons were thus acquired just as high-speed trains, *minitel*, and supersonic passenger aircraft were developed to turn France into a truly modern power (toilets with hand wash basins have always come distinctly further down on the list). More still, France, like a jealous younger sibling, wanted everything her big sister America had. She is thus the only second rank nuclear power which developed almost the entire range of nuclear weapons which the USA and the USSR developed and deployed, with both a strategic and a tactical triad of air-, land- and sea-based weapons.[19] If any connection was made between France's nuclear weapons and their benefits for other countries, however, it was in a non-tangible way. Vague phrases were used to deflect allied criticism of French selfishness, such as that France's nuclear weapons, by virtue of being in Europe, were European nuclear weapons, and thus of benefit to everybody in Europe.[20]

France, like Britain, the US and indeed NATO, adopted a deterrence posture, but she clung more firmly to the belief than other countries that the threat of massive nuclear retaliation to *any* attack (including a purely conventional one) was sufficient for deterrence to work. There has consistently been a pronounced disinclination among French strategists, both within and outside government, to discuss what would happen if deterrence ever failed, and all declarations simply reiterated without cease the conviction that it would not. More than anywhere else, the atom bomb was thus, in France, a 'weapon of non-use'.[21] Instead, they were predominately 'a political weapon', in the words of historian Cyril Buffet,[22] designed to buy France great power status. This matched the sentiments of many in France, who were raised on the notion that the French were leaders of nations, and that France was predestined through her history of greatness to play a great-power role.

Infinitely more than in Britain, and similarly to the US and to Russia after the end of the Cold War, nuclear weapons also became in France the symbol of a political order. French proclivities for a monarchic democracy, in which the president (as formerly the king) holds in his hands the power over life and death, is admirably summed up in his command over nuclear weapons, supreme symbols of state sovereignty, but also of the life and death of his subjects and their enemies. In France great significance is thus attached to the handover of the control over nuclear release from president to president. It is commented upon in the media as though it were the passing on of the Revelations of Our Lady of Fatima from pope to pope, an initiation into sacred Elysian rites. The air of quasi divinity thus given to the French president, who as representative of the entire nation is supposed to stand above party politics, was a welcome replacement of the strife and instability of the much more democratic, parliament-oriented Fourth

Republic with its series of short-lived governments, and remains a stabilising factor in French politics even today.

Thus nuclear weapons have provided solutions to important internal problems of France. Another one of these concerns the retrospective compensation of what is seen as great French failures: the inner divisions of the nation ever since the French Revolution and the factional strife which is believed to have contributed to the great defeat of 1940 has already been alluded to. Nuclear weapons in the hands of one determined president are the perfect replacement for an unwieldy military apparatus with conscript soldiers who never again want to suffer the trench warfare of World War I. The latter wonder whether they should rise up in arms against their class enemy or the immigrants who are believed to have done them out of a job, rather than again attacking forces from without. Nuclear weapons take the decision whether to stand up and fight and die away from those suspected of preferring to surrender and live.

However, the imagery and myths surrounding nuclear weapons in France appeal also to French beliefs of a more romantic kind. The sacredness of France, untouchable behind her nuclear shield, appealed to French mentalities in a singular way. It married itself perfectly with a historical heritage of metaphors drawn from the Old Testament, from the medieval philosophy of kingship, and from ideas of the *volonté générale* as embodied in France's elected representative as developed by the *philosophes* of the Age of Enlightenment.

In these beliefs, allies play no part, or at best that of traitors, from perfidious Albion to the American usurper of France's place in the Middle East and in South-East Asia. French thinkers and practitioners mistrust alliances, and this is perfectly reflected in French nuclear strategy.[23] France's nuclear weapons, unlike those of Britain and the US, are *not* assigned to NATO, and France's semi-detached position in NATO continues to be part of the articles of faith of the Fifth Republic. From the late 1960s until the mid-1990s, a series of attempts by France's allies and by a small band of Atlanticists within France to bring France back into the integrated military structure failed, as across any party divides, France's independence is treasured more than any security that could be derived from allies.

The paradoxical nature of France's relationship with her former 'hereditary enemy' Germany is again fully reflected in her nuclear posture. This shows that despite the rhetoric and gestures of Franco-German reconciliation, Frenchmen continue to think in terms of exclusive nationhood when it comes to the most vital aspects of self-defence.

This paradox also extends to France's relationship with the European

Union, sometimes regarded as a synonym for 'we-ness' by the French. When (what French writers themselves define as) the ultimate test of defence is applied, France's nuclear umbrella does not cover Finland or all the other members of the EU, but only France, and at most the access routes leading to France. Benevolent minds can interpret these to mean the inclusion of parts of Germany, Belgium and Luxembourg under France's nuclear umbrella.

Nuclear weapons, and the doctrines in which they were clad, were thus in many respects the perfect reflection of many beliefs of the French about themselves, their society, the world around them. They hold the answer to many French psychological problems arising from having been raised to believe in the incomparable greatness of France and the chosenness of the French people, and the bitter experience of defeat and occupation in World War II, of decolonisation and marginalisation by the competition coming from the 'Anglo-Saxon' cultures. The consensus within her population on the need for France to own nuclear weapons has therefore been staggeringly great.[24]

At the same time it seems that only one of the many reasons why France acquired nuclear weapons is directly to do with the sheer necessity of defence, and with the obsession of preventing a repetition of 1940. One cannot help thinking that if Britain and the US had systematically treated France differently, if other symbols had been found for France's internal unity, if European integration had not faltered (due in large part to one French culture undermining it), France might have been able to achieve all she wished for without acquiring a purely national nuclear force.

The Non-Nuclears: The Federal Republic of Germany (FRG)

On the other end of the spectrum, there are the powers who, although they might have contributed to nuclear proliferation, eventually chose not to. There is no doubt that it would have been feasible technically also for Germany, Italy and Japan after the World War II to acquire nuclear weapons. German and Italian nuclear scientists had been prominently involved in nuclear research, and governments of both countries showed a lively interest in nuclear weapons from the mid-1950s. Nevertheless, both German and Italian governments decided not to move behind the backs of their major allies, and to try to enhance their security through close co-operation with the US rather than the French way.

In terms of pure geostrategy, West Germany more than any other country in Western Europe could have seen hard reasons to develop a nuclear deterrence stance to keep any invasion at bay. As front-line states, both East and West Germany would have been affected most even by a purely conventional attack from the Warsaw Pact, either by being defended (with massive nuclear or even just conventional ordnance used on West German territory), or by being the first to be overrun by Soviet forces, if the US commitment were not honoured. Yet Bonn chose alliance loyalty above anything else, including any option of constructing nuclear weapons.

In the FRG, the shock of the defeat of 1945, of the total vanity of all sacrifices made, and of the confrontation with the horrors of Auschwitz, created a deep allergy to all things military. In the mid-1950s, the campaign against the creation of an army in the FRG came close to leading to a defeat of this policy in the parliament in the mid-1950s, even though it was strongly supported by the NATO countries who had agreed to integrate the FRG into their ranks. The waves of protests against NATO's nuclear strategy, and more specifically against the stationing of NATO nuclear forces on the territory of the FRG, only followed a more general pattern of rejection of the use of force.

This was also amply demonstrated by German popular reactions to the prospect of involvement in the 1991 Gulf War, which hardly created the risk of a nuclear retaliatory Iraqi attack on Germany. In the culture of the Bonn Republic, the use of force was from its creation regarded an absolute evil, and anything symbolising this use of force, above all nuclear weapons, has been thought of, literally, as diabolical. Throughout the Cold War, nuclear weapons were thus rejected as totally immoral by an important section of the West German population, to the point where it would have been out of the question for any government to procure nuclear weapons – their own population would not have allowed them to. Mutual suspicions among the population, the Left was forever suspecting the Conservatives of neo-Fascist tendencies, the Right forever accusing the Left of selling out to the Soviet Union, created a culture rife with press investigations and scandals about government officials purportedly overstepping the limits of their competences. This was not a society in which a government could have pursued a clandestine nuclear programme, as the British government virtually did from 1947 until the first British nuclear test in 1952.

A slim majority of West Germans did, however, accept the need for NATO to have nuclear weapons, grudgingly, as a necessary evil, rather than joyfully, as a guarantor of national independence as in France. Like most of their NATO allies, this culture within West Germany was persuaded that nuclear weapons could ban *all* war and were thus a blessing in a very repugnant disguise, if treated with an appropriately critical distance. Like their more purist countrymen and -women (and indeed very much like the French), they never again wanted to contemplate involvement in any war, but for them it was precisely through nuclear weapons – and total integration, absorption into a greater whole (NATO, 'the West') that they could assure this. This went along with a willing as much as exacted surrender of responsibility to the Alliance, above all to the US. All that was completely taboo in France (the stationing of foreign forces on her soil, American supreme command and political leadership in the alliance) was thus positively welcomed in the FRG, where it was seen as the best guarantee against any return of the past. Uncertain about themselves, more uncertain still about their countrymen, West Germans were reasonably happy to follow the lead of countries which in two world wars had demonstrably been on the right side – that of the victors.

Certainly, there was and is a small group of defence experts in the FRG, who, educated in British and American thinking, occasionally use terms such as 'national interest' and 'political realism', copied out of Anglo-American IR textbooks. These they read with all the admiration of those who know that a German would be positively pilloried if he or she wrote after 1945 the sort of things which a Hans Morgenthau, a Henry Kissinger, a Hedley Bull or a John Mearsheimer published. Yet their final conclusion is always that it is in Germany's deepest, profoundest interest, 'never to stand alone'.[25] Germany's interest is thus always to have the alliance alongside, it is *by definition* a collective, not a national interest, as there must be something wrong with it if it is not supported more generally by the allies.

The same attitude obtains with regard to Europe – Germans, like Italians, actually think of themselves as Europeans almost as much as they think of themselves as Germans and Italians, and for similar reasons. For them it is thus just about *credible* that another nation's government would use nuclear weapons in their defence, and they place greater faith in the alliance's collective nuclear deterrence posture, hinging, always, on the willingness of the nuclear powers unilaterally to honour their nuclear commitments.

Nevertheless, nuclear weapons, even if owned by other powers who were trusted more by the Germans than the Germans trust themselves, sit uneasily with the beliefs of the citizens of the Federal Republic of Germany. Most see them as the weapons of a Beelzebub whose dubious services are enlisted to keep the Devil at bay, and the abrogation of responsibility to handle them by leaving it to other powers in the alliance to assume – the moral burden of nuclear ownership fits the German post-war mentality perfectly. The beliefs prevalent in the Bonn Republic are a stronger hedge against nuclear proliferation here than any external pressures.[26] It is thus absurd to waste time on speculations about whether Germany will 'go nuclear'.[27]

Other Examples

The case of Italy has already been mentioned: it has much in common with that of Germany. In Italy, too, the use of force is seen as morally suspect after the abuse of force by Mussolini, and Italy plays a disproportionally small role in military affairs, in relation to its size and economic potential. This does not mean that Italian governments were always immune to 'me-too-ism', or that their analysis of American reliability, or of the Russian threat was fundamentally different from that of other European allies. Italy, like the FRG, was deeply divided politically between the Christian Democrats and an assortment of Leftist parties, which long focused their opposition to the Right on the issue of nuclear weapons. Nevertheless, as in other Catholic countries, interest in the moral dimension of nuclear weapons was much smaller in Italy than in Germany, for example.

Where it comes to relations with America, many Italians, not unlike Germans, see these as an anchor that will protect their country from any political drift into radicalism or adventurism, as a healthy counter-balance to the inner problems of their country. They welcome nuclear weapons as an additional bond between the US and Italy, forcing the US to pay attention to Italy, as America's most loyal ally in the Mediterranean.[28] It is important for Italy's attitude to nuclear weapons that they are not valued as symbols of statehood, just as the state as such plays a much smaller role in Italy, and commands much less loyalty, than in most other European countries. All the mystique which nuclear weapons give to the French state and president would thus be lost on Italians, whose cultural loyalties are more regional and local.

Like Italy, Norway and Sweden had advanced nuclear research programmes on the eve of World War II. Both countries decided, however, not to pursue further research into nuclear weapons options. In Sweden, the decision-making process was, typically for Swedish culture, a slow and tacit one – it seems difficult to point to any one occasion when the decision was actively made to abandon the option of developing nuclear defences. They militarily might have made more sense in Sweden, as in the Italian Alps, than in most other parts of Europe. Nevertheless, in an unspoken consensus, Sweden backed away from nuclear weapons in the early 1960s, while developing secret contacts with the US that created the option of abandoning Swedish neutrality and enlisting US military support – and nuclear weapons – virtually overnight.[29]

In Sweden as elsewhere in the Protestant cultures of Europe, a strong puritan strand saw nuclear weapons as particularly immoral, which reinforced the government's reluctance to pursue an active nuclear option any further. Like Norway and Denmark, Sweden thus constitutes a 'nuclear-free zone', but unlike Norway and Denmark, Sweden's long-standing historical commitment to neutrality – after an equally long period of aggressive expansionism – created a taboo even with regard to any formal and open association with the US as a nuclear ally. While Norway and Denmark thus became allies of the nuclear power USA in NATO, Sweden's defence connections with the US were kept secret even from the Swedish population.[30]

A nuclear taboo can also be found outside Europe, in Japan. The Japanese, seeing themselves as standing in the tradition of the victims of Hiroshima and Nagasaki, have a strong nuclear allergy. Their alliance relationship with the USA is more difficult than that of the Europeans, as they tend to feel quite alone in a heavily unbalanced relationship, while the Europeans can complain to each other about their rather imposing big sister America. Their dependence on the atomic shield provided by the very power which used atomic weapons against them must be a very difficult one to handle psychically. It may account for much of the suppressed contradictions in the Japanese attitude to their own World War II past.[31]

A different case is that of Israel, where we encounter very distinctive beliefs, which form the basis on which Israel is founded, particularly where defence is concerned. The firm pledge never again to allow Jews to become passive victims of murderous persecution, especially in the hostile environment of the Middle East, has given an edge and a desperation to Israel's defence culture which is well captured by the mystique of Masada. Most Israeli conscripts are sworn in on this dramatic site on which in the first century AD, a whole community committed suicide rather than surrender to the Romans who were besieging this rock fortress in the desert. Masada is the symbol of Israel's nuclear posture, one designed to insure that Israel cannot possibly be conquered and victimised by any other power. In that Israelis would not again intend to sacrifice themselves without inflicting equal doom on their enemies, Israel's posture has also been likened to a 'Samson option', a commitment, *in extremis*, to bring down the enemy, even if it means one's own destruction.[32] It is difficult to think of a nation that is more committed to its defence, or that has a more credible deterrence posture. One can speculate as to how far contemporary Germans, Frenchmen or Italians would ever be prepared to go, if a conflict arose which threatened them directly, and NATO's nuclear deterrence was brought into play. In the case of Israel, there is less doubt that the peacetime defence posture would translate into an equally serious wartime attitude to the use of nuclear weapons.

These are just a few examples in which we can show the diversity of beliefs held in different cultures, and the importance of such beliefs in shaping attitudes towards nuclear weapons. This is not to deny factors such as geographic situation, economic resources, technological capabilities and a host of other factors that matter in the decisions of governments of the countries discussed either to opt for the acquisition of nuclear weapons, or not to pursue such an option. The very specific beliefs of these countries, which have their roots in historical experiences and cultural traditions, emerge quite clearly.

It is not unimportant in this context to ask how widely the repugnance of WMD and of killing civilians in massive numbers[33] is shared outside the 'Western' Liberal super–culture (which on this point includes Australia and New Zealand as much as Japan). The impact on most European, North American and some Commonwealth countries of particularly traumatic conflicts, including the American Civil War, the two World Wars, and for the United States, the Vietnam War, are unparalleled, it seems, in the collective psyche of some other cultures. While the Soviets and Yugoslavs, to give just two examples, had also experienced extremely high-casualty conflicts within the last half-century, they reacted to it quite differently from the Western Liberal culture.

Despite the trauma of the Great Patriotic War, until the decline and fall of the Soviet Union, Soviet military doctrine prepared for even higher casualties in an all-out nuclear war, so that Socialism might survive (even among a very much reduced population).[34]

The extremely high casualty figures of World War II in Yugoslavia – surpassed only by casualty figures in the USSR, and largely inflicted on Yugoslavs by Yugoslavs – might have given way, as in Europe at the end of the Thirty Years War, to a determination to live and let live, based on mutual tolerance. Indeed, during the decades of Tito's rule, the experiment seemed to promise success, but the bloody explosion of Yugoslavia in the 1990s, with the deliberate genocidal massacres of civilians which accompanied it, went precisely the opposite way.

One cannot, therefore, extrapolate that the experience of a war with particularly high casualties leads *any* culture to react in the medium- to long-term with abhorrence of high casualties. Additional cultural factors were apparently necessary to produce the reactions of the Western Liberal culture, and we can almost take for granted that its views on mass civilian casualties are not universally shared, with the obvious implications that has for the future use or abstention from use, of nuclear weapons.

BELIEFS INSIDE AND OUTSIDE OF WAR

I have argued that the beliefs of any particular culture are useful indicators of attitudes to war, and to the acquisition and use of nuclear weapons, but, as I have pointed out at the beginning, these cultural indicators also have their limits. Few states contain just one culture, and just one homogeneous population with shared values, traditions, and attitudes to life, death, and the use of force. Even countries with a strong consensus on its nuclear policy such as France or (with an opposite orientation) Sweden have dissenting minorities.

It is thus not possible to exclude the possibility that regimes will come to power within nuclear-weapons owning states whose attitudes to WMD will differ from those of the regimes which first procured them (e.g. the main procurement motivation may have been more for deterrence or status reasons, the new regime might consider their actual use in a concrete military situation). This is particularly easy to imagine in states where two or more significantly different cultures exist side by side, for example one close to that of the Western Liberal culture, one extremely focused on nationalism (and a wish to avenge centuries of colonial oppression by acquiring attributes of 'great power status'), and one extremely focused on religion, to the point of basing arguments on the assumption of an afterlife, which can compensate for any human sacrifice in this life. Pakistan can serve as an example of such a mix of cultures.

A second limitation of our prediction arises from the structural secrecy of government apparatuses, even within the Western Liberal culture. The revelations about Sweden's secret operational alignment with the US are so shocking, not because of any criminal or dangerous content, but because they show that an otherwise well functioning democratic state can develop secret policies which are totally concealed from its citizens, and about which it can systematically lie to them. The secrecy with which British and French governments decided to procure nuclear weapons should also be mentioned in this context.

Another factor that has to be considered here is the importance of the existence of a distinct culture within the military of a state, particularly if the distinctness concerns attitudes towards inflicting and incurring mass casualties. I have shown elsewhere that the 'strategic' city bombing of World War II had explicit pre-war advocates not only in the persons of National Socialists and Fascists like Ludendorff and the Italian Giulio Douhet, but also in the person of A. I. Egorov, Chief of the Red Army Staff, and, perhaps most significantly in the person of Sir Hugh Trenchard, revered to this day as the founder of the British Royal Air Force (not to mention Sir Arthur Harris, whose controversial practices are more widely known). The flip-side of this coin is that in the interwar years, we can identify opponents of area bombardment in the air forces of the US (where we might expect it), but also in the British Royal Air Force and, surprisingly, in the German *Luftwaffe*.[35] While a variety of reasons and rationalisations of the respective stances can be put forward,[36] the fact remains that proponents of both views were aware of the ethical (or, to be more precise, legal) problems posed by area bombardment, and that proponents of both views (or adherents of both cultures) could be found *within* the air forces. It is thus not enough to say that the respective militaries (or here: air forces) were a culture within a culture:[37] the cultural split went right through the institutions, and yet transcended national frontiers.

Applied to the nuclear age, this is of extreme importance, as within the Western Liberal culture, there were proponents of nuclear war (and indeed of nuclear pre-emption) even within the executive, within the highest ranks of the very forces that would have carried out such a strategy. The supreme example is US General Curtis E. LeMay, whose enthusiasm for attacking the Soviet Union with nuclear weapons before the latter was strong enough to retaliate in kind had to be stamped on by the US President.[38] It is true that all Western nuclear powers (and, from what we know, the Soviet Union and the People's Republic of China) have gradually ensured maximum political control over nuclear weapons, so that these cannot be released, today, without an explicit order from the supreme political leader. Yet control was less effective when these respective nuclear forces were in their infancy, and unauthorised use of nuclear weapons would have been a real possibility.

Finally, in a prolonged war, an abandonment of any moral restraints can take place. This was most notably the case in World War II. Upon starting the war against Poland, the German Air Force set aside its earlier, quite ethical doctrine on the use of the air forces, and bombed Warsaw without provocation and with the explicit intention of instilling terror, which had been ruled out by its doctrine of 1935. The Royal Air Force experimented with a whole series of different target sets, only to find that technological constraints as much as preferences such as Trenchard's and Harris's pushed it towards area bombing even in 1941. The US Army Air Forces clung to the targeting of specific industries or transport nodes for longest, but by early 1945, the effects of its bombing raids on the civilian populations were much the same as those of British air raids. Thus the air power strategies even of the Western Liberal cultures degenerated in the course of the war, in so far as they ever had been a reflection of their humanitarian values (which could be said categorically only about US strategy). The culmination of this degeneration was the bombing of Tokyo, Dresden, Hiroshima and Nagasaki.[39]

Beliefs or principles developed and held outside of an actual ongoing war thus cannot be seen as ultimate indicators of how a government with nuclear weapons at its disposal would act if driven to desperation *in* war. What can, however, be said to some extent is that Britain, and more clearly still, France acquired nuclear weapons in the belief that these would prevent all major war. Thus the issue of whether nuclear weapons had be used would not arise, and in those two cases, the proliferation of nuclear weapons was hardly an inherent threat to any other power, nuclear or non-nuclear.

Even the colossal war machine of the US only came down on the side of nuclear use after America had been attacked by Japan (nuclear use would have been contemplated also against Germany which had declared war on the US, had Germany's surrender not preceded the production of the world's first atomic bomb). The subsequent debates within America about the problems of nuclear use indicate that a US government would hesitate to use nuclear weapons once more. Although the Western nuclear powers in and of themselves pose no nuclear threat to any other state, the very fact that they own nuclear weapons, and have the mechanism to use them, makes their behaviour unpredictable in a war in which their leaders of the day might feel driven to take a desperate measure. This factor of unpredictability was arguably particularly great during the first decade or two during which they owned nuclear weapons and were still thinking through the implications. This same unpredictability clearly also applies to any new nuclear powers, and is a destabilising factor in and of itself, whatever the beliefs underpinning the prevailing culture.

CONCLUSIONS

I am not a specialist on the beliefs and culture of India, Pakistan, or of other states that are working to acquire nuclear weapons and their means of delivery. But the above reflections on the causes of proliferation in other countries indicate the sort of questions that should be on the research agendas of specialists who can study and evaluate the decisions taken in these countries. Do the leaders who wish to acquire nuclear weapons wish to do so for mere deterrence purposes? How generally held is the belief in the cultures concerned that actual use of such weapons, particularly in ways that would result in very many deaths among non-combatants, is repulsive in principle? How credible is deterrence in their countries, that is how close to credible implementation is the threat contained in deterrence, and thus how open to accidents, or to a breakdown of deterrence resulting in catastrophic use of nuclear weapons?[40]

Even if the leaders who decided to build nuclear weapons have done so with the wish to create deterrent relationships with potential adversaries, how stable is the political structure of their state? How unlikely or likely is it that they will be replaced by religious fanatics – not madmen, but people whose confidence in their religion and its teaching about an afterlife determines their attitude towards sacrificing lives in this world – or risk-prone leaders like Saddam Hussein who used missiles against Tel Aviv?

While studies of regional power relationships, economic needs, long-standing territorial disputes and competition for national resources are certainly factors that will give valuable clues as to the likelihood and implications of further proliferation, they are unlikely to be sufficient on their own. As inter-state conflicts seem to be occurring slightly less frequently while intra-state conflicts continue unabated, classic '*international* relations theory', particularly the sort focusing on the 'state system', seem less and less adequate as analytical framework.[41] Nor can the importance of WMD in intra-state conflicts be denied: chemical weapons have been used by Iraq against its Kurdish minority, and it has been used, admittedly by an intervening outside power, the US, in the internal wars of Greece and Vietnam. It is still not wholly clear how the previous South African governments intended to use their nuclear weapons. And the sect which successfully used chemical agents to kill people in the Tokyo underground transport system in 1995 had previously tried to use biological weapons in the same context. Many other scenarios, from terrorist use, to intra-state forms of nuclear deterrence or even use, can be imagined.[42]

A study of the beliefs specific to cultures that may be considering the acquisition of nuclear weapons is thus greatly to be recommended, if we hope to be able to assess the implications and consequences of such policies.[43] Indeed, by studying these, we may even be able to find policy-relevant ways in which these tendencies can be contained, and culturally-conditioned quests for additional security or status etc. can be satisfied in other ways.

If the procurement of nuclear weapons is to a large extent being contemplated by a regime for status reasons or as a political bargaining chip (as which they have been used, particularly, by North Korea), then alternative ways of satisfying this regime's quest for status or leverage, and proliferation might yet be stopped or reversed.

If the intention is to have an enhanced war-making capability, one might well find that the quest for a nuclear option goes along with attempts to develop other WMD or even 'conventional' weapons systems like Saddam Hussein's project of a super-cannon. In the latter case, other governments would be mistaken to give attention only to the possibility of nuclear proliferation, and should be as wary of the development of other weapons.

If nuclear proliferation could occur primarily as the function of the perception of a threat to one's vital security that cannot be met in any other way, then the only answer is a reliable commitment by the powers that have chosen to play the role of world policemen to the defence of the state feeling threatened in this way. They must engage in the delicate balancing act of preventing that state from taking advantage of this protection to resort to aggressive or otherwise provocative action *vis-à-vis* its antagonist(s). In such a context, nuclear proliferation might again be reversible. While these propositions may sound like a statement of the obvious, they are neglected by any reflection of how to prevent nuclear proliferation, and thus ultimately, nuclear use, that does not start with the assumption that the particularities of any case, the beliefs and the cultural varieties, must be examined to the full. There is no one common answer to all potential cases of such proliferation.

NOTES

Helpful comments on this study by Eric Herring and Yannis Stivachtis are gratefully acknowledged.

1. Arthur Koestler, *Janus: A Summing Up* (London: Hutchinson 1978) p.15.
2. R. Jeffrey Smith, 'Clinton Directive Changes Strategy on Nuclear Arms', *Washington Post* (7 Dec. 1997). The negative security assurances were conditional upon other factors, but threatening to retaliate with nuclear weapons against biological weapons use would constitute a clear departure from the US engagement, as indeed it would for the engagements of Britain and France.
3. For a figure for Dresden, see *Der grosse Ploetz: Auszug aus der Geschichte von den Anfängen bis zur Gegenwart*, 31st edn. (Würzburg: Verlag Ploetz 1991) pp.876–916; for figures for Tokyo, Hiroshima and Nagasaki, see Laura Hein and Mark Selden, 'Commemoration and Silence', in idem (eds.), *Living with the Bomb: American and Japanese Cultural Conflicts in the Nuclear Age* (NY: East Gate Books/M.E. Sharpe 1997) p.4.
4. The South African case shows that nuclear proliferation is not an irreversible process, as does the abandonment of chemical weapons by several states who owned stocks at some point.
5. Ken Booth means similar things when he writes about 'strategic culture', but his point of departure is a 'nation', the 'traditions, values, attitudes, patterns of behaviour, habits, symbols, achievements' of which influence the way it will threat or use force, see Ken Booth, 'The Concept of Strategic Culture Affirmed', in Carl G. Jacobsen (ed.) *Strategic Power: USA/USSR* (London: Macmillan 1990) p.121.
6. Kenneth Waltz, *Man, the State and War* (NY: Columbia UP 1959).
7. Karl Deutsch and Dieter Senghaas, 'A framework for a theory of war and peace' in A. Lepawsky (ed.) *The Search for World Order* (NY: Appleton-Century Crofts 1971).
8. *Hitler's Secret Book*, trans. Salvator Attanasio (NY: Crove Press 1961) p.14f.
9. Erich Ludendorff, *Der Totale Krieg* (Munich: Ludendorffs Verlag GmbH 1935).

10. This was first developed in the seminal book by Robert J.C. Butow, *Japan's Decision to Surrender* (Stanford UP 1954).
11. Morale Division, *The United States Strategic Bombing Survey: The Effects of Strategic Bombing on Japanese Morale* (Washington DC: 1947) contains significant statistics on Japanese motivations for supporting the war effort.
12. Carl von Clausewitz, *On War*, Book VIII Chapter 3.B – my translation from the 19th ed. by Werner Hahlweg (Bonn: Dümmler 1980) p.962.
13. Vladimir Iljich Lenin, 'War and Revolution', in *On War, Army and Science of War* (Moscow: Prospekt 1957) p.100.
14. For British, French and FRG official nuclear strategy, perceptions of the Soviet threat and of US reliability, see Beatrice Heuser, *NATO, Britain, France and the FRG: Nuclear Strategies and Forces for Europe, 1949–2000* (London: Macmillan 1997). For the underlying beliefs in these three countries, see Beatrice Heuser, *Nuclear Mentalities? Strategies and Beliefs in Britain, France and the FRG* (London: Macmillan 1998).
15. Sir Michael Quinlan, 'Defence planning in a changing world', *The World Today* (July 1992) p.3.
16. See Heuser, *Nuclear Mentalities?* (note 14) Ch.2.
17. Malcolm Chalmers, '"Bombs Away"? Britain and Nuclear Weapons under New Labour', forthcoming in *Security Dialogue*.
18. For US concessions since the 1950s, see Marc Trachtenberg, 'La formation du système de défense occidental', in Maurice Vaïsse, Pierre Mélandri and Frédéric Bozo (eds.) *La France et l'OTAN, 1949–1996* (Brussels: Complexe 1996) pp.115–28, and Paul Buteux, *The Politics of Nuclear Consultation in NATO, 1964–1980* (Cambridge: CUP 1983).
19. This was only reduced to a double dyad in the mid-1990s, when France's short- and medium-range nuclear missiles were scrapped.
20. Prime Minister Pompidou during the debate in the Assemblée Nationale, quoted in *Le Monde*, 3 Dec. 1964.
21. *arme de non-emploi*.
22. Cyril Buffet, 'De Gaulle and the Second Berlin Crisis, or how to use a political weapon', in idem and Leopoldo Nuti (eds.) *Dividing the Atom*, Special issue of *Storia delle Relazioni Internazionali* (Autumn 1998).
23. See Beatrice Heuser, 'Dunkirk, Dien Bien Phu and Suez, or why France does not trust allies and has learnt to love the Bomb', in Cyril Buffet and Beatrice Heuser (eds.) *Haunted by History: Myths in International Relations* (Oxford: Berghahn 1998).
24. See Heuser, *Nuclear Mentalities?* (note 14) Ch.3.
25. Michael Stürmer, 'Deutsches Interesse ist es, niemals allein zu stehen', *Frankfurter Allgemeine Zeitung*, 11 July 1988.
26. See Heuser, *Nuclear Mentalities?* (note 14) Ch.4.
27. For such a classic case of total disregard of any beliefs and cultural proclivities, and of speculation deduced from absurdly inapplicable political science theories, see John J. Mearsheimer: 'Back to the future: Instability in Europe after the Cold War', *International Security* 15/1 (Summer 1990) pp.5–56.
28. Leopoldo Nuti, '"Me too please": Italy and the Politics of Nuclear Weapons, 1945–1975', *Diplomacy and Statecraft* 4/1 (March 1993) pp.114–48.
29. Tor Larsson, 'The Swedish Nuclear and Non-Nuclear Postures', in Buffet and Nuti, *Dividing the Atom* (note 22); Wilhelm Agrell: *Alliansfrihet och atombomber: kontinuitet och förändring i den svenska försvarsdoktrinen, 1945–1982* (Stockholm: Liber 1985); *Had there been a war... Preparations for the reception of military assistance 1949–1969* (Report by the Commission on Neutrality Policy, Stockholm, 1994, SOU 1994:11).
30. Ingemar Dörfer, 'La Skandinavie ou la défense de la virginité nucléaire', in Pierre Lellouche (ed.) *Pacifism et Dissuasion* (Paris: IFRI 1993); Ann-Sofie Dahl, 'The Myth of Swedish Neutrality', in Buffet and Heuser, *Haunted by History* (note 23).
31. Ian Buruma, *The Wages of Guilt: Memories of War in Germany and Japan* (NY: Meridian 1994).
32. As Lawrence Freedman first called it. See also Seymour Hersh: *The Samson Option: Israel, America and the Bomb*, 2nd rev. ed. (London: Faber 1993).

33. On the gradual development of this rejection among Western cultures, see Beatrice Heuser, *The Bomb: Nuclear Weapons in their Historical, Strategic and Ethical Context* (London: Longman's, forthcoming 1999) Ch.4.

34. Cf. Beatrice Heuser, 'Warsaw Pact Military Doctrines in the 70s and 80s: Findings in the East German Archives', *Comparative Strategy* 12/4 (Oct.–Dec. 1993) pp.437–57.

35. Heuser, *The Bomb* (note 33) Ch.2.

36. Reasons for this can be constructed around vested institutional interest not only for separate sections of the air force, but also for other sections of the armed forces, such as the navy, see e.g. Fred Kaplan, *The Wizards of Armageddon* (NY: Simon & Schuster 1983) p.235 on the fluctuations of US Navy support for city-targeting with nuclear weapons as functions of whether or not the US Navy had such weapons at its disposal.

37. The armed forces of the Weimar Republic, which did not support the values of that Republic, have been called 'a state within a state', see Francil L. Carstens, *The Reichswehr in Politics*, (Oxford: Clarendon Press 1966).

38. Kaplan, *Wizards* (note 36) p.134.

39. Tami Davis Biddle, 'British and American Approaches to Strategic Bombing: Their Origins and Implementation in the World War II Combined Bomber Offensive', *Journal of Strategic Studies* 18/1 (March 1995) pp.91–144; W. Hays Parks: '"Precision" and "Area" Bombing: Who did Which, and When?' ibid. pp.145–74.

40. It is worth remembering in this context that in the view of many experts from Thomas Schelling to Michael MccGwire, it was only incredibly good luck which prevented the East-West nuclear deterrence relationship from blowing up into nuclear catastrophe on several occasions. See Thomas Schelling, 'Nuclear Deterrence: The Case of Many Near-Catastrophes?', Dept. of War Studies Annual Lecture, 1994, unpublished MS; Michael MccGwire, 'Nuclear Weapons Revisited: Is there a future for nuclear weapons?', *International Affairs* 70/2 (April 1994) pp.211–28. Milton Leitenberg, however, argues that mutual restraint led to the suppression of a very large number of small crises, each of which could have triggered nuclear responses, 'Nuclear Weapons and 50 Years of International Political History: Risks, dangers, threats, crises, proposals and consideration of use', unpublished MS (1997).

41. Martin van Creveld, *On Future War* (London: Brassey's 1991).

42. For example, there has been much speculation and few convincing conclusions about South African planning for the use of the nuclear arsenal acquired there.

43. For an excellent collection of articles, which follow precisely this route, see Nuti and Cyril Buffet, *Dividing the Atom* (note 22).

6

The International System and the Use of Weapons of Mass Destruction

YANNIS A. STIVACHTIS

The proliferation of Weapons of Mass Destruction (WMD) – nuclear, chemical, and biological – and the means for their delivery at longer ranges has emerged as a leading issue in the post-Cold War debate about international security.[1] The greatest concern, however, is related to their use.

The purpose of this study is to examine whether there is any relationship between the various features of international system on the one hand, and the use of WMD, on the other. In so doing, it will compare the bipolar Cold War international system with the multipolar post-Cold War one. It aims at answering questions such as do structural differences between the two systems imply the creation or disappearance of opportunities and constraints that encourage or discourage the choice of the decisions makers to use WMD, or does this choice remain unaffected by changes in the structure of international system? Is it necessarily the existence of structural differences between the two systems that determines whether and to what extent WMD would be used, or there are other factors that could also influence the choices of the decision makers?

THE INTERNATIONAL SYSTEM

Examining the international system, one should focus on three issues: first, the structure of the system; second, the processes that take place within it; and third, the rules and norms that seek to regulate the actors' behaviour in the system. The structure of international system tells one first, how the component units (states) of the system are related to each other (hierarchy versus anarchy); and second, how power is distributed within the system (polarity).[2] The processes tell one how the units interact with one another.

The rules and norms function as guidance devises for states.³ Structure, processes, and norms and rules define the overall character of the system. The following subsections are designed to show whether, and if yes, how these systemic features are related to the use of WMD.

International Anarchy

International anarchy implies the absence of any superior authority above the states. Thus, both the Cold War and post-Cold War international systems have been anarchical in nature. This implies that if there is any relationship between the anarchic structure of the system and the use of WMD, then, this relationship remains unaffected by the passage from the Cold War system to the post-Cold War one. This also means that the conditions under which WMD are produced, acquired and might be used are common to both systems. But what are these conditions?

International anarchy imposes competitive, self-help conditions of existence on the states within the system. Under anarchy, states need to look after themselves to ensure their survival and welfare. However, in seeking power and security for themselves, states can easily threaten the power and security of other states. Thus military measures undertaken by one state, even if they are defensive in character, may be seen as offensive by other states. This security problematique under anarchy is known as the power-security dilemma.⁴

The security problem becomes more complicated when states have different foreign policy objectives. Although survival is a common goal to all states, beyond that, not all of them have the same foreign policy goals. Some of them prefer to maintain the *status quo* while others wish to alter it to their favour. Since armaments are needed to maintain as well as alter the *status quo*, states are not sure about the incentives of their neighbours. As a means to deter their opponents, redress military imbalances, and achieve their foreign policy objectives, some states have sought to acquire WMD thereby creating the WMD proliferation problem.

PROLIFERATION OF WEAPONS OF MASS DESTRUCTION:
SYSTEMIC MOTIVES

Although both the Cold War and post-Cold War international systems are anarchical in nature, there are quantitative differences in the proliferation trends and qualitative differences in the motives that lie behind the acquisition of WMD. The issue of proliferation is not the same with that of the use of WMD. However, it has been argued that the two issues are interrelated and that the proliferation of WMD in conjunction with the absence of mechanisms for crisis avoidance and crisis management as well as the domestic instability facing the possessor states increase the chances of their use.[5] The purpose of this section is not to discuss the logic of these systemic motives but simply to state them.[6] They may vary according to the status of the international actors (great and lesser powers) or may be similar.

The first of these motives is that WMD may give a decisive advantage to their user. The atom bombs used by the United States against Japan, for instance, led to the surrender of the latter, while the possible acquisition and use of nuclear bomb by Germany could have given a decisive advantage to Hitler's forces. This motive is common to both systems under discussion. The difference is that since more states acquire WMD, the possibility that they might use them whenever they wish to achieve a decisive advantage increases.

Although there has been always a fear that great powers might use WMD against each other, this is not very likely for three reasons. First, great powers possess safety mechanisms and procedures designed to prevent accidental use of WMD as well as crisis management mechanisms that reduce the possibility of accidental wars with WMD. Second, some great powers possess second strike capability that serves as a means of mutual deterrence. Third, power disparities between the great powers themselves prevent the weaker of them from hurting the more powerful ones, while the latter are conscious that any effort to dominate the system would most certainly attract the combined reaction of the other great powers.

The real concern is whether lesser powers would use WMD against other lesser powers accidentally or intentionally. Lesser powers have neither established procedures dealing with crisis situations nor mechanisms to prevent accidental use of WMD or accidental wars with WMD. More importantly, they do not have second strike capability; a fact that would provide the first user of WMD with a strategic advantage in a case of war.

About the use of WMD in a conflict situation between a great and a lesser power, two things can be said. First, it is very unlikely for a great power to use WMD against a lesser power because it possesses enough conventional power to achieve its ends. Second, because lesser powers do not possess second strike capability, it is highly unlikely that they would use nuclear weapons against great powers. Nevertheless, due to differences in the mode of combat between nuclear weapons, on the one hand, and chemical and biological weapons on the other, it is very likely that lesser powers might use chemical and biological weapons against great powers if and whenever they consider it necessary. However, they need to think whether such a use would be outweighed by the costs associated with the response of the great power that would be hurt as well as the reaction of international community as a whole.

A second motive, common to Cold War and post-Cold War systems, is that possession of WMD by great powers is seen as providing a low-key element of insurance in support of world order. The contribution of the great powers to international order derives from the inequality of power between the states that make up the international system. This implies that usually great powers are all in the front rank in terms of military strength.[7] The main objective of great powers is the preservation of a general balance of power throughout the international system and as a means to prevent the system from being transformed by conquest into a universal empire.

Great powers also seek to preserve regional balances of power in order to protect the independence of states in particular areas from domination by a locally preponderant power. Both general and regional balances provide the conditions in which other institutions, on which international order depends, are able to operate.[8]

In this context, war serves both as an instrument of policy and as a determinant of the structure of international system. It is war, or the threat of war, which determines whether there is a balance of power or a particular state becomes predominant. Therefore, adequate military power is needed to prevent any state dominating the international system.[9] WMD are thus viewed as non-conventional means aimed at preserving both regional and global balance of power. For example, it has been suggested that if there were only one nuclear superpower, it would be possible to impose its rule over the other states.[10] However, possession of nuclear weapons by other powers and the possibility of their use in case of war seek to prevent any state from attempting to transform the international system to an empire. Relevant to this argument is the idea that WMD, and especially nuclear weapons, are needed to prevent a state from the temptation to make a clandestine dash to sole nuclear possession, or, in other words, to close off nuclear adventurism.[11]

Third, WMD are considered as necessary for redressing imbalances in military capabilities. This is another element common to both systems. For example, during the Cold War, the US policy of extended deterrence aimed at reducing European insecurity stemming from the fact that the Soviet Union had conventional superiority on the continent. Currently, the superiority of India in conventional weapon systems has convinced Pakistan to see the nuclear option as a means to balance the power of its neighbour.

The difference between the two systems is that today, more than in the past, WMD are increasingly seen by certain regional powers as a political-military quick way to overcome the Western powers' significant qualitative advantages in conventional military forces. As American officials have recognised, WMD 'may directly threaten US forces in the field and threaten the effective force employment by requiring dispersal of those forces. Potential Adversaries may use WMD to deter US power projection abroad'.[12] This is a qualitative difference in the sense that during the Cold War the main conflict was between two ideologically opposed camps, while today certain states tend to see a conflict between the 'West and the rest'.

Fourth, it has been claimed that WMD can be used as a means of deterrence either by denial or by retaliation. Deterrence by denial means that a state will not initiate an attack because the use of WMD against its forces and territory will raise the costs and minimise the benefits of this attack. Deterrence by retaliation means that, despite the high cost, the opponent decides to attack with WMD but the defender is able to strike back. The motive for acquiring WMD for deterrence purposes is common to both systems. There is only a quantitative difference: the number of states possessing WMD has significantly increased since the 1980s.

Fifth, unlike during the Cold War, today many Third World states see WMD as a means of achieving their strategic objectives on the cheap, especially when compared to the costs of conventional forces that might be able to achieve comparable results. As American military officials have claimed, 'rogue regimes may try to use these devastating weapons as a relatively inexpensive way to sidestep the US military's overwhelming conventional military superiority'.[13] However, a similar strategic judgement was made during the Cold War by all major nuclear powers in their acquisition of nuclear weapons. The difference between the two systems is both quantitative and qualitative. It is quantitative because more states are prepared to achieve their strategic objectives on the cheap; and it is qualitative because these states are not among the traditional powers.

Sixth, it has been argued that many regional powers see the intimidating psychological effects of even small quantities of WMD and are prepared to go further. This thinking was summarised by the former Indian Army Chief of Staff who said, 'the next conflict with the United States would involve weapons of mass destruction'.[14] In this context, nuclear weapons in the hands of Western states are seen as a means for deterring the use of WMD by other states. Once again, the difference between the Cold War and post-Cold War international systems is qualitative. While during the Cold War the main conflict was between the Soviet Union and the US and it was ideological in nature, today this conflict has been substituted by a cultural one: that of between the 'West and the rest'.

Seventh, the acquisition of WMD has been seen by certain states as a means to maintain or strengthen their power status and national prestige both at regional and international levels and as a leading vehicle for assertiveness and attention in the post-Cold War world.[15] An illustration of this is the celebrations in India following its May 1998 nuclear tests and the demand of that country to be included in the club of nuclear powers, as well as to obtain a permanent seat at the UN Security Council. Another example is provided by an Algerian analyst who has stated that 'in ten years time there will be two countries in Africa which are taken seriously by the United States – South Africa and Algeria – both will be nuclear powers'.[16] This statement was not meant as a reference to nuclear weapons. It was rather intended to highlight the significance of civilian nuclear power programmes for international prestige and the capacity of states in peripheral locations to be taken seriously by the West. In this context, civilian nuclear power and dual-use chemical and aerospace projects provide ample opportunities for some states to build international prestige.

Eighth, many analysts believe that WMD may give opportunities to certain states to alter the regional *status quo* to their favour and become regional hegemons. As it has been argued, 'for rogue nations these weapons are a ticket to power, stature, and confidence in regional war'.[17] The difference between the Cold War and post-Cold War systems is not that there were not tendencies for regional hegemonies before, but that states are now prepared to acquire WMD as a means to this end. WMD can give certain regional powers qualitatively superior military and political options for intimidation, especially if combined with standoff delivery systems.[18] Thus states with even small quantities of WMD and limited numbers of delivery systems may be able to exert a high degree of strategic leverage against other states by threatening to attack their vulnerable civilian populations.

Ninth, some analysts see the acquisition of WMD as the result of regional powers search for strategic weight after the end of the Cold War. For example, countries like Iraq, Syria and Libya saw their relationship with the Soviet Union weaken and finally dissolve. They were, therefore, forced to rely on indigenous political and military power and to search for new sources of geo-strategic weight.

Tenth, unlike during the Cold War, today, the pursuing of WMD capabilities provide a basis for diplomatic blackmail. The best illustration of this is the attitude of North Korea that relates its nuclear programme to the increase of Western aid to meet its economic problems, but diplomatic blackmail is used even in cases where the potential possessors have extensive ties with the West. The primacy of proliferation concerns provides considerable scope to signal, implicitly or explicitly, that Western states should pay more attention to regional security issues and development requirements.

Eleventh, another difference between the Cold War and the post-Cold War systems is that today transfers of WMD and their associated technologies, including co-operative development programmes, serve to cement strategic alliances across or within regions and contribute to the general level of Third World development.[19] This possibility is highlighted by the growing ties between leading proliferators in the Muslim world (Syria, Iran, Algeria and Libya) and suppliers of nuclear and ballistic missile technology in East Asia.[20]

The character of the post-Cold War international system provides powerful long-term motives for acquiring WMD but regional motives will continue to be leading factors in the proliferation dynamic, often reinforcing or outweighing systemic motives. Those flowing from regional security concerns vary considerably from state to state, but at least three generalisations can be made.[21]

First, some states that face serious internal and external challenges are highly insecure and, in some instances, highly militarised societies. Under these conditions, the acquisition of WMD offers special advantages. Yet, there are states that find themselves in a highly militarised environment, such as that of the Middle East, with significant interstate challenges. In this case, WMD capabilities are clearly linked to military imbalances and strategic competition.

Second, the internal environment of some states also contributes to proliferation dynamics. The obsession with security, both internal and external, gives the military and associated industrial establishments considerable weight. State-directed development and purchasing programmes for military technology, nuclear research, and dual-use chemical facilities offer high prestige vehicles for individual and bureaucratic activity.[22]

Finally, many politicians and analysts have focused on the issue of terrorism.[23] For instance, the former United Kingdom Secretary of State for Defence Malcolm Rifkind has stated that 'the increasing threat from WMD is introducing an entirely new dimension into the world, and is relevant not only to threats from states but as a potential threat from terrorist organisations'.[24] Although the seriousness of WMD terrorism is disputed,[25] it is possible that a terrorist group would try to purchase WMD, as the Japanese Aun Shiinrikyo cult apparently tried to do in Russia, or build a device on its own. A small device could be used by terrorist groups for achieving political objectives, or for obtaining economic benefits through blackmail. Indeed, the March 1995 terrorist attack on the Tokyo subway, that left 12 civilians dead and a significant number of people injured, demonstrated the vulnerability of urban populations to attacks by WMD. Although this attack did not achieve its objectives, it manifested the relative ease with which subnational groups can acquire and use WMD without being detected.

Although the power-security dilemma operates similarly in the Cold War and post-Cold War international systems, the risks associated with the use of WMD are higher in the post-Cold War system. The reason is that the proliferation of WMD together with the absence of crisis avoidance and crisis management mechanisms and the domestic instability facing the possessors of WMD increase the chances that they might be used. The following section will discuss the conditions under which the use of WMD might take place in such a system.

THE USE OF WEAPONS OF MASS DESTRUCTION

Historical experience has shown that the employment of WMD is possible. Nuclear weapons, for instance, were used at the end of World War II. The employment of chemical weapons is dated back to the pre-World War I era, while in the 1980s, chemical agents were used at least in two occasions: first, during the Iran–Iraq War; and second, by the Iraqi government against Iraqi citizens of Kurdish origin.

The use of WMD may occur through purposeful choice, through miscalculations, or through a variety of accidents. It may be decided by a political leader, by a military commander, or by a group of terrorists. It could come as a sudden surprise in a time of peace or as the seemingly inevitable culmination of a prolonged conflict between states that at least one of them is armed with such weapons.[26] It could be invited by systemic or domestic conditions. This section focuses on two types of WMD warfare: deliberate use and accidental use.

Deliberate Use

Deliberate use of WMD involves the intentional and informed decision and action of the national command authority, that could take the form of a surprise attack, pre-emption in anticipation of an attack by an actual or potential enemy, or escalation of conventional wars to wars involving WMD. The most interesting type of deliberate use is the inadvertent war.

There is not a precise definition of inadvertent war. Actually, there is a question whether there is any meaningful distinction between accidental and inadvertent war. What the two terms have in common is that neither is premeditated war as exemplified by the classical preventive war. The latter is associated with the hypothetical possibility that one state might plan and initiate an unprovoked war, most likely under peacetime conditions in order to achieve surprise, so as to destroy its opponent's war-making potential and to eliminate or significantly reduce its ability to compete in the international arena.

Accidental war can be defined as one that occurs as a result of a wholly erroneous or significant misinterpretation of tactical warning that the opponent has launched a substantial strike which leads, in turn, to prompt launch of major retaliation with WMD. The term prompt launch includes both launch-on-warning of an attack that is underway and launch-under-attack.[27] Included in this definition is the possibility that what is in fact a small attack is misjudged in early attack assessment to be a substantial one.

Inadvertent war differs in that it is not tied to misinterpretations of tactical warning or to erroneously early attack assessment. The term 'inadvertent war' refers to the scenario in which a crisis gets out of control and escalates to the point at which one or the other side, or both, come to believe that war is now inevitable and seemingly imminent. It is considered, therefore, better to initiate a pre-emptive strike before the opponent does so.[28]

Inadvertent war is an unwanted one in that at the outset of the crisis neither side wanted or expected a war with WMD. However, both sides entered into it as a result of provocative coercive bargaining, misperceptions, misjudgements and perhaps accidental or unauthorised actions, all of which feed escalation to the point at which conventional conflict might have begun and time-urgent decisions whether to pre-empt seem to be necessary.[29]

By definition, pre-emption is undertaken on the basis solely of strategic warning without waiting for tactical warning that the opponent's attack is already under way. In practice, a pre-emptive war can be initiated on the basis of a combination of strategic warning with some partial but inconclusive tactical warning indicators or on the basis of a mixture of equivocal strategic and tactical warning.

Many people may think of this example of inadvertent war as one of pre-emptive or deliberate war, since the attack is launched without sufficient evidence that an attack by the opponent was inevitable. Nevertheless, there is a possibility that 'hot lines' would be ineffective or unavailable and the decision would have to be made on the basis of strategic and tactical information or misinformation. The Indian-Pakistani case is illustrative of this fact. The absence of safety valves, similar to those existing between the US and Russia, makes both India and Pakistan to rely heavily on strategic and tactical information. If this information is incorrect, then, these countries are running into the risk of being engaged into an accidental war. This type of WMD warfare can be also called 'incidental' because the likelihood of happening is built into the structure of the broad military policy and strategy.[30]

Many of the technical issues related to accidents that could contribute to crisis escalation that results in inadvertent war are covered by the discussion of accidental war that follows. But this risk is fundamentally a political one since it depends on a decision to pre-empt made by top-level responsible civilian authority. Therefore, it is essential to avert conventional war for that would provide highly fertile ground for escalation leading to a possible pre-emptive strike. By the same token, it is also essential to prevent political differences from escalating into dangerous crises.

Since the early 1960s there has been a reduction in the chance of deliberate nuclear war due to the effects of deterrence, especially mutual deterrence via the threat of a retaliatory second strike. The logic of deterrence, however, applies more to the great powers that have significant nuclear capabilities (especially to those possessing a second strike capability) and not to states that have a limited number of nuclear systems or only chemical and biological weapons in their disposition. In this case, deterrence may not work.

On the other hand, there are several significant factors pointing to an increase in the chance of accidental wars that may involve WMD.[31] There is, first, the growing complexity of the systems that protect and control such weapons involving many components, any of which could fail.[32] A second factor is the greater automation and technological sophistication and the resulted shorter decision times for strategic warning and command and control systems, which are potentially susceptible to false alarms, computer failure, and human error.[33] In fact, stopping a disaster may have become almost impossible due to shorter warning times, greater use of computers and accelerated communications, and the potential interactions between the command, control, communications, and intelligence systems of opposing states, which could possible lead to cascading instability.

A third, and perhaps the most important factor, is the possibility of a launch-on-warning system either in place, or a *de facto* one that is in place during a crisis or alert situation. In such a system, vulnerable land-based missiles are launched on the warning of an enemy attack to avoid their being destroyed on the first strike. The rationale behind this launching is reflected in the doctrine 'use them or lose them'.

Accidental Use

The custodianship of WMD, and all that goes into preventing accidental explosions, or any other mishap that could lead accidentally to disaster or war, has been of profound military as well as civil concern. This is not a small responsibility, and the only 'acceptable record for the discharge of that responsibility is the perfect record in which nothing went badly wrong'.[34] The success of the military organisations in handling their responsibility have given many people a false sense of security, enabling them to ignore the accidents that have occurred, some of which could more likely have led to accidental nuclear war.

Others, who are aware of the immense complexity of modern military organisations, of command and control, communications, and intelligence systems, of human fallibility, of the complex phenomena of crisis, and of unforeseen failures in the best-designed technical systems, do not share this feeling of security.[35] Serious accidents that have occurred did not result in accidental explosions or war, but did give rise to international tensions, or even crises.

What are the chances of an accidental use of WMD or of an accidental war where WMD would be used? At one extreme, there are those who have tended to exaggerate the chances of such an event going so far as to suggest that it is a virtual certainty. At the other extreme, military and political leaders have tended to minimise this problem.[36] The view presented here is that the chances lie between the two extremes and that accidental use is an issue that should be addressed in a serious way rather than to be ignored either as certainty, or as something impossible.

Accidental war is defined as any war without a deliberate and properly informed decision to use WMD on the part of national command authority or the legitimately pre-delegated authority.[37] A point to be emphasised is that accidental war is a systems problem more than a numbers problem. The most serious accidents involving WMD, and especially nuclear weapons, have had, in fact, relatively little to do with the numbers of such weapons and thus would not be mitigated by a reduction in these numbers. Rather, they depend on a set of critical relationships in a very complex system involving on the one hand, people who are subject to stress and fatigue and who have to deal with procedures in situations not experienced before, and on the other hand, equipment that is subject to failure or overload.[38]

There are four critical relationships.

First, there is a relationship between the warning system sensors and the sensor system operators that can lead to potential accidents in warning systems.

Second, it is the relationship between the sensor system operators and the national command authority, and between the national command authority and weapons operators, leading to potential accidents in these systems and potential accidents with pre-delegated authority.

Third, there is a relationship between weapons systems operators and the weapons themselves, which could lead to accidents with actual or potential weapons carriers and to accidents with weapons.

And fourth, it is the relationship between states armed with WMD and national or sub-national terrorist groups, leading to potential accidents involving third parties. An accidental or intentional launch by third parties could, particularly in a crisis, lead to an accidental war.

The initiating accident, that would lead to an accidental war, could occur in any part of the warning and decision system, starting with warning systems, continuing through communications links at the level of the national command authority, and again continuing through communications links to field commanders. It could also occur in weapons carriers, in the weapons themselves, in delegated or pre-delegated authority, or in third parties.[39]

Warning systems, involving sensors detecting an enemy attack, must cope with two possible types of error. The first is the failure to detect an actual enemy attack due to system malfunction, or the destruction of its weak links by the opponent, as in a decapitation strike that destroys the national command authority.

The second type of error is the false signal of an enemy attack when there is, in fact, no such an attack. Since further action is based on the warning systems signalling an enemy attack, the most important accidents in terms of a possible accidental war are those involving a false signal of an enemy attack.[40] If such a mistake were made in a crisis, there is the possibility that weapons would be launched in the mistaken belief that an enemy attack is under way. In fact, there are many cases in which such an error took place.[41]

Another type of accident involves systems of command, control, communication, and intelligence.[42] For a state planning a deliberate attack such systems form the link between the national command authority and the operational units that would conduct an attack or a retaliatory strike. For a state intending solely to retaliate against an enemy first strike, the command, control, communications and intelligence systems is the link from the warning system to the national command authority, and then from the latter to the operational units responsible for the retaliatory strike. In either case, accidents in such systems could lead to a launch.

These types of accidents are particularly serious during a crisis situation or during high-level alerts when the next step may involve one's own launch, or may trigger the other side to launch. They are also particularly serious when decisions are automated in a launch-on-warning system.

Historical examples include accidents with computers, misread or misinterpreted signals, and losses of electrical power. These accidents have not led to accidental war for three reasons. First, due to the redundancies in the system; second, due to the requirements of confirmation by independent systems; and third, because they have not occurred in crisis or high-level alert situations.

Accidents with actual or potential nuclear carriers involve the operational units responsible for launching nuclear weapons. The term 'carriers' includes planes, ships, submarines, and missiles. This type of accident is particularly serious during a crisis.[43] Yet, accidents with WMD include accidental launches or firings of warheads. The explosion of such weapons in a third country may trigger a response in the mistaken belief that it was a strike on them.[44]

Accidents may have also to do with pre-delegated authority. The latter involves the authority of field commanders to launch weapons at their own discretion in certain situations. With such pre-delegated authority the possibilities of accidents increase dramatically. Accidents in communications links could in crisis lead to accidental launch. Similarly, early release of tactical nuclear weapons to battlefield commanders in time of crisis could lead to accidental use of such weapons.

There are two types of accidents in peacetime: accidents at low alert status and accidents at high alert status.[45] Most people believe that the likelihood of serious consequences of an accidental launch when both sides are in peacetime posture, or at a low alert status is minimal. However, it is not obvious that this confidence is justified for the following reasons.[46]

First, it appears unlikely that a breach of the complex safeguards could occur only at the level of a single target. Therefore, an appreciable number of missiles might be fired in the event, to which low probability is attached, of an accidental launch.

Second, by the same token, accidental launch from a ballistic missile submarine might involve more than one missile.

Third, such an accident could involve casualties that dwarf human experience. Even if the accidental launch did not trigger a launch-on-warning or launch-under-attack response, it seems unjustified to ignore the possibility that it would lead to demands for revenge, extremely tense international relations, and the fall of governments. All these could lead to war that might begin at the conventional level but that would later escalate to a point where the national authorities may consider the use of WMD.

The risk that an accidental launch would lead to war is far greater in the context of a crisis sufficiently severe to stimulate a high level alert of nuclear forces.[47] No nuclear power has so far placed its nuclear forces on a high alert status. In peacetime, it is only possible to test the command, control, communications, and intelligence systems, and its personnel, to a limited degree by simulating high stress conditions. There is a good reason, therefore, to be concerned that under highly stressing circumstances decision-makers may not be able to choose the best option available.[48]

Considering the various critical relationships and the type of possible accidents, one should be aware that accidents would continue to happen. It is impossible to design a system completely free of the potential for accident, and the larger and more complex the system the greater the potential for accident.[49] The chances of an accident increase significantly in a time of crisis or in a period of international tension. In a crisis, weapons systems may be on an alert status; the national command authorities, field commanders, and sensor operators may all be under stress; there may be delegation of authority to launch weapons; and there may be a possibility of a launch-on-warning system put in place.[50]

One of the most important features of the post-Cold War international system is the growing domestic instability facing states. Instability exists not only within small states, but also, within great or middle-range powers, such as Russia and Pakistan. Because they are possessors of WMD, instability in these states poses major threats to international community. Domestic instability may lead either to the coming on power of nationalistic leaders with assertive policies, or to foreign intervention, or to war with neighbouring states as a means to unite the domestic front. In any case, crises may arise that could provide the fertile ground for the use of WMD, deliberately or accidentally.

Having discussed the conditions under which WMD might be used in an anarchic international system, it is imperative to examine whether, and if yes, how the power structure of this system is related to the use of WMD.

THE POWER STRUCTURE OF THE INTERNATIONAL SYSTEM

Discussing polarity, the first methodological question that needs to be addressed is: how can power be measured? Power has many different aspects that make it difficult for one to provide a reliable assessment about the power capabilities of states.[51] Additionally, the importance of particular aspects of power does not remain constant over time. From the beginning of the Cold War and until the late 1970s, military power was the most important aspect of national power. Thus, during these years the international system was bipolar in the sense that the military power of the US and the Soviet Union was overwhelmingly superior to the military power of the other states. Since the late 1970s, however, economic power started to increase in importance. Power calculations were, therefore, affected by this change.

In the 1980s the international system was gradually transformed from a high-density bipolar to a low-density bipolar system. The collapse of the ideology and the political framework of the Soviet Union opened a way not toward a unipolar system, but toward a low-density multipolar one. This time, however, multipolarity is occurring on a global scale.[52] At the moment, this system has the tendency to become a high density multipolar one.

This section attempts to sketch the main features of the new pattern of global security relations that has emerged after the end of the Cold War and which are associated with the multipolar structure of the post-Cold War system. In so doing, it distinguishes between the 'centre' that is composed of the major powers (US, Russia, China, Japan, Canada, Germany, Britain, France, and the European Union as a whole) and the 'periphery' that includes a set of financially and politically weaker states. Certain states of the periphery form a 'semi-periphery' whose aspiration is membership of the core.[53] Acquisition of WMD by some states that belong to the periphery or semi-periphery is seen as a way to upgrade their international status.

Shifting from a bipolar to a multipolar system raises questions like: how stable can a multipolar system be? Is war with WMD more likely to occur in a multipolar world where an increasing number of states are armed with such weapons? There has been an extensive debate as to whether bipolarity or multipolarity represents a more stable system. This debate, however, has produced inconclusive results. The best-known statements on this matter are coming from Kenneth Waltz, David Singer and Karl Deutsch.[54]

All three agree that the amount of uncertainty about the consequences of a particular action taken by a decision-maker increases as the number of international actors increases. The logic of this assumption is that as the number increases, a decision-maker has to deal with a greater quantity of information. More international actors means more information is generated that needs to be taken into account in the formulation of foreign policy. Thus, as an international system moves from bipolarity to multipolarity, the amount of overall uncertainty increases. Where they part company is on the matter of whether an increase in the number of actors, and hence uncertainty, makes war more or less likely.

Waltz argues that greater uncertainty makes it more likely that a decision-maker will misjudge the intentions and actions of a political opponent. Hence, a multipolar system, given its association with higher levels of uncertainty, is not desirable because uncertainty makes the probability of war greater. It has been therefore argued that we may come to regret the passing of a stable bipolar world.[55]

Singer and Deutsch make the opposite argument. They believe that a multipolar system is more conductive to stability because uncertainty breeds caution on the part of decision-makers. Hence, as the system moves from bipolarity to multipolarity, the frequency and intensity of war is expected to diminish. They assume that coalitions reduce the freedom of alliance members to interact with outside countries. The greater the number of states that are not alliance members, the greater the number of possible patterns for interaction in the international system. Although alliance membership minimises both the range and intensity of conflict among the alliance members, the range and intensity of conflicts with states outside the alliance are increased. Although interaction among states is as likely to be competitive, as it is to be co-operative, the more limited the possibility of interaction, the greater the potential for instability.

Deutsch and Singer assume that one of the greatest threats to stability is the shortage of alternative partners. Interaction with a great number of states produces cross-cutting loyalties that induce hostility between any single dyad of states. Furthermore, they argue that the increase in the number of actors diminishes the share of attention that any state can allocate to any other single actor. This, it is argued, also reduces the probability of war because a state's attention is allocated to a larger number of actors.

The above arguments have been subject to criticism. Richard Rosecrance, for instance, argues that although the intensity of conflict may be lower in a multipolar world, the frequency of conflict will be greater because of a greater diversity of interests and demands.[56] Bruce Bueno de Mesquita claims that uncertainty is not higher in a multipolar world because learned patterns from prior behaviour will aid decision-makers to anticipate the likely consequences of similar behaviours under similar circumstances.[57]

Hence, the level of systemic uncertainty neither increases nor decreases the likelihood of war.

Empirical studies yielded conclusions that do not fully support the hypotheses regarding the power structure of the system and its relationship to war. Findings pointed out first, that there is a tendency towards equilibrium and stability in multipolarity; second, that the alignment of two or more states with each other heightens the opposition of others and enhances the risk of war; and third, that interactions between the alliance members and outside members increase.[58]

The emergence of multipolarity has spurred some scholars to examine earlier periods of similar system structure. Work on alliance formation has concluded that while democratic states are not particularly less inclined to go to war than other forms of government, they are disinclined to go to war against each other.[59] Focusing at the state-societal level of analysis, scholars have examined domestic factors, such as the economy and concern for domestic political stability, that may influence foreign policy choices. This approach attempts to correct the traditional work on alliances that tends to assume that external threats virtually alone determine a state's international alignment.[60]

What is the relevance of the above arguments to the use of WMD? Since there is not an agreement about the relationship between polarity and stability, what conclusions can be drawn regarding the use of WMD? What are the conditions that determine the use or the non-use of WMD in a multipolar world? Do these conditions apply exclusively to a multipolar system or can they be equally applied to a bipolar one? To arrive to some conclusions, one should focus on the war participants. In this context, three types of warfare can be identified. First, war between the major powers of the system; second, war between the major powers on the one side, and the powers of the periphery and semi-periphery on the other; and third, war among the powers of the periphery and semi-periphery.

War with WMD among the major powers seems unlikely for six reasons.

First, there are not currently strong causes that can justify a resort to arms.

Second, major powers are armed with significant numbers of WMD that provide credible deterrence.

Third, power disparities between the great powers themselves prevent the weaker of them from hurting the more powerful ones, while the latter are conscious that any effort to dominate the system would most certainly attract the combined reaction of the other great powers.

Fourth, great powers have established crisis prevention and crisis management mechanisms that reduce the possibility of inadvertent or accidental wars.

Fifth, increasing interdependence and globalisation brings major powers closer to each other.

And sixth, it is difficult for a state, even if it is a major power, to commit a breach of international law by using WMD; especially when it has enough conventional power in its disposition. The only possibility for a major power to resort to the use of WMD is when it evaluates that this use is imperative for achieving its goals and that the benefits it obtains from it are not outweighed by the costs.

As during the Cold War, armed conflict between a major power and a lesser power is difficult but not impossible. In case of such conflict, WMD are more likely to be used by the lesser power in order to outweigh the advantages that the conventional superiority gives to the great power. Whether the lesser power will use WMD depends on the specific strategic conditions and the costs associated with the expected reaction of the international community and more importantly on the response of the major power that will be hurt. Indeed, if WMD were used against it, the major power might find it less difficult to initiate a retaliatory attack with similar weapons. Such an attack, however, is subject to two conditions: first, whether enough conventional power is available to defeat the opponent; and second, whether the benefits of this retaliatory strike are higher than the costs associated with the expected reaction of the international community.

The possibility of war among states of the periphery and semi-periphery seems to increase in the multipolar system. The multi-centred core seems to offer more competing points of contact for the periphery, while the existence of several great powers has led to both a reduction in the intensity of global political concerns and a reduction in the resources available for sustained intervention.[61] This in turn points to the rise of regional politics.

During the bipolar world, there existed a general balance of power operating in the international system as a whole, as well as various regional balances of power that supported the general balance of power. Regional balances of power, however, were subordinated to the general balance in the sense that the latter affected them much more than they affected it.[62] In other words, it was the nature of the American-Soviet relations that generally affected developments in the various parts of the world and not the other way around.

Currently, because the great powers are spread across several regions and have a less dominating ideological or power rivalry among them, they project their own conflicts into the periphery less forceful and systematically than during the bipolar world. Therefore, the degree to which regional balances affect the general balance of power is much greater than in the bipolar international system. Because regions are less constrained by the impact of their conflicts on the centre, local rivalries have more autonomy. However, not all regions are equally important for the maintenance of the general balance of power. For instance, the Middle East and East Asia are currently far more important than Africa or Latin America.

Multipolarity at a global level implies that the great powers want to have an exclusive say in what happens in their own regions or those regions geographically close to them, and therefore, attempt to minimise any other power's involvement that could threaten their interests there. Thus Russia wants to keep the US and NATO away from the Baltic States, while China wants to be the main actor in East Asia. Multipolarity at a global level also means absence of a dominant power at the international level as a whole, but this does not preclude either possibilities of regional hegemonies or a struggle to preventing them.

Since the local balances of power during the Cold War were subordinated to the general balance of power, that meant that the actions of lesser powers were largely determined by the relationship between the superpowers. Although there was always the possibility of political blackmail, international conditions generally prevented smaller powers from changing camps.

In the post-Cold War system, the states of periphery and semi-periphery have far more opportunities for political manoeuvring. Since war remains a political option, these states may find it convenient to exercise their military power as a means for achieving political objectives. Thus international crises may increase in number.

This has two important implications for the use of WMD. First, they may be used deliberately to offer a decisive victory to the striker, or for defensive purposes when imbalances in military capabilities are significant; and second, crises increase the possibilities of inadvertent or accidental wars involving WMD.

The above scenario, however, depends on five factors. First, the region in which these states are situated; second, the character and power of those states; third, the interests of the great powers; fourth, the possible constraints posed by the systemic processes; and fifth, the determination of the international community not to accept the breach of rules and norms related to the use of WMD.

Although many factors contribute to the enhancing of the possibility for the WMD to be used, there are certain systemic processes that pose serious constraints to the potential user, while the breach of international rules and norms may lead to political, military, and economic reprisals imposed by the international community. Thus, states need to judge whether advantages and benefits related to the use of WMD are outweighed by costs. The purpose of the following sections is to discuss how systemic processes and international norms and rules can restrain the use of WMD.

SYSTEMIC PROCESSES

The use of WMD seems to be affected by two distinctive, though inter-related, systemic processes: interdependence and globalisation. The effects of these systemic processes on the use of WMD, however, have been to a great extent conditioned by the retreat of ideology which used to underline the conflict between the great powers as well as their respective allies.

The Retreat of Ideology

The post-Cold War international system is characterised by a much lower degree of ideological division and rivalry among the great powers. The defeat of fascism and communism as alternative ideologies for advanced industrial societies has made liberal capitalism, identified with political pluralism and market economy, to be seen as the most effective and desirable form of political economy. This, however, does not mean that an ideological homogeneity has been reached, or it is about to be achieved. Nevertheless, in conjunction with multipolarity, the retreat of ideology reduces, but does not eliminate, great powers' political and military incentives for competing intervention into the periphery. Whether such intervention would take place depends on the region, the interests of the great powers, and the costs associated with this intervention.

The low degree of ideological conflict makes the possibility of war between the core powers of the system highly unlikely. For reasons explained before, the possibility of use of WMD in a war between major powers is even more unlikely. The low degree of ideological rivalry, however, does not necessarily minimise the possibility of war occurring between the states of the periphery, or between them and those of the core. It is worth noting that the majority of the peripheral states not only do not share all the ideas about liberal capitalism, political pluralism, and market economy, but in fact, they also oppose to them in their theory and/or practice. In this case, the use of WMD by either side would be determined by the specific strategic conditions and the costs associated with the expected reaction of the international community.

Although there have been strong signs that the reduction of the ideological conflict among the major powers would serve as the foundation for a global concert, the military, economic and technological superiority of the United States has pushed great powers, like Russia and China to resist American leadership in military and political operations that could in the near future transform the United States into a global hegemon. The summer 1998 events regarding the problems between the UNSCOM and the government of Iraq as well as the events related to the Kosovo conflict are illustrative.

A low degree of ideological rivalry, therefore, does not imply the absence of major conflicting interests among the core powers of the system. In contrast, since each of those powers seeks to enhance its political, economic and other interests, it is inevitable that some of these interests will conflict. However, they do not expect, or are prepared for, the use of military force in their relations with each other. Thus the possibility of use of WMD diminishes.

Interdependence

One of the most important characteristics of the post-Cold War international system is the increasing interdependence among international actors. Although interdependence existed even during the Cold War, its current degree is substantially higher than before. Interdependence implies the existence of reciprocal, although not necessarily symmetrical, costly effects of transactions among states or among actors in different states. However, it is asymmetries in dependence that are most likely to provide sources of influence for actors in their dealings with one another.

According to Barry Buzan, the principal force behind interdependence is the rising density of the interaction networks that ties the international system together.[63] Rising density is driven by increasing technological, organisational, and financial capabilities and incentives for action. Rising density has important consequences for the international system. At the political level, for example, due to advanced communication systems, ideas circulate globally and the model of liberal democracy has been seen by many states as the ideal form of government. In the economic field, the world is increasingly tied into a global market of production, trade, and finance, whose circulation system is an even more efficient transportation network. Thus the principal impact of rising density is to increase the level of interdependence among states.[64] In military terms, given the existence and continuing proliferation of WMD, interdependence means that states depend for their survival on the restraint of their rivals, while in economic terms, states depend for their welfare and development on access to external markets, credit and resources.

Interdependence has three main characteristics.[65] First, the agenda of interstate relationships consists of multiple issues that are not arranged in a clear or consistent hierarchy. This absence of hierarchy means, among other things, that military security does not consistently dominate the agenda. Different issues generate different coalitions across the governments and involve different degrees of conflict. Indeed, as non-military issues have risen in importance, the great powers worry less about their military and more about their economic competitiveness. At the same time, the ideological landscape is dominated by the relative success of market economics and pluralist politics.

Second, resort to military force is far more difficult when interdependence prevails. Military power, for example, is irrelevant to resolving disagreements on economic issues. This does not mean that military force has ceased to be a central component of national power, or that it cannot be used at all. It rather means that force is not always the most appropriate way of achieving important foreign policy goals.[66]

Third, there exist multiple channels that connect national societies especially in the economic field.[67] Thus, foreign economic policies touch more domestic economic activity than in the past, increasing the number of issues relevant to foreign policy. The existence of these channels imposes limits on the ability of statesmen to calculate the manipulation of interdependence or follow a consistent strategy linkage.[68] Governments must consider differential as well as aggregate effects of interdependence strategies and their likely implications for politicisation and agenda control.[69]

The existence of multiple channels gives a different and significant role for international institutions in world politics. Contemporary international society consists of a whole range of global and regional institutions and regimes with which states co-ordinate their behaviour in pursuit of common goals. In a world of multiple issues imperfectly linked, in which coalitions are formed transnationally and transgovernmentally, the potential role of international institutions is greatly increased and their operation assists the strengthening of international society.

The three main characteristics of interdependence give rise to distinctive political processes that translate power resources into power as control of outcomes. This implies the existence of linkage strategies where militarily and economically strong states will dominate a variety of issues, by linking their own policies on some issues to other states' policies on other issues.

As military force is devaluated, militarily strong states find it more difficult to use their overall dominance to control outcomes on issues in which they are weak. Dominant states may try to secure much the same result by using overall economic power to affect results in other issues.

Interdependence seems to have a mitigating effect on the possibility of armed conflicts. This does not, however, mean that the possibility of war is eliminated. Interdependence is not only unlikely to reduce conflict, but it may even increase it by giving states several issues on which their interests and circumstances will differ. But where interdependence is strong, it seems that reduces incentives to resort to armed force. Interdependence makes relationships costly to disrupt. Force is increasingly costly not only in itself, but also in its consequences regardless of whether the motive for using it is expansion or justice. Moreover, interdependence makes it more difficult for states to pursue national security by seeking unilaterally to reduce their vulnerabilities to outside pressure. In contrast, states are pressured by circumstances into relying more and more on collaborative arrangements to reduce threats by dealing with them as multilateral international issues.[70] In this context, the use of WMD, which has become a multilateral security issue, would be determined by strategic considerations including the calculation of the costs that the disruption of relations under interdependence entails.

Globalisation

Globalisation refers to a process where 'people, activities, norms, ideas, goods, services, and currencies are decreasingly confined to a particular geographic space and its local and established practices'.[71] As a result of this process, politics, economics, culture, and ideology are interwoven. Manifestations of the globalisation process include the inter-penetration of industries across borders, the spread of financial markets, and an emerging world-wide preference for democracy. Globalisation is rendering boundaries and identity with land less salient and encompasses the expansion of production, trade, and investments beyond their prior locales.

Although globalisation does not constitute a post-Cold War phenomenon, its degree has considerably enhanced in the post-Cold War era. This can be mainly attributed to increasing interdependence and rising density in the international system. Among other things, the dynamics of the globalisation process have been cited as explanations for the post-Cold War efforts in various parts of the world to redefine the meaning of security in the absence of superpower rivalry. Consequently, security is now seen as having economic, social, political, environmental and military aspects, while concerns about the security of the individuals, as opposed to that of states, have increased in importance.

One of the most important consequences of increasing globalisation is the diminishing role of military force as a means to solve international disputes. War is seen as disrupting economic and financial processes necessary for the development of states and, therefore, as affecting the well-being both of states and individuals. Depending on the state, globalisation has further increased the importance of national pressure groups. The interests of those groups are related to the function of international markets, as well as to international economic and financial processes. Thus, they see the resort to military force as endangering their interests.

In this context, the use of WMD and the war itself appear to be highly unlikely among states that are involved in, and affected by the globalisation process. On the other hand, war between states armed with WMD is easier to occur among those that are not participants to this process. In any case, the use of WMD will depend on the specific strategic conditions and calculations, as well as on the costs associated with globalisation and the expected reaction of the international community.

INTERNATIONAL RULES AND NORMS

The commitment of states to the observance of international rules regarding warfare varies from period to period and not from system to system. However, one can identify a qualitative difference between the Cold War and the post-Cold War international systems. This difference is mainly due to the diminishing of ideological rivalry among the great powers.

Specifically, the eighteenth and nineteenth centuries, which saw the abandonment of any attempt by international law to restrict the right of states to go to war, also saw the growth of rules regulating the way in which wars should be fought.[72] This was not a coincidence. In the age of just war, each side had usually considered that the other side's cause was unjust, and it had, therefore, tended to treat the other side as a mere outlaw, lacking any right to fair, if not to human treatment.

During the said period, states did not regard themselves as fighting for survival. Wars were seldom fought for ideological reasons and tended not to rouse the same intensity of passion as twentieth century wars. The balance of power system necessitated flexibility in political alignments and meant that a state's enemy today might be its ally tomorrow. This had a restraining effect on the degree of brutality practised in wars, because states did not want to arouse undying bitterness among potential allies.[73]

Even more important than these political considerations was the fact that laws of war were designed mainly to prevent unnecessary suffering.[74] Unnecessary suffering meant suffering that would produce no military advantage or a military advantage that was very small in comparison with the amount of suffering involved. Theoretically, violations of the laws of war were expected to be rare, because it was thought that the military advantage to be gained by breaking those laws could be outweighed by disadvantages such as reprisals, loss of neutral good will, and so on. In practice, however, the laws of war were frequently breached.

During the eighteenth and nineteenth centuries, wars were regarded by military theorists and officers as armed conflicts between armed forces, rather than wars between people. For instance, Clausewitz claimed that the destruction of the enemy's military force is the foundation-stone of all action in war. In other words, the purpose of all war activities was to disarm the enemy so not to be able to prosecute the war and not to destroy the physical base of the rival state.

Consequently, rules grew up to protect the armed forces not only in battle, but also when soldiers were sick, wounded, or prisoners of war. Although Clauzewitz argued that the laws of war were 'almost imperceptible and hardly worth mentioning', the reason for their imperceptibility was that they accorded perfectly with the limits of military necessity. Hence, the conception that civilised states do not put their prisoners to death and do not devastate towns and countries. According to Clausewitz this was because, 'their intelligence has taught them more effectual means of applying force than these crude acts of mere instinct'.[75] This approach to war made it easy for international law to protect not only the members of the armed forces, but also civilians. In practice, nevertheless, this protection was never absolute and several times the actions of European armies had had devastating effects upon the civilians of the opponent country.

In the second half of the nineteenth century, states began to issue manuals of military law, while laws of war which had been derived almost entirely from customary law, began to be codified and extended by treaties. Despite the existence of international treaties and conventions, states have several times broken the rules of armed conflict since then.

Particularly, there are two factors that have encouraged violations of the laws of war during the twentieth century.

First, the two great wars produced more bitter feelings than previous ones. They were fought for ideological reasons, and for virtually unlimited objectives. Belligerent states sought no longer to achieve a delicate adjustment to the balance of power, but adopted a policy of unconditional surrender.

Second, economic and technological changes vastly increased the military advantage to be gained by breaking the laws of war. In particularly, the distinction between the armed forces and civilians is largely illusory, now that the whole of a country's economy is geared to the war effort. Destruction of state infrastructure, and even the killing of people associated with it, produces a military advantage that would have been inconceivable a century ago.

The end of the Cold War and the diminishing of the ideological rivalry among the great powers have led the international community to adopt a more combative stance against the proliferation and use of WMD. Economic sanctions, diplomatic isolation, and possible military reprisals may serve as a means for international society to achieve compliance with international rules and norms. Thus states may find it more difficult than before to use WMD since the costs related to this use might be far higher than the benefits derived from it. On the other hand, it seems that states rely more and more on collaborative legal arrangements to secure themselves against the use of WMD. The creation of zones free of WMD is illustrative.

CONCLUSION

A set of conclusions may be drawn from the above analysis. First, the anarchical structure of the international system is irrelevant to the use of WMD. Since both the Cold War and post-Cold War international systems have been anarchical in nature, the conditions under which WMD are produced and acquired are common to both systems, while the probability of their use remains unaffected by the passage from the one system to the other.

Second, it is not clear whether, and how the power structure of the international system is related to the use of WMD. It seems that war with WMD between the major powers in the multipolar post-Cold War system is very unlikely; a situation that is not very much different than that existing in the bipolar Cold War system. Apart from strategic factors, the low probability of a war between the major powers is conditioned by the operation of the forces of globalisation and interdependence as well as by the retreat of ideology as the driving force of great power conflict. One of the most important consequences stemming from the retreat of ideology is that the definition of, and adherence to international rules and norms by major powers has become easier than before.

Third, the low degree of ideological rivalry, however, does not necessarily minimise the possibility of war between the core and peripheral states. In other words, armed conflict between a major and a lesser power, although difficult, is not impossible. War between states armed with WMD appears to be unlikely if the rivals are involved in, and are affected by the globalisation process, but war is easier to occur when one of them is neither involved in, nor affected by this process. Yet, growing interdependence between the core and peripheral states does not eliminate the possibility of a war between them.

In sum, war between major and lesser powers armed with WMD and the use of those weapons depend on the particular strategic conditions facing the rival states; their associated calculations; the costs which the disruption of relations under globalisation and interdependence entails; the costs associated with the reaction of the international community to the breach of international rules and norms; and the response of the state that has been hurt by this use.

Fourth, the possibility of war among the peripheral and semi-peripheral states seems to increase in the multipolar system. This is because the low degree of ideological rivalry among the major powers has little effect on the relations among the lesser powers. However, the probability of war among lesser powers armed with WMD and the probability of the use of those weapons are conditioned by factors identical to those regarding the conflict between major and lesser powers.

Fifth, although the power-security dilemma operates similarly in the Cold War and post-Cold War international systems, the proliferation of WMD in the post-Cold War era in conjunction with the absence of crisis prevention and crisis management mechanisms and the domestic instability facing the possessors of WMD increase the chances that these weapons might be used intentionally or accidentally. The chances of intentional or accidental use increase significantly in a time of crisis or in a period of international tension.

The above conclusions have five important policy implications.

First, the international community should be more concerned with the proliferation of WMD and should, therefore, devise additional mechanisms for controlling it.

Second, the possessors of WMD should establish the necessary mechanisms that would help to avoid or manage crises that might lead to inadvertent or accidental wars.

Third, states that possess WMD should design policies aimed at increasing domestic stability.

Fourth, all states alike should coordinate their efforts for addressing adequately the problem of terrorism. Finally, the international community should be prepared to enforce the rules regarding both the proliferation and use of WMD.

The question, however, is what measures should be taken to control the proliferation of WMD and penalise their use, and what are the implications of these measures? For example, cases have shown that diplomatic isolation is either not entirely possible or not enough to change the minds of national decision-makers. Although economic or other sanctions are still considered as an acceptable means for penalising the offender, there is an increasing number of voices that argue that such actions hurt only the population of the offending state and not the leadership that is responsible for the particular decisions and actions. They, therefore, suggest that sanctions should be instead regarded as another type of WMD that should be prohibited and those using it should be penalised. Similar concerns apply to the use of military reprisals. Are those reprisals morally justified? If yes, then, under which conditions and to what extent are they justified?

If the effectiveness and morality of the above means is disputable, then, what should be done? What should the international community as a whole and the individual states that compose it do to prevent the use of WMD? What guarantees can the international community give to individual states that they will not be victims of an attack with those weapons? The absence of credible answers to these questions has led the individual states to devise their own military mechanisms aimed at deterring their actual or potential rivals.

The main concern for the international community is that national policies might jeopardise the international legal order related to the use of WMD. For example, the decision of the United States to produce and deploy anti-ballistic missiles as well as to demand the revision and modification of the Anti-ballistic Missile Treaty (ABM) may provide other states with an excuse to produce and deploy weapon systems that are currently prohibited and then ask for the revision and modification of the relevant treaties. This may lead to the paradox of revising a legal order that, in fact, does not exist. Perhaps more important is the fact that such actions may lead to arms races and the re-opening of the power-security dilemma that might make the definition of new international rules very difficult, if not impossible.

The International System 129

NOTES

1. See the special section on Proliferation in Asia, *Survival* 38/3 (Autumn 1996) and Ian Lesser and Ashley J. Tellis, *Strategic Exposure: Proliferation Around the Mediterranean* (Santa Monica, CA: RAND Corp. 1996).
2. See Kenneth Waltz, *Theory of International Politics* (Reading, MA: Addison-Wesley 1979).
3. Friedrich V. Kratochwil, *Rules, Norms, and Decisions* (Cambridge: CUP 1989) p.10.
4. Barry Buzan, *People, States, and Fear*, 2nd ed. (London: Harvester Wheatsheaf 1991) p.295.
5. See Daniel Frei and Christian Catrina, *Risks of Unintentional Nuclear War* (Geneva: UNIDIR 1982) Ch.7. See also Ike Jeanes, *Forecast and Solution* (Blacksburg, VA: Pocahontas Press 1996).
6. For a discussion concerning the logic of some of the stated motives see Michael MccGwire, 'Is there a future for nuclear weapons?', *International Affairs* 70/2 (April 1994) pp.211–28.
7. Hedley Bull, *The Anarchical Society* (London: Macmillan 1977) Ch.9.
8. Ibid. p.106.
9. Ibid. p.189.
10. Michael Quinlan, 'The future of nuclear weapons: policy for western possessors', *International Affairs* 69/3 (1993) pp.485–96.
11. Ibid. p.496.
12. Cited in Robin Ranger and David Wiencek, *The Devil's Brews II: Weapons of Mass Destruction and International Security*, Bailrigg Memorandum 17 (Centre for Defence and International Security Studies, Lancaster Univ. 1997) p.19.
13. Ibid. p.8.
14. Cited in Samuel Huntington, 'The Clash of Civilizations?', *Foreign Affairs* 72/2 (Summer 1993) p.46.
15. Lesser and Tellis, *Strategic Exposure* (note 1) pp.6–7.
16. Ibid. p.7.
17. Cited in Ranger and Wiencek, *Devil's Brews II* (note 12) p.7.
18. Ibid. p.16.
19. See Leonard S. Spector and Nancy Blabey, 'Nuclear Proliferation Threats in the Islamic Middle East', *New Outlook* (Sept.–Oct. 1991).
20. Huntington, 'Clash of Civilizations?' (note 14).
21. Lesser and Tellis, *Strategic Exposure* (note 1) p.16.
22. Ibid. p.16.
23. See Richard A. Falkenrath, 'Confronting Nuclear, Biological and Chemical Terrorism', *Survival* 40/3 (Autumn 1998) pp.43–65 and Paul Wilkinson, 'International Terrorism: New Risks to World Order', in John Baylis and Nicholas J. Rengger (eds.) *Dilemmas of World Politics* (Oxford: Clarendon Press 1992) pp.228–60.
24. Cited in Ranger and Wiencek, *Devil's Brews II* (note 12) p.2.
25. See Karl-Heintz Kamp, Joseph F. Pilat, Jessica Stern and Richard A. Falkenrath, 'WMD Terrorism: An Exchange', *Survival* 40/4 (Winter 1998–99) pp.168–83.
26. See Harvard Nuclear Study Group, 'The Shattered Crystal Ball: How Might a Nuclear War Begin?', in Melvin Small and J. David Singer (eds.), *International War* (Homewood, ALA: Dorsey Press, 1985).
27. Alexander L. George and Kurt Gottfried, 'Accidental and Inadvertent War: Definitions and Scenarios' in Derek Paul, Michael D. Intriligator and Paul Smoker (eds.) *Accidental Nuclear War* (Toronto: Science for Peace/Samuel Stevens 1990) p.31. See also Kurt Gottfried and Bruce G. Blair (eds.) *Crisis Stability and Nuclear War* (NY: OUP 1988) pp.83–9.
28. George and Gottfried, 'Accidental and Inadvertent War' (note 27) p.41.
29. Ibid. p.41.
30. Horst Afheldt, 'Matching Strategy to the Needs of Security', in Paul, Intriligator and Smoker, *Accidental Nuclear War* (note 27) p.92.
31. Michael D. Intriligator and Dagobert L. Brito, 'Accidental Nuclear War', in Paul, Intriligator and Smoker, *Accidental Nuclear War* (note 27) p.15. See also M.D. Wallace, B.L. Crissey and C.I. Sennott, 'Accidental Nuclear War: A Risk Assessment', *Journal of Peace Research* 23/1 (Feb. 1986) pp.9–27.

32. See Herbert L. Abrams, 'Component Failure in the Military and Accidental Nuclear War', in Paul, Intriligator and Smoker, *Accidental Nuclear War* (note 27).
33. See C. Perrow, *Normal Accidents: Living With High-Risk Systems* (NY: Basic Books 1984).
34. Derek Paul, 'Introduction' in Paul, Intriligator and Smoker, *Accidental Nuclear War* (note 27) p.1.
35. See Daniel Frei, 'Command, Control, Communication, Intelligence and Crisis Stability', in Joseph Rotblat and Laszlo Valki (eds.) *Coexistence, Cooperation and Common Security* (London: Macmillan 1988).
36. Frei and Catrina, *Risks of Unintentional Nuclear War* (note 5) pp.1–2.
37. Intriligator and Brito, 'Accidental Nuclear War' (note 31) p.6.
38. Frei and Catrina, *Risks of Unintentional Nuclear War* (note 5) pp.4–9.
39. Intriligator and Brito, 'Accidental Nuclear War' (note 31) pp.7–13.
40. See P. Bracken, *The Command and Control of Nuclear Forces* (New Haven, CT: Yale UP 1983) and Daniel Frei, *Risks of Unintentional Nuclear War* (London: Croom-Helm 1983).
41. See Intriligator and Brito, 'Accidental Nuclear War' (note 31) pp.8–9.
42. Frei and Catrina, *Risks of Unintentional Nuclear War* (note 5) pp.50–8. See also S. Briton, *The Invisible Event* (London: Menard Press 1983); B.G. Blair, *Strategic Command and Control: Redefining the Nuclear Threat* (Washington DC: Brookings 1985); D. Ford, *The Button: The Pentagon's Strategic Command and Control System* (NY: Simon & Schuster 1985).
43. Intriligator and Brito, 'Accidental Nuclear War' (note 31) pp.10–11.
44. Ibid. p.12.
45. Frei and Catrina, *Risks of Unintentional Nuclear War* (note 5) pp.16–22.
46. George and Gottfried, 'Accidental and Inadvertent War' (note 27) pp.33–4.
47. Frei and Catrina, *Risks of Unintentional Nuclear War* (note 5) pp.10–5 and 23–30 and Ch.5.
48. See Ole R. Holsti, 'Theories of Crisis Decision Making', in Paul Gordon Lauren (ed.), *Diplomacy: New Approaches in History, Theory and Policy* (NY: Columbia UP 1979); Robert Jervis, *Perception and Misperception in International Politics* (Princeton UP 1976); and Michael Wallace, 'Human Performance Under Stress: A New Scenario for Accidental Nuclear War', in Paul, Intriligator and Smoker, *Accidental Nuclear War* (note 27).
49. See B. Ramberg, 'Lessons from Chernobyl', *Foreign Affairs* 65/4 (Winter 1986/87) pp.304–28.
50. See Bruce B. Blair, *The Logic of Accidental Nuclear War* (Washington DC: Brookings 1993).
51. See Hans Morgenthau, *Politics Among Nations*, brief edition, revised by Kenneth W. Thompson (NY: McGraw-Hill 1993) Chs.8–10.
52. Barry Buzan, Charles Jones and Richard Little, *The Logic of Anarchy: Neorealism to Structural Realism* (NY: Columbia UP 1993) p.13.
53. See Barry Buzan, 'New Patterns of Global Security in the Twenty-First Century', in William Clinton Olson and James R. Lee (eds.) *The Theory and Practice of International Relations*, 9th ed. (Englewood Cliffs, NJ: Prentice-Hall 1994) p.207.
54. Kenneth Waltz, 'The Stability of a Bipolar World', *Daedalus* 93 (Summer 1964) pp.881–909 and 'International Structure, National Force and the Balance of Power', *Journal of International Affairs* 11/2 (1967) pp.215–31; and Karl W. Deutsch and J. David Singer, 'Multipolar Power Systems and International Stability', *World Politics* 16 (April 1964) pp.390–406. See also Arthur Lee Burns, 'From Balance to Deterrence: A Theoretical Analysis', *World Politics* 9 (July 1957) pp.494–529; Stanley Hoffmann, 'Weighing the Balance of Power', *Foreign Affairs* 50 (July 1972) pp.618–43; and Ronald Yalem, 'Tripolarity and the International System', *ORBIS* (Winter 1972) pp.1051–63.
55. Kenneth Waltz, *Theory of International Politics* (note 2) p.170 and John J. Mearsheimer, 'Back to the Future: Instability in Europe After the Cold War', *International Security* 15/1 (Summer 1990) pp.5–56.
56. Richard N. Rosecrance, 'Bipolarity, Multipolarity, and the Future', *Journal of Conflict Resolution* 10 (Sept. 1966) p.318.
57. Bruce Bueno de Mesquita, 'Systemic Polarization and the Occurrence and Duration of War', *Journal of Conflict Resolution* 22/2 (June 1978) pp.245–56 and 'Risk, Power Distributions, and the Likelihood of War', *International Studies Quarterly* 25/4 (Dec. 1981) pp.541–68.

58. See J. David Singer and Melvin Small (eds.) *Quantitative International Politics* (NY: Free Press 1968) and Brian Healy and Arthur Stein, 'The Balance of Power in International History: Theory and Reality', *Journal of Conflict Resolution* 17/1 (March 1973) pp.33–61.

59. See Melvin Small and J. David Singer, 'The War-Proneness of Democratic Regimes, 1816-1965', *Jerusalem Journal of International Relations* 1 (1976) pp.50–69.

60. See Thomas J. Christensen and Jack Snyder, 'Chain Gangs and Passed Bucks: Predicting Alliance Patterns in Multipolarity', *International Organization* 44/2 (Spring 1990) pp.137–68 and Steven R. David, 'Explaining Third World Alignment', *World Politics* 43/2 (Jan. 1991) pp.233–55.

61. Buzan, 'New Patterns of Global Security in the Twenty-First Century' (note 53) p.209.

62. Bull, *Anarchical Society* (note 7) pp.102–3.

63. Barry Buzan, 'Is International Security Possible', in Ken Booth (ed.) *New Thinking About Strategy and International Security* (London: HarperCollins 1991) p.41.

64. Ibid. p.42.

65. Robert O. Keohane and Joseph S. Nye Jr, *Power and Interdependence: World Politics in Transition* (Boston: Little, Brown 1977) pp.8–11.

66. See Klaus Knorr, *The Power of Nations: The Political Economy of International Relations* (NY: Basic Books 1975).

67. See Robert O. Keohane and Joseph S. Nye Jr (eds.) *Transnational Relations and World Politics* (Cambridge, MA: Harvard UP 1972); Richard Rosecrance and Arthur Stein, 'Interdependence: Myth or Reality?', *World Politics* 26/1 (Oct. 1973) pp.1–27 and Peter Katzenstein, 'International Interdependence: Some Long-Term Trends and Recent Changes', *International Organization* 29/4 (Fall 1975) pp.1021–34.

68. Robert O. Keohane and Joseph S. Nye Jr, 'Transgovernmental Relations and International Organizations', *World Politics* 27/1 (Oct. 1974) pp.39–62.

69. Branislav Gosovic and John Gerard Ruggie, 'On the Creation of a New International Economic Order', *International Organization* 23/2 (Spring 1969) pp.205–30.

70. Buzan, 'Is International Security Possible?' (note 63) p.43.

71. James Rosenau, 'The Dynamics of Globalization: Toward an Operational Formulation', *Security Dialogue* 27/3 (1996) pp.247–62 on p.247.

72. For the development of laws related to armed conflict see L.C. Green, *The Contemporary Law of Armed Conflict* (Manchester UP 1993) Ch.2. See also Malcolm N. Shaw, *International Law*, 3rd ed. (Cambridge UP 1995) pp.729–36.

73. Michael Akehurst, *A Modern Introduction to International Law*, 6th ed. (London: Unwin Hyman 1987) p.270.

74. Green, *Contemporary Law* (note 72) p.28.

75. Cited in Akehurst, *A Modern Introduction* (note 73) p.271.

7

The Impact of the Revolution
in Military Affairs

PATRICK M. MORGAN

Judging by the record, avoiding the use of Weapons of Mass Destruction (WMD) has thus far not proven to be very difficult. Nuclear weapons have not exploded in a war since 1945 and we have no evidence that numerous occasions have arisen in which their use was seriously considered.[1] Chemical weapons have been used by Iraq and Iran, and earlier by Egypt in Yemen, but otherwise not in interstate warfare and rarely in internal warfare.[2] Biological weapons have apparently been used only once in combat, by Japan in China during World War II.[3] We have virtually no instances of mass destruction from CB weapons, in a century crammed with mass destruction. Thus this study is on doing something about a plausible but almost hypothetical problem.

How was this record achieved? Deterrence is perhaps the favorite answer, particularly deterrence via threats of a response in kind. Antipathy born of political and moral considerations is another, states were reluctant to violate thresholds on nonuse of these weapons because setting such precedents seemed likely to have bad consequences. A third answer is insufficient military utility, the weapons were too gross or imprecise in their effects to suit most objectives; they were bad weapons militarily and therefore politically and morally as well.

Why worry about preventing the use of WMD now?[4] One concern is that it is unrealistic to expect states to practice deterrence successfully with WMD forever; sooner or later there will be a disaster. There is also fear that for many states today deterrence will not work as well as it did for the superpowers during the Cold War. Many conflicts are less 'controlled' or 'contained' – the Cold War, and particularly the superpowers, used to keep them in check. Included here is fear that the end of the Cold War has whet the appetites of would-be (or actual) regional hegemons who are 'rogue' in their ambitions and willingness to ignore taboos and other rules of the game. There is also great interest in forestalling WMD proliferation, in part to prevent use of these weapons, and thus heightened concern that WMD taboos not be violated. These concerns are all widely expressed in the West. Elsewhere, there is considerable anxiety that without the Cold War little can now deter states like the US from using WMD, if they feel like it, in the Third World.

This contribution considers potential effects of the injection of the 'revolution in military affairs' (RMA) into this mix of fears and difficulties. The idea that an RMA is upon us can be traced back to the 1970s, when notions of an electronic battlefield emerged alongside early versions of relevant technologies in the Vietnam War – people sniffers, air-dropped battlefield sensors, early smart bombs. This was also when Marshal Ogarkov and other Soviet military analysts saw such a revolution coming, saw the US pursuing it, and predicted eventual Soviet military obsolescence.[5]

The US was indeed at work. The Vietnam War suggested that the American public, and opinion elsewhere, would resist any use of enormous amounts of force and would probably not support any long war with substantial casualties. It also provoked marked reductions in US military spending, forces, and procurements, making it necessary to find ways to make war with smaller forces and limited costs/casualties on both sides.

First results were on display in the 1991 Gulf War. The US drew heavily on satellites (some 64 in all)[6] to provide intelligence plus precise guidance for allied forces and weapons. It employed very sophisticated aiming and guidance systems on tanks, planes, ships, bombs, and cruise missiles. It used stealth aircraft, advanced electronic warfare, possibly some computer viruses. And the alliance won easily and quickly, with minimal casualties.

There were immediate effects. American efforts to develop such weapons and related capabilities were reinforced. Prior to the war advanced systems and 'smart' weapons were sharply criticized as too expensive, too complicated to maintain under the stress of combat conditions, too unreliable in their availability and their effects. The Gulf War gave them a good name. It therefore also stimulated a torrent of analysis about what was termed the coming RMA. And that incited numerous analyses challenging the whole idea on grounds that such revolutions are frequently sighted but rarely appear, that much of the supposed RMA rests on hypothetical capabilities, that there will be effective military responses to it, and that it is another manifestation of the American technology mania.[7]

The 1999 war over Kosovo further boosted attention to the RMA. The percentage of 'smart' weapons used rose greatly, as did their effectiveness. Collateral damage or damage from mistakes was, though highly publicized, remarkably light given the number of attacks. The allied losses were one stealth aircraft. The 'American' technological mania will therefore spread, and this will become the warfare of choice for those who can afford it.

This analysis begins by sorting out the nature of the RMA, summarizing the existing or emerging capabilities involved as well as analyzing what it entails. Then the focus turns to how these developments will affect the future of the last revolution in military affairs – the development of nuclear weapons and long-range delivery systems. The point is to see whether that revolution might now be canceled, superseded, supplemented, or even enhanced by the RMA. Along the way, the RMA's potential impact on the use of other weapons of mass destruction is also explored

REVOLUTIONS IN MILITARY AFFAIRS

We cannot be *certain* an RMA is occurring or will.[8] Analysts disagree sharply and the evidence is mixed or ambiguous.[9] In my view, the revolution is inevitable and has already begun. Still, the specific course of technological change and its military applications is never precisely known, so any discussion is unavoidably speculative.

What constitutes a revolution in military affairs? There are several possibilities.[10] Normally, these revolutions are seen as arising out of a major shift in military technology that greatly alters weapons and their effects. One view is that the technological shift constitutes the revolution. Changes in the effectiveness, range, and scope of weapons and forces can have a great impact, altering the nature, utility and outcomes of war. This happened when changes prior to 1914 came to favor the *defense*, turning Word War I into an unprecedented, largely unanticipated slaughter and stalemate, a war of attrition/exhaustion. After 1945 nuclear weapons had a revolutionary effect by favoring the *offense*. Only a few were needed to do terrific damage and no defense could ward off all those that could be fired. This was revolutionary – eventually even the greatest powers could not militarily guarantee their survival against all opponents or even guarantee to limit damage from a war to acceptable levels. The best they could do was practice deterrence and hope for the best.

However, a major technological shift normally has to be accompanied by sufficient recognition of new possibilities and by other steps to bring them to fruition. A second view, therefore, is that a revolution in military affairs is the fortunate conjunction of a major shift in technology with new *social and organizational* arrangements to exploit it, producing a great change in warfare. The technological changes might even be incremental, so that the social/organizational arrangements really drive the revolution. In blitzkrieg warfare it was not the tank that was crucial (tanks were around long before it emerged) nor the realization that something new could be done with tanks. It was the development of a new sort of military organization and command system, and related training, that generated a new way of war.

I am partial to a third view: the revolution lies in existing or new technology along with new social and organizational arrangements plus *a new strategic approach* to the use of force, a greatly altered, highly successful, conception of how to use war or threats of it and of how to win wars. The nuclear revolution was fully with us only when the theory and strategy of deterrence came to drive much rearranging of military forces, training, procurements, etc. and encapsulate why and how the nuclear age must profoundly alter our way of thinking about war and the utility of large capacities for destruction. This is a stiff definition; the implication is not just that such revolutions are rare but that they seldom take place fast.

Additional points need emphasis. A military revolution need not take place quickly because its nature lies in its *impact*, not necessarily the rate it takes hold. The coming of gunpowder had massive effects, but only eventually. Some analysts believe the RMA will take at least 50 years to develop, that we are in roughly its first decade. This is probably wise and is not at odds with referring to it as 'revolutionary.' A military revolution is also not necessarily a surprise. Strategic analysts and other observers often anticipate many of the changes and some of the larger implications, especially when the revolution rests on broad new developments in science and technology or in society and its organizational components.

The revolution also need not benefit a few at others' expense, giving them a 'commanding lead' or an 'unmatched capability.' Unfortunately, there is more than a whiff of this in American discussions. While unilateral advantage is one possible outcome, a revolution might diffuse easily; since such revolutions often take a good deal of time, diffusion can be expected. Hence any unilateral advantage might be temporary and thus cannot be the heart of these revolutions.[11] However, we can hardly identify as a revolution a set of changes that do not disadvantage those who fail to either embrace or offset them. Thus the important point is that what can be done in and with war (or threats of war) shifts a great deal, not the degree to which this occurs in an unevenly distributed way.

The current RMA consists of interacting military developments, which in turn grow out of large changes in many facets of society, and which are likely to lead to significant adjustments in strategy.[12]

Technological Changes

The RMA is the product, initially, of a confluence of three streams of technological change. The first has to do with *surveillance*, with detecting, observing, tracking things and people of military concern. For some time now, the developing ability to find things or people has been outrunning the ability to hide them. Improvements in surveillance have multiplied at a rising rate and indications are that this will continue. The improvements come at all levels, from outer space to the platoon. This is of great benefit to military forces in planning, capability assessments, avoiding surprise attacks, etc. For the RMA its significance comes primarily in *targeting*, in being able to track potential or actual targets under all sorts of conditions no matter what their speed. This is being steadily enhanced and shows up on multispectral satellites, drones, enhanced listening equipment, night vision technology, etc., and especially in connection with links to global positioning satellites, advanced rangefinders, and other means for exactly detecting objects.

The second stream feeding the RMA lies in *information processing and presentation*. Surveillance can now generate prodigious information, which must be delivered in readily usable form to those who need it. It has to be timely in arrival, easy to comprehend, and simple to plug into both decision making and implementation. Information about possible targets must be meshed with information about the user (location, readiness). It must be packaged for ready comprehension by each level of command, and there must be suitable systems for passing and processing it among command levels and field units.

The enormous progress here needs no discussion. Computers grow in capabilities almost daily, even as they shrink in size and weight. The ability to tap directly into satellites, planes, and other sensor platforms is proliferating – to units, tanks, soldiers and sailors. Commanders can have the proverbial bird's-eye view of both an entire combat arena and small unit situations. Maps can be generated on call and are far more precise, simulations are much more accurate for training and planning, displays of information are more elaborate and flexible, more readily generated on command. Information can now be readily, often continuously, transferred directly to weapons.

This rising capacity to process information reinforces the impact of the third stream, the heightened ability to hit targets precisely. Advanced forces have a steadily rising ability to hit what they aim at. Enhanced surveillance and information processing have much to do with this, but much more is involved. Getting to the exact spot at the right time involves the speed and flexibility provided by enhanced guidance and propulsion systems or by new principles for projecting mass and/or energy. With stationary targets, this means the ability to hit just where it will do the most good; with moving targets, it is the ability to hit them no matter how abruptly or rapidly they move. This comes in ballistic missile defenses, exotic weapons, smart weapons, tanks and artillery, plus the aiming and rangefinding for weapons of individual soldiers

Social and Organizational Changes

Significant social and organizational changes are required to fully exploit these developments. People are needed who can develop, but particularly operate, maintain, and repair advanced surveillance, communications, and information processing systems and particularly advanced weapons. This requires changes in recruitment, training, advancement, and organization and will culminate in shifts in the relative status of military career lines, an armed services' version of what has been occurring in many industries and professions for some time.

The technological shifts are greatly enhancing the firepower and other capabilities available for even small military units, which can be more effective with weapons they carry and also call in extensive firepower from elsewhere. Small units can access exact information on where they are, what they will encounter in any direction, what weather is brewing. Soon they will use computer simulations to comparatively evaluate alternative solutions to decision problems. In effect, small units can operate more independently. Some analysts suggest that soon there will be nothing but small units because large units will make large and less mobile targets. Thus there is both a push and a pull away from mass hierarchical forces and toward small, dispersed, highly mobile units backed by ample firepower on call. Large weapons platforms (carriers close to shore, tanks, big bombers) may have to be abandoned due to their excessive visibility and insufficient mobility.

Having smaller units operating on their own would not, in itself, be radical. This has been the essence of blitzkrieg as well as guerrilla warfare, and is a common feature of terrorist groups. The contemporary twist is that new technologies can vastly enhance the commander's detailed knowledge as well as the his ability to give detailed direction to specific units or individual soldiers. This has been done only in recent years and only for specific, very sensitive, one time operations (such as the hostage rescue attempt in Iran). Now it can be done all over the battlefield, and even by civilians in overseeing military operations.

This invites information overload at the command level and excessive civilian interference in command decisions and unit actions. Running everything from headquarters will be a terrible temptation (well illustrated in modern diplomatic negotiations), one that could maximize the impact of any centrally held misperceptions and misjudgments. In civilian organizations the information revolution has reduced hierarchy, in organizational design and operations, in favor of lateral networks in management and operations. For the armed forces the trouble is that they must retain a significantly hierarchical element, and the consequences of military actions are so significant and sensitive that top commanders or civilian overseers cannot readily accept extreme decentralization. Governments and services will have to work out creative, flexible ways to mix central command with local initiative and expertise.[13]

Central guidance will have to blend in with field units that supply detailed information to superiors but also tap into centrally held, strategically supplied information on their own, with the information helping to turn 'orders' into something more like 'assistance' and 'local responsibility' into skill in taking good advice from above. As a result, an effective operation will show fewer instances of orders issued above and carried out below. It will be powered instead by the efficient conduct of a vast multilayered conversation.

NEW STRATEGIES

It is too soon to identify with precision the strategic implications of these shifts. The 1991 Gulf War displayed new capabilities but they were used in pursuit of a traditional strategy, that is, fix the opponent in place with firepower and then maneuver around him. However, there are indications of the direction in which strategy will move.

Since much surveillance can be performed at a great distance, and since some advanced precision weapons also operate at great ranges, the scale on which military operations are designed and conducted will likely shift strategy to a scale reserved in the past for grand strategy. For a country with a full range of RMA capabilities, strategy will likely turn on pinning down an opponent throughout an entire theater or his entire country, not concentrating at one isolated point for penetrating attacks and breakthroughs. It will be possible to attack an opponent over a much broader area, looking to flatten or shock the opponent's entire system or forces. It will also be possible to have such flexible forces that the point of an attack can shift whenever gaps in enemy capabilities appear.

Strategy will likely turn on disruption more than destruction. It will be appealing to use (nonnuclear) electromagnetic pulse effects and other communications disruptions, precision targeting to break down transportation, communication, surveillance, information processing, and command systems, or the systematic overloading and distortion of such systems. The more advanced these systems are, and the greater the dependence on them, the more important disruption becomes – the strategy may work best against complicated societies and political systems with elaborate external interactions. This is not a new approach but may now be attainable at much lower levels of casualties and destruction and may have significant strategic, as opposed to what were formerly tactical, consequences.

Strategy will turn on doing harm from a distance, beyond the reach of the opponent's forces if that can be achieved. The object will be to inflict considerable harm and leave the opponent no way to disrupt or punish in return, weakening his incentive to continue fighting and negating the bargaining leverage that would otherwise accrue to him from his being able to continue to fight.

Next, strategy will probably involve concentrating attacks on the elite or leadership, in the way that attacks on Indian tribes often focused on chiefs. The goal would be to make war *personally* costly by threatening their lives, their hold on power, their elite structures, etc. This became a US preoccupation relatively late in the Cold War, on the (unverified) expectation that it would enhance deterrence, but the weapons for carrying it out were very indiscriminate. Now it will be possible to attack such targets, when identified, much more precisely.

Finally, RMA capabilities will probably turn out to be most supportive of *defensive* operations, eroding the advantage of the offense. This is a complicated subject and certainly debatable, particularly since the early advantage from such things as smart bombs, stealth technology, and very accurate cruise missiles has appeared to go to the offense. However, it is hard to see how the ability to track and destroy with ever greater precision will not over time be of most value to the defense. To begin with, modern success on offense has often been associated with achieving surprise. As advanced surveillance capabilities continue to develop, they will be more likely to frustrate attempts to achieve surprise and make it especially difficult to pull off strategic surprise attacks. Attacking will also be more difficult when long-range defensive forces can disrupt or destroy attackers at a distance and when accurate weapons destroy a much higher percentage of the attacking forces as they approach their targets.

The chief advantages of the offense in the twentieth century have been weapons too difficult to detect, or too mobile to hit, and with rising explosive power. This promoted offensive strategies as the way to carry the war to the enemy in hopes of ending it before weaknesses in one's own defenses became clear, and was ultimately the basis on which to threaten retaliation so as to deter. The RMA is about new technologies for detecting and tracking, and for hitting whatever can be seen and tracked. This applies, for instance, to ballistic missile defense (BMD), there will be a very large increase in BMD capabilities in the next two decades. The battlefield will become steadily more lethal for anything that can be detected, concealment will become ever more difficult. Many relevant systems will operate automatically, to shorten the reaction time required. This bundle of enhanced capabilities will reinvigorate defensive strategies.

WHY IS THIS A REVOLUTION?

This is not the place for an answer in detail, but an outline of one will help. To start with, critics have emphasized that having better information has always contributed to chances of victory in war (Sun Tzu, for instance, stressed intelligence as a key), so what is new? What this misses is the combination of greater information with the greater accuracy of weapons. Having better information has not always been crucial. The British could read German codes and controlled the German spy network in Britain, and they were in desperate military shape by 1942. Being able to exploit information with precise weapons makes information dominance likely to be crucial now.

Next, the RMA should deeply affect the ways force can be used. Force has normally been a blunt instrument. It could readily be carried too far because of the extreme effort involved, the intensity of the commitment required, and the size of the stakes. In addition, the gaps between commanders and units in the field has made precise battle management only an ideal. Despite the best of intentions (and often they are not 'best'), commanders have seen their forces inflict indiscriminate harm or engage in mistaken military action. Clausewitz's 'fog of war' is generated by a poor grasp of one's own behavior, not just enemy actions, concealment and deception, and communication or the overloads due to stress and the fighting itself.

The bluntness extends to civil-military relations. Armed forces are deeply attached to autonomy, in operations and in peacetime decisions about equipping, training, and deployments. One result is a gap between the plans civilian leaders approve and what armed forces actually do. Even when states do not order atrocities they often occur. Leaders never order friendly fire deaths but they happen. Leaders put targets off limits which are destroyed nonetheless, while others identified for attack are left alone. Armed forces ignore politically or professionally unwelcome orders, or exceed their orders and confront their superiors with *faits accompli*. They also honestly misinterpret orders.

Force has also been a blunt instrument because military resources have made it so. To compensate for difficulty in finding and hitting targets, military forces have often settled for saturating the target area or using huge explosions. Many weapons are inherently indiscriminate: anti-personnel mines, chemical weapons, a hydrogen bomb. One complaint about chemical and biological weapons has always been that they are difficult to use with precision. It has always been difficult to do target location and damage assessments precisely, leading to random shelling, redundant attacks, and other indiscriminate methods. In land warfare, this has strongly encouraged use of mass attacks – hardly precise, especially when implemented via firepower.

Indiscriminate effects have made war difficult to encompass within systems of law and morality. The implements have not lent themselves to limitations like using only the force necessary or hitting only military targets. Restraint has often been an early casualty in modern war and this helped generate reliance for security on nuclear deterrence threats that promised to ignore all limits.

The RMA makes it possible to envision war and lesser military actions as more precise in terms of damage done. That may challenge inhibitions on the use of force. The primary impact of the nuclear revolution was to make total war so grossly destructive (and lesser wars so dangerous) as to be unusable among great powers. This might now change; the RMA might make even great power warfare tolerable, or possible to contemplate, again. War as controlled and precise, even among great powers, would be a radical change from the nuclear era.[14]

This would occur if the RMA makes it possible eventually to mount successful *strategic* attacks without WMD.[15] The target would be the enemy's capacity to engage in serious military efforts, including the capacity of the nation to sustain itself. In the past this required repeated strategic attacks on a large scale and was nonetheless far from successful. Efforts at strategic attacks were modestly more successful during the 1991 Gulf War, and much was learned then about how to improve while the necessary equipment is only getting better. (For instance, cruise missiles already have better guidance systems.)

The modern history of great power warfare has often turned on the search for a cheap victory strategy, some way of fighting another great power and not having to bear very high costs (in winning or losing) – from Napoleon's decisive grand battle to preemptive nuclear strikes. Rarely have such strategies taken on a defensive cast, but the RMA promises to turn this search in that direction for those suitably equipped. (Imagine, for instance, having to mount the D-Day invasion against a force with modern surveillance and targeting capabilities.)

This will do for defenses what nuclear weapons initially did for offenses, revive dreams of a war that need not be particularly costly to oneself, via defenses so effective that hardly anything can get through. That would be a revolutionary shift. The modern approach to war has had a primarily offensive cast due to the desire to force the opponent to give up, so offensive success, especially strategically, seemed best for achieving this but usually required overwhelming the enemy. Now this might be sought by frustrating him and disrupting his national functions, leaving him with pain and no gain.

It is impossible here to do RMA critics justice but a couple of comments are in order. First, many critics see little utility in the capabilities described above because they will not fit common kinds of contemporary wars, in Bosnia, for example, and expect opponents to pick ways of fighting that minimize Western advantages. The defects in this view are clear. If an RMA leads 'rogue' states and others to avoid totally outright military challenges of a conventional sort (no more Gulf Wars) and confine provocations to much smaller military activities, that would amount to a significant improvement. Resorting to terrorism, for instance, is now often the result of conceding overwhelming conventional military superiority, a superiority that rests in part on the RMA. One critic notes that opponents will not choose the form of conflict the West prefers and that

> The permutations of enemies and modes of warfare are endless: terrorists might gain access to WMD, renegade states might plant

bombs in public places, a mischievous hacker might insinuate himself into the computer networks of a country's military establishment, while drug cartels might arm themselves for pitched battles.[16]

All true, but this treats all security threats as equivalent; the ones cited are annoying but hardly momentous in comparison with threats of interstate war in the past. It is equivalent to suggesting we are very unhealthy because steps that eliminated standard diseases have left us vulnerable to the ravages of old age.

In addition, gains from the RMA *will not be confined to large-scale warfare*; in some ways, better surveillance and precision in weapons are most radical in their implications for subconventional warfare or peace enforcement/peacekeeping. The chief recourse of guerrillas, urban terrorists, and the like is concealment, the ability to move with stealth, the ability to move away before a response arrives, the ability to provoke slaughter that erodes political support for their opponents. All these tactics can be made far more difficult to achieve with RMA capabilities. Thus the *long-term effects* of the RMA are likely to be just as great at subconventional conflict levels. This is not yet appreciated because we have not seen a full scale deployment of the relevant capabilities.

Most critics of the RMA display a poverty of imagination and an excessively short timeframe in their thinking. The proponents can point to the existing *trends* and extrapolate whereas the critics readily cite some potential shortcomings but not serious trends moving in the opposite direction.

THE RMA AND PREVENTING THE USE OF WMD

We now turn to the main topic, the potential implications of the RMA for the use of nuclear, chemical, and biological weapons. We can start by reviewing possible effects of the RMA on WMD use, and then look at the approaches being taken by various states. Thinking abstractly about the relationship between the RMA and WMD, the following possibilities come to mind. The RMA could *supersede* the use of WMD, or *stimulate* their use, or *deter* their use, or *preempt* their use, or possibly even *become a new* version of WMD. We can consider each in turn.

(1) RMA to supersede WMD

The revolution could put weapons of mass destruction in the shade, superseding them as weapons of choice and causing them to be gradually discarded as an outmoded form of military power. The easiest way to outmode a weapon or a way of war is to outgrow it. As this implies, superceding weapons or a way of war is apt to be slow and uneven, the history of the cavalry being a leading example. But it does take place, in at least three forms. The first is to find something that militarily works better. Almost no weapon has ever ceased to be of any value by itself.[17] Knives are as capable of inflicting lethal results as ever, as are Mauser rifles. The same is true about ways of making war. A cavalry charge today could do as much harm as in the past. What has outmoded them is weapons and forces that are so much better: more lethal, or more efficiently or reliably lethal.

The second way to outmode weapons, forces, or ways of making war is to have something appear that permanently negates their effectiveness. That is what happened to spears and clubs and shields or propeller driven strategic bombers, cavalry charges, and armies marching forward on the battlefield while firing volleys. Their intrinsic ability to inflict harm, or to give protection from it, has been interfered with in a decisive way.

The third way is to arrive at a situation in which what they were intended to do is no longer needed. This means finding a *nonmilitary* recourse that is better or even abandoning the goal for which force was required. Iraq seemed quaint in wanting to seize Kuwait's resources to enhance its national power and economic strength. Seizure was a common practice for centuries but is now considered far less reliable than economic development via participation in the global economy. States no longer need the distinctive military capabilities employed for maintaining colonial empires because they have given up empires.

Outmoding weapons or tactics and strategies is a good deal easier than outmoding a revolution in military affairs, such as the nuclear revolution. Such revolutions have long echoes and are not readily superseded. They are roughly equivalent to a paradigm shift in intellectual and cultural life, have deep roots in societies and are thus very resistant to change without the immense pressure of wartime necessity. Outgrowing or outmoding such a revolution is therefore apt to take time. Completely negating its effectiveness in short order is most unlikely. And displacing the necessity for a way of war is truly rare in the history of international politics.

Taking up the first of these three options, if we think about outmoding WMD by coming up with something better, the first question is: outmoded as to what? Those weapons have hardly ever been used in wars. This suggests that when it comes to actual warfare, finding something that works 'better' should not be hard. By the same token it should not be all that important if WMD have rarely seemed very useful for killing people.

Those weapons are primarily used as *deterrence*, to ward off attacks by such weapons or by those who are, or might soon be, more powerful.[18] For credible deterrence it has to be conceivable that they could be used in a war but their actual use is not (hopefully) necessary. They are also used as indicators of achievement and tokens of prestige and status. How are weapons used for these purposes outmoded? Alternative ways of performing these functions must appear ones that are better, cheaper, easier, more practical, or the weapons must become unfashionable. They become symbols not of prestige or achievement but of being backward.

Thus to have them superceded would mean that fewer governments find them suitable for purposes of deterrence in comparison with other weapons, and that they also find them unattractive in terms of prestige and status, due to the RMA. This could happen.[19] After all, a majority of the states that could build such arsenals have chosen not to develop them, including some with serious security problems, presumably because they seemed unsuitable. The weapons are not readily usable, which can cripple the perceived credibility of WMD threats and invite reliance on other weapons. Having little credibility would also make them impractical, a lot of expense for weapons of little use. The RMA, on the other hand, could provide weapons that are quite useable, with plenty of credibility for purposes of deterrence.

The one difficulty would be the 'existential deterrence' nuclear weapons, and possibly chemical and biological weapons, are said to possess. This is an argument developed to cope with the serious credibility problems attached to WMD. Much of the support behind the chemical and biological weapons conventions reflects the paucity of good ways to use them in combat. It is hard make an extended deterrence threat to use WMD credible, particularly if the 'challenger'is also armed with them. During the Cold War American allies continually suspected that the US commitment to use nuclear weapons on their behalf would not be upheld. The British, French, and Israelis responded by developing their own, while the South Korean and Taiwan governments once tried to do the same. This is partly due to broad inhibitions like the 'nuclear taboo' and other political/psychological thresholds that states are reluctant to cross. These restraints have had a powerful impact, leading states to forego use of WMD under very trying circumstances. The thresholds may have a strong grip even on weaker states that confront strong states. A weak state that chose to use nuclear weapons against a strong state would not automatically enjoy support from other weak states; they have no reason to feel safer if thresholds are violated and it becomes easier or more acceptable to use

WMD. The restraints may be even greater if the opponent is a collective actor such as the Organization of American States or the Security Council which is important to other small states.

On the other hand, in the Cold War many analysts seized on the view that nuclear weapons carry an inherent credibility since their use might not be rational or sensible but a government might use them anyway, and the consequences would be so awful that its opponents would not take that chance. If this view is widely held, then nuclear weapons will not readily be outmoded in deterrence. Colin Gray, for instance, argues on this basis that nuclear weapons will not readily be superceded.[20]

However, the existential deterrence argument is not impressive on the record. Israel was attacked in 1973 and again during the 1991 Gulf War despite being known to have nuclear weapons. Britain was attacked in the Falklands. Iraq was known to have WMD and was ousted from Kuwait with no real hesitation. China and the Soviet Union engaged in nasty conventional battles in 1969 despite the presence of nuclear weapons on both sides. India and Pakistan daily shell each other, and sometimes have come very close to war since each established a nuclear weapons capability. The US was prepared to invade Cuba in 1962 knowing that Soviet nuclear-armed missiles there might be fired and fully appreciating the Soviet strategic nuclear capability. And Soviet forces in Cuba initially had orders to use tactical nuclear weapons to stop the invasion regardless of the American nuclear threat. It would be wrong to suggest that existential deterrence does not exist because at times it does. For instance, retrospective analyses of the Missile Crisis strongly suggest that the two leaders were highly concerned about getting into a process they could not control that would culminate in nuclear disaster.[21] Still, it is not always a determining factor.

WMD could also turn out to be so unacceptable and so clearly *passé* that they have little use as tokens of prestige and status, being taken instead as unusable, backward, uncompetitive, or ineffective. This would be a replay of the standard appeal of technologically advanced capabilities to states seeking both modernization and a modern image, with 'image as everything'. The weapons might exist in arsenals without being functional any longer. States often have outmoded weapons laying around. Thus the likelihood of their use would decline even more but the possibility would not vanish completely for some time to come.

Lest outgrowing the weapons seem far fetched, most states already find WMD unusable, irrelevant, outmoded, or deficient as tokens of status and prestige, and have said so in the Nuclear Proliferation Treaty and the chemical and biological weapons conventions. The RMA might eventually convince the rest, particularly if the greatly enhanced defensive capabilities emerge for states that WMD powers were hoping to deter or coerce.

The second way to outmode a weapon or way of warfare is to have developments cancel its effectiveness, which is what a marked improvement in defensive capabilities would do. The RMA could produce a situation in which to deter via retaliation would decline in appeal while deterring via defenses would rise. If the expense was not prohibitive many states might settle for strictly or primarily defensive postures, something strongly encouraged now in Europe, as highly practical, moral, and unprovocative. The RMA would make for a far more robust defense.

Both possibilities would greatly enhance the likelihood that WMD would not be used and would eventually be discarded, but only if the RMA generates capabilities of greater or offsetting effectiveness that readily spread. If it does not easily spread to states that have WMD capabilities or want them, then it cannot supersede their functions in deterrence or enhanced national status and prestige. We will take up the degree to which the RMA can spread later.

The third way of outmoding WMD would require a sharp improvement in the general political or security circumstances of those who possess or might want them. They become outmoded because there is little or no need to practice deterrence and there are better routes to national status and prestige. For great powers, this requires that their current relative amity continue and their interaction and cooperation expand so that they all no longer anticipate becoming serious enemies. It also means not having to confront other states as enemies that would require deterrence. For smaller states, this means either the absence of very serious conflict with any powerful or WMD-armed states, or the emergence of a regional or global security management that can guarantee their safety. All these are only possibilities at the moment, but they are not implausible.

(2) The RMA Provoking or Stimulating WMD Development and Use

The second possible relationship between the RMA and WMD is that the former could provoke or stimulate the development, proliferation, and even use of the latter. This is a major concern among security analysts, who argue roughly as follows. The RMA is being pursued primarily by the rich and powerful; it mainly enhances the ability of the US, the West, and the UN they control, to use force against any state or society that they dislike. The one recourse weaker states that do not see eye to eye with the US or the West had in the past was their ability to inflict casualties and other costs in a war, and the West threatens to eliminate this. Their logical, perhaps only, recourse is try to use WMD to negate the effects of the RMA by still confronting the US and its friends with threats of unacceptable harm. In short, for them deterrence now becomes even more important and WMD even more vital for achieving it. The more effective the RMA looks the more this will be true. Commonly cited are the remarks of (India's) General Sundarji that the first lesson of the 1991 Gulf War was to never fight the US without having nuclear weapons.[22]

That states want WMD to offset US military superiority is not surprising, but the desire could become stronger if the RMA thoroughly negates older conventional military capabilities. One appeal of nuclear weapons is as an equalizer, and under 'existential deterrence' small nuclear arsenals can be roughly equivalent to big ones. Small states, even poor and weak ones, can achieve 'unacceptable damage' against very powerful states with only a small number of weapons. Their concern then is with achieving a second strike posture and acquiring a suitable delivery system suitable. That concern grows with other WMD, which are difficult to dispense in an effective way and hard to deliver.[23] What is unclear is whether willingness to use those weapons would rise with the development and enlargement of such arsenals. The superpowers did not find this to be the case. Having more, and more kinds, of WMD did not make it any more attractive to use even one. In addition, the RMA may result in a nuclear or other WMD response being disproportionate to the damage suffered by a weaker state, making the onus for such a response severe.

It seems likely that incentives to acquire and use WMD would rise for states that saw themselves facing steadily rising threats and hostility from neighbors or the great powers, saw their costs from potential military defeat rising, and had no way to imitate the RMA or borrow its important components. It follows that if, instead, they do not see their security deteriorating, if their anticipated costs of being defeated are not going up and even an outright defeat is becoming more bearable, and particularly if they believe the RMA can readily diffuse and help them strengthen their security, then the desire to offset the RMA need not rise. Or, as noted above, the RMA could make a state like Iraq find that an RMA-based military attack or even defeat is relatively bearable, while a response with WMD would be widely deemed disproportionate, making the onus for resorting to WMD more severe.

All this is possible. Many smaller and weaker states are busy investing in advanced technology, particularly tactical missiles and avionics, equipment to use global positioning satellites, night vision equipment, etc., to enhance their military effectiveness. As for states having no need for deterrence, for many states this will not come about soon unless the 1991 Gulf War turns out to exemplify how the Security Council treats all cases of aggression.

(3) RMA as a Deterrent to WMD

To deter the use of WMD requires a severe threat, and it is often assumed that it must be on a par with the threatened attack, namely, only a threat of retaliation in kind will deter their use with high certainty. On the other hand carrying out the threat may expose the threatener to severe retaliation. There are also the many inhibitions on using WMD noted above, particularly if the situation is not a last resort requiring desperate measures. Many analysts believe it would be extremely difficult for the US to use WMD, even after its forces had been attacked by such weapons, because the US would still have all the necessary conventional capabilities to defeat the attacker and would be expected to use them instead. The US confronted this possibility in the 1991 Gulf War and had given it much thought in connection with its commitment to South Korea. In both cases the US threatened indirectly to retaliate with WMD, but in the Korean case the US eventually withdrew its nuclear weapons from the ROK because it did not envision any occasion when it would have to use them, even though the North Korean threat remained potent. The implication was that there could be a fully effective conventional US response.

Thus the RMA can have mixed results as an a deterrent. It might successfully be used by great powers to practice extended (or even direct) deterrence by supplying a huge capability to retaliate in a much more acceptable way than with WMD, lending their retaliatory threats much more credibility even when the target states have WMD. It might also be used as a deterrent to WMD proliferation by giving great powers better military tools for disrupting a state's progress toward it. Threatening would become easier since the potential costs to both sides would be lower than with even standard conventional forces. (This will be enhanced by steadily better surveillance capabilities for sustaining verification or other inspection systems to detect violators of a proliferation regime early on.) The US was planning precise strikes on North Korea when it was using threats to induce negotiations to halt the North's nuclear weapons program.

On the other hand, the threat to use RMA-related capabilities may not be effective precisely because the magnitude of what is threatened is within 'bearable' limits. A challenger may more readily decide that implementation of the threat would not bring disaster, and thus more inclined to gamble that the threatener will not go through with it. Precisely because RMA resources are more useable, therefore, chances would go up that they would have to be used. If so, deterrence or compellance would culminate more often in having to carry out threats, much as has been the case for the Security Council in dealing with Iraq.

(4) Possibilities for Preempting WMD Use

At present, the US enjoys enhanced offensive capabilities from the RMA but also an enhanced ability to protect its forces from everything except ballistic missiles. (If RMA capabilities readily disperse this would likely erode much of this advantage.) As long as this is true, the US and some other states may be able to use conventional forces to attack sites that would have been, in the past, targets for nuclear weapons, in particular an opponent's WMD sites and command centers. As noted above, analysts anticipate that high-tech capabilities will someday be suitable for strategic purposes, such as preemptive attacks on WMD and related installations. The idea of using nonnuclear forces for this is not new: the Soviets worked hard toward such a capability in the 1970s and 1980s in Europe. What is new is the rising capacity for doing it through very precise weapons.

However, many important targets for preemption would normally be hardened or well below ground and perhaps not readily destroyed by RMA resources. In addition, those capabilities are still not reliable enough, the US could not find and destroy Iraqi Scud launchers, for example. Thus the ideal preemption capability for some time to come will probably have to be multi-tiered: initial attacks that destroy enemy weapons and other important targets, and some advanced defenses against those enemy weapons that emerge unscathed. This requires much greater enhancement of defenses than has taken place thus far but it is not improbable over the next decade and beyond. Thus RMA capabilities effective for preemption against WMD are likely to develop down the road, but are not yet sufficiently developed to rely on.

(5) RMA as a WMD Extension

Thus far the RMA involves capabilities not designed with mass destruction in mind. This may not always be the case. For instance, there is no reason to confine precise attacks to military targets. They could just as an easily be used against targets that have much to do with maintaining civilian life, with large casualties as a result. Or there could be simple extensions of R & D for the RMA that produce new, much more lethal, forms of WMD. One possibility would be the use of myriads of tiny vectors not just to flood an area with reconnaissance devices but to dispense biological weapons.

There is also a possible synergy between the two. For instance, the more precise the delivery of weapons and the more accurate surveillance is, the more appealing it may be to use highly tailored packages of WMD, particularly on things like deep underground bunkers. The RMA might, in other words, erode some of the norms that have helped preclude WMD use. This is already a realistic possibility technologically, and must be kept in mind when the RMA is championed only as an alternative to WMD.

THE RMA AND RELEVANT STATES TODAY

We can continue the analysis by exploring the impact thus far on the states that now possess WMD or might. We start with those with superpower-level capabilities, then turn to other well established arsenals (Britain, France, China, Israel), then to ones with significant but lesser capabilities (India, Pakistan, Egypt, Iran, North Korean), and to states just on the edge (like Japan).

SUPERPOWER-LEVEL STATES

It is easy to see what the United States is up to. First it is pursuing the complete spectrum of enhanced military capabilities the RMA involves. It has by far the largest research and development effort, has gone farthest in incorporating these capabilities in its forces, and has generated the most speculation about the implications for weapons, forces, and strategy. Ideally, this will extend to a very substantial preemption capability against WMD, as in the effort to devise a conventional option for hitting the Libyan underground chemical weapons facility. The US intends to have the RMA provide a highly effective and credible deterrent, including one against any use (even development) of nuclear weapons.

Second, the US advocates a marked deemphasis of WMD for itself and in the international system. Hence the Strategic Arms Reduction Treaty (START) agreements and other arrangements to sharply reduce its nuclear stockpile, its belated agreement to a comprehensive test ban, its readiness to destroy its chemical and biological weapons and subscribe to the conventions on those weapons, its moratorium on fissile materials production and its proposed permanent international moratorium, its removal of most of its nuclear weapons from abroad and at sea, and its endorsement of a NATO strategy and a national strategic posture in which using nuclear weapons is a very last resort (though stopping short, so far, of no-first-use). While taking many steps unilaterally, the US is vigorously trying to get other states to do the same if they have not already done so and through international agreements where possible. Third, the US has become the foremost advocate and enforcer in nuclear nonproliferation efforts – playing a large role in the regimes for limiting sales of WMD-related technology or delivery systems, leading the efforts to halt North Korea's nuclear weapons program and repress Iraq's programs, etc.

Clearly the US hopes to avoid ever having to contemplate using WMD to respond to an attack of that sort by shrinking the world's nuclear arsenals and eliminating CBW stocks. While it is not committed to complete elimination of nuclear weapons soon, and does not regard this as feasible now, that would be the logical culmination of its policies. The US regards the RMA as an alternative, far more acceptable, version of the military superiority it now enjoys and considers necessary to uphold its security responsibilities.

Military domination of this sort of world would provide the US with numerous benefits. It could reinforce benign relations among the great powers by removing WMD as sources of fear and resentment. It would strip nuclear weapons from governments not fully reliable, in judgment, control, experience, safety, and political moderation, and leave no one with WMD-based deterrence against US or UN forces, thereby enhancing the possibility of reliable security management. It would contribute to keeping those weapons out of the hands of terrorists. The US would also again be essentially militarily invulnerable to an attack on its homeland. Finally, the US would have a highly useable military capability, acceptable in terms of the casualties the US would suffer and the casualties and destruction it would have to inflict. This would reverse the impact of WMD on war.

The last part of the US strategy is to reduce sharply the need for nations to be concerned about deterrence, making it easier for them to abandon WMD. This is one objective of the democratization campaign (since democracies do not go to war with each other) and also of the American push for multilateral security management. By urging that NATO have more peace enforcement responsibilities, by leading the Security Council intervention against Iraq, by having eventually organized the NATO interventions in Bosnia and Kosovo the US is demonstrating that it wants a multilateral approach to providing security.

The US is often accused of now lacking a grand strategy, equivalent to containment, but it is hard to see why. The above amounts to a rather breathtaking grand strategy. It would be universally condemned as self-serving were it not for the heavy emphasis on multilateralism, the benign state of great power relations which it intends to reinforce, the clear benefits for most of the world of the elimination of WMD, and the fact that prime targets of the strategy now are among the least popular regimes in the world.

The US has already moved a good way down this road. By committing itself to elimination of its chemical and biological stockpiles it has only nuclear weapons for a WMD response to that sort of attack. While it threatened a nuclear response against Iraq in the 1991 Gulf War, many analysts doubt that it would have followed through. Even as North Korea was developing nuclear weapons the US was moving to remove its nuclear weapons from the ROK and signal that it did not intend a nuclear response to a North Korean attack. The US is clearly counting on an RMA-enhanced military superiority to enable it to drop nuclear weapons from its military menu for all but the most extreme circumstances.

It is also hoping to utilize the fruits of the RMA to achieve an effective regional anti-ballistic missile system (ABM). It is almost certainly going to deploy one early in the twenty-first century, intended to negate the most effective delivery systems available. The end result, ideally, would also be to dilute the deterrence capacities of WMD powers *vis-à-vis* the US and its friends.

The US clearly also intends to make its military capability available for UN operations, and since the RMA will likely to spread furthest among other Western powers the UN and NATO will end up with considerably enhanced capabilities. They could be used for military pressure or intervention to uphold international restraints on WMD, as with Iraq. If the great powers ever agree to really outlaw nuclear weapons, this will almost certainly be done on the basis of an RMA-based Security Council enforcement.

One caveat is in order. The point of US policy is to achieve a more acceptable and usable military capability for upholding its obligations and responsibilities, but that capability may eventually by employed by a neoisolationist US to retreat behind its defenses and abandon many of its current responsibilities. This would reduce chances that the US would ever be using WMD, but some analysts contend that it would *increase* the chances of WMD use by others.

As the only other nation with a superpower nuclear capability, Russia has faced serious decisions. It has agreed to dispense with chemical and biological weapons (with the West sometimes wondering about its compliance), has made great reductions in nuclear weapons and wants further cuts. Yet it currently has little ability to pursue the RMA and is now living on past technological achievements; its conventional forces are seriously deficient, particularly in advanced high technology areas, and are now prostrate like the rest of the nation. To compensate, Russian reliance on nuclear weapons has grown. Russia has abandoned the former Soviet commitment to no-first-use, has expanded the role of nuclear weapons in its national security strategy, and has maintained the Soviet-era reliance on a launch-on-warning (LOW) posture.

Dating from Gorbachev's reign is a substantial official commitment to multilateral security management, which means opposing all unilateral or non-Security Council endorsed military interventions (except its own!), as well as a strong bias against using force unless unavoidable. This is combined with very strong official opposition to WMD proliferation, support for an end to nuclear testing, the nuclear nonproliferation treaty and other nonproliferation regimes, whatever the US concerns about Russian sales of nuclear-weapons-relevant technology to states like Iran. Russia now aims to try to outmode nuclear weapons for most states, while at the same time restraining US use of its advanced military capabilities so that collective security management is really the prime beneficiary of the RMA. Russia can appreciate uneasiness about American military power elsewhere, such as in states not currently on good terms with the US, a view strongly reinforced by the war over Kosovo.

Thus in Russia, the RMA has had the effect of *increasing*, however marginally, the potential use of WMD because it is leaving Russia behind. An important offsetting factor is that Russia currently has no serious enemies, no likely war, and thus the matter of possible use of its nuclear weapons is unlikely to come up. However, this is not guaranteed to last.

In the meantime, another important factor is at work. The Russian government now *cannot sustain its nuclear forces at levels which existing agreements allow,* and will have to make significant cuts. American arms-control advocates have been pushing for unilateral US reductions, and the administration has committed itself to significant cuts in a prospective START III, so as to make it easier (politically) for Moscow to reduce its nuclear forces to a level more in keeping with the threats it faces and its resources. There are also signs that the Russian early warning system is defective, undermining the technical basis for a LOW posture. Apparently its satellites cover US missile sites only about 2/3rds of the time or less and cannot cover some ocean sites at all. As a result Russia is likely to eventually move to a smaller nuclear force tailored for nuclear retaliation, not LOW.[24]

It does not seem that Russia will be able to pursue the RMA seriously, on other than a very selective basis, for years to come. Thus it could eliminate any Russian inclination to use WMD only if Russia abandoned any unilateral approach to security by relying heavily on a collective security management, as bolstered by Western RMA capabilities. This would shed the last vestiges of its superpower status, quite appropriate in terms of Russian resources but maybe impossible in Russian politics; nuclear weapons are now, for many in Russia, a matter of national status. Yet Russia has made a great shift, however, away from nuclear weapons as overwhelming vital for security and a Russia at peace may become steadily more willing to set them aside as tokens of national status, but not soon.

As for other states with significant WMD capabilities of long standing, Britain, France, China, and Israel show no signs of giving up their nuclear arsenals though they have agreed to not maintain chemical and biological weapons. They seem committed to the view that nuclear weapons will be vital, as an ultimate recourse, for their security for years to come (with France still ready to use nuclear weapons first if necessary). There is a mix of status and security concerns involved for Britain and France, while security seems the dominant concern in China and Israel. In neither Britain nor France has it been widely suggested that the RMA could allow them to abandon this posture; the argument for nuclear disarmament is more likely to be made on moral grounds. Both countries are very interested in RMA capabilities, particularly as their forces shrink and they want maximum effectiveness from those that remain. Yet neither can keep up with the US, and European cooperation on military research and development does not take the weapons very seriously as yet. Thus the most potent justification for giving up WMD completely is likely to be that the weapons are outmoded by Europe's security situation (a lack of serious security threats). Given the situation in Russia and the troubles in the Middle East and North Africa this justification is unlikely to seem sufficient any time soon.

Israel is not likely to find the enhancements associated with the RMA enough to permit an end to its nuclear arsenal; it will continue to suggest that only a general political settlement in the Middle East can do this. Israel has worked hard to incorporate advanced technology into its forces and has pioneered some of it (such as using drones for reconnaissance). However, as long as the grave threats for which its nuclear arsenal was built continue to exist, Israel will not consider giving it up.

China continues to maintain an unconditional no-first-use policy on nuclear weapons and also foreswears any use or threat to use nuclear weapons against non-nuclear weapons states and in nuclear-free zones.[25] It will continue to find that RMA improvements in American forces make American hegemony ever more apparent and potentially threatening, possible to offset only by a nuclear arsenal. The Chinese concluded after the

1991 Gulf War that they were in roughly the situation Russia finds itself now, that is with a large conventional capability much less useful than expected so greater reliance on nuclear forces is necessary. Hence it is not surprising that China was the last to test nuclear weapons before joining the test moratorium and is the only great power with a growing nuclear arsenal.[26] Here is another example of the RMA acting to stimulate reliance on WMD. This situation is offset only by the fact that China now has a benign security situation and no serious military conflict on the horizon, certainly not one that might call for WMD. China is, however, very concerned about the possibility of effective ballistic missile defence (BMD) and of it being available to Japan and would be greatly disturbed by heavy Japanese investment in other aspects of the RMA.

It is hard to know what these states would do if the US and Russia invited them to join in complete WMD disarmament, but the differential impact of the RMA would probably have the following effect. Evidence of an immense US military advantage due to the RMA, confidence it is available for their protection, and in particular evidence of a highly effective regional ABM (and other delivery system) defense that the US will deploy to protect them, might bring France, Britain, and even Israel to join. Under its current political system, China will take a lot more convincing and remain inclined to see the enhanced US capability as an increasing threat, making it important to retain nuclear weapons for years.

This brings us, finally, to other states with lesser WMD capabilities or the ready capacity to create them (Iraq and Iran, Libya, Egypt, India, Pakistan, Japan). How will the RMA affect the likelihood that they will ever end up using such weapons? There are two possible ways it might reinforce Japan's allergy to WMD. US capabilities will be extended to protect Japan, and if effective missile defense is included this would erase any serious Japanese interest in someday becoming a nuclear power. This is plausible given the recent refurbishing of the US-Japan alliance and the strong possibility that the US and Japan will soon agree to cooperate on BMD development. Or Japan might decide to delve into the RMA to develop suitable defense forces for itself – Japan being one of the few that might seriously imitate the US in this regard if it chose to. This seems very unlikely unless Japan's security situation deteriorates badly. If it does, then a military buildup that emphasized RMA would have strong appeal as less provocative to the neighbors than to build nuclear weapons.

Of course, Japan is committed to trying to preclude situations in which the probability of WMD use would rise. It also presses for complete nuclear disarmament and is a member in good standing of numerous arms control regimes. It calls for calm political dialogue on conflicts and is now able to participate in peacekeeping operations to strengthen security management. It wants reduced salience for all highly destructive weapons in international affairs, within a smaller role for force and conflict in general.

For others on the list, the RMA is more likely to be seen as a serious threat by allowing the US and its friends to more readily intervene militarily in their affairs and sometimes dominate security management in their regions. This applies directly to Iran and Iraq in particular; the RMA will continue to serve as an incentive for these states to maintain or enlarge WMD capabilities and then to threaten their use for purposes of deterrence. They will feel that something is better than nothing, that in a confrontation with the US it is better to have some WMD capabilities to brandish. The war over Kosovo will only exacerbate this. Rather than American military intervention, India and Pakistan fear American-led pressure to deny or strip them of military capabilities they have deeply desired for both status and security purposes. Egypt has no reason to expect that its neighborhood will soon be free of WMD and feels the need for some offsetting capability. All these states have serious concerns besides the United States for which they consider those weapons potentially useful and they have no prospect of being able to use RMA capabilities as a reliable substitute. Unless these political threats can be eliminated or until international security management becomes much more reliable, these states are not going to give up WMD. And that means they will be possible users of them in the years ahead.

DIFFUSION OF THE RMA?

What about the possibility that the RMA will readily diffuse, so that states can use elements of it to better fend off the US and its friends, to redress an imbalance that seems adjustable now only via WMD? It is often suggested that the technologies involved make it easy to spread, and thus any advantage it conveys will be fleeting. Examples include the ways commercial satellites can now be used for surveillance, the ready access to the Global Positioning System, the performance of much of the world's computer production, maintenance, and programming in Third World countries, the ease with which advanced avionics, radar systems, and weapons can be bought, etc. Particularly emphasized is the fact that this is technological change driven by the civilian sector and global markets. Often the best available technology can be bought off the shelf or is coming out in civilian industries and therefore is not secret or exotic or difficult to obtain. For instance, US supercomputers sold to India probably contributed significantly to India's missile development program.[27]

A related set of arguments has to do with the ways in which an ability to readily obtain relevant technologies can sustain penetration and disruption of RMA-based military systems. Anything (nuclear or nonnuclear) which could induce electromagnetic pulse effects might completely paralyze an RMA-dominated military force with inadequate protection. The biggest concern now is the vulnerability of computer systems to hacking, viruses, and other manipulation. There is also speculation that satellites will be vulnerable and everything depending on satellites will be subject to disruption; this is why there is top-level US concern about China's work on anti-satellite laser systems. Finally, there is the dreadnought example; when a major technological shift outmodes existing capabilities it outmodes the inequities in those capabilities, making it easier for those who were behind to catch up now.

While it is certainly true that the technologies of the RMA are, in many instances, quite approachable, the overall argument is not impressive. Since not simply technology but better arrangements, organizationally and strategically, for using it are involved, unless the latter accompany diffusion of the technology the advantages supplied by the RMA will not be readily lost. And the necessary arrangements are not easy to graft onto a society or a military force; in fact, they are almost certainly more difficult to embrace than the technology itself. States that feel threatened by advanced conventional capabilities are not likely to find it easy to import the RMA to make up the difference.

In addition, we will be subjected to waves of technological change in military matters and repeated adjustments in social, organizational, and intellectual spheres to embrace them. This is already obvious in civilian spheres. The RMA will be hard to keep up with, even if mastered for a particular purpose in some early version. And one of the foremost targets of the later waves will be ameliorating the vulnerabilities associated with earlier versions. Thus the US is busy developing ultralight solar-powered drones that, at high altitudes, do the work of satellites. Almost all the advanced fighters, tanks, artillery, radar systems and other resources imported by Iraq turned out to be almost useless because of changes introduced by the RMA in just its very earliest phase. The most distinctive feature of the RMA may well be that it is a continuous revolution rooted in a larger also continuous technological upheaval, and if so only those political, military, and social systems configured for and comfortable with constant change will be able to embrace it effectively.[28]

As for one other concern, many of the most interesting criticisms of the

RMA suggest that it is not appropriate for coping with terrorism, insurgencies, domestic unrest, etc., for the kind of conflict endemic today.[29] That may be true now, though there is a good chance it will not be in the future, but that sort of conflict is largely irrelevant to the threat of WMD use which is of concern here.

CONCLUSION

The threat of WMD use is primarily long-term. At present there are few cases where it seems likely to become imminent on short notice (India–Pakistan being the primary one). The RMA is currently having a beneficial effect in several ways. States which depend on the US for security can be more confident of sufficient protection, with sufficient credibility, from major conventional attacks. They are confident enough to forego developing nuclear weapons (the chief cases being Japan and South Korea). The RMA also makes it easier for the United States and others to be confident of a successful intervention in cases of aggression, which also works to encourage states with serious security threats to forego WMD. Finally, the RMA makes it much easier for the US and others to be confident that they need not resort to WMD to counter attacks by even states with major conventional forces. In turn, this has made it easier to justify cutting nuclear weapons and eliminating chemical and biological weapons.

In the long run, the RMA may be very beneficial by lending powerful support to a multilateral security management focused on curbing aggression and enforcing restrictions on the proliferation of weapons of mass destruction. The gravest problem in multilateral security management is finding ways to use force that have few casualties for the participants and fit the expectation that multilateral actors will not use force extravagantly and indiscriminately. The RMA offers a potentially durable solution. And a suitable military capability in support of security management would greatly reduce the pressures for WMD proliferation and use, and over time would add greatly to the pressures for elimination of those weapons. Looked at in another way, associating the RMA with multilateral security management may be the best way for many states to contain, exploit, and utilize American military superiority, research and development, RMA innovations, etc. so as an to minimize the US as an a potential threat. The leading long term problem in the international system at the moment is keeping everyone reassured about America's unique military strength and this may be the best way to do that.

In the longest run, the RMA may greatly enhance defense at the expense of offense. For years there has been speculation that the most stable international systems are defense-dominant. We may get a chance to find out. The RMA may make it easier for major states to provide themselves (and clients) with very effective protection, outmoding the effects of the nuclear revolution and adding to the possibility of doing away with those weapons.

However, these are speculative comments and depend on developments in more than military affairs, and in the meantime there are several serious short-term difficulties. The RMA is now stimulating efforts by some states to enhance their nuclear capabilities and/or their reliance on those capabilities (Russia, China) and helping incite efforts at nuclear proliferation and the like in other states (Iran). This is not going to change in the near future. The RMA cannot be used by these states to offset their perceived need for WMD capabilities. As it stands, it cannot be used to guarantee that states cannot be successfully attacked with WMD, which encourages WMD proliferation as well.

NOTES

1. The US put its strategic nuclear forces on high alert only twice, the Soviet Union apparently only once. There are conflicting reports as to whether India and/or Pakistan put nuclear forces on high alert in 1990. The Soviet Union hinted at using nuclear weapons against China in 1969 (but this may have been a bluff), and possibly Chinese nuclear weapons were on high alert as a result. Israel has not indicated whether its nuclear weapons were ever on high alert, for example in 1973 according to some reports, because it never admits to having the weapons.
2. This does not cover accidents with CW. Also, on a possible use I side with the skeptics on the 'yellow rain' controversy about the Afghanistan War.
3. Apparently as many as 250,000 people were killed. See the brief report in *NAPSnet Daily Report*,18 Aug. 1998, available at ftp://ftp.nautilus.org/napsnet/othnaps.html
4. An example of worrying – the US Department of Defense in Oct. 1998 established a Defense Threat Reduction Agency (merging three existing units) with over 2000 employees and a $2 billion budget to deal with emerging WMD threats. Laura Myers, 'Pentagon Launches New Nuke Agency', Associated Press, in *NAPSnet Daily Report* 1 Oct. 1998, available at: ftp://ftp.nautilus.org/napsnet/othnaps.html
5. Ogarkov's resulting insistence on heavy spending for this new round of the East–West arms race was one reason he was forced to retire.
6. Lawrence Freedman, *The Revolution in Strategic Affairs*, Adelphi Paper No. 318 (London: IISS 1998) p.30.
7. As in '…American culture…loves the latest technology, believes it enjoys a long lead in exploiting that technology, and yearns to find clean, discriminate, (American)-casualty-minimal modes of war. Cyberwar is particularly appealing to a mind-set that seeks to avoid war's brutal realities, instead finding ways to play at war in cyberspace'. Colin Gray, 'Nuclear Weapons and the Revolution in Military Affairs', in T.V. Paul, Richard Harknett, and James Wirtz (eds.) *The Absolute Weapons Revisited: Nuclear Arms and the Emerging International Order* (Ann Arbor: U. of Michigan Press 1998) p.120.
8. The term is usually traced back to Geoffrey Parker, *The Military Revolution: Military Innovation and the Rise of the West 1500–1800* (NY: Cambridge UP 1988), who in turn cites a lecture by Michael Roberts in 1955 as its origin. The ensuing debate about it is covered in Clifford Rogers (ed.) *The Military Revolution Debate* (Boulder: U. of Colorado Press 1995).

9. For challenges to the idea that the RMA exists see Jeremy Shapiro, 'Information and War: Is it a Revolution?', in Zalmay M Khalilzad and John P. White (eds.) *Strategic Appraisal: The Changing Role of Information in Warfare* (Santa Monica, CA: RAND 1999) pp.113–53; also Michael O'Hanlon, 'Can High Technology Bring US Troops Home', *Foreign Policy* No. 113 (Winter 1998–99) pp.72–86 and the attached bibliography.

10. For discussion and examples see: Andrew Krepinevich, 'Cavalry to Computer: The Pattern of Military Revolutions', *The National Interest* 37 (Fall 1994); Freedman (note 6); Martin van Creveld, *Technology and War: From 2000 B.C. to the Present* (NY: Free Press 1989); and Jeffrey Cooper, 'Another View of the Revolution in Military Affairs', in John Arquilla and David Ronfeldt (eds.) *In Athena's Camp: Preparing for Conflict in the Information Age* (Santa Monica, CA: RAND 1997) pp.99–140.

11. This is not necessarily the case when the revolution builds on a civilization's overall advantages, as when the military revolution in the West gave Western forces the power to seize the colonial empires.

12. The literature on the RMA is piling up and includes: International Institute for Strategic Studies, 'Is There a Revolution in Military Affairs?', *Strategic Survey 1995–96* (London: OUP 1996) pp.20–40; Alexander Bevin, *The Future of Warfare* (NY: Norton 1995); John Arquilla and David Ronfeldt, 'The Advent of Netwar', in Arguilla and Ronfeldt, *In Athena's Camp* (note 10) pp.275–93; George Millburn, 'New Technologies: An Overview', in Desmond Ball and Helen Wilson (eds.) *New Technology: Implications for Regional and Australian Security* (Canberra: Australian National U. Strat. and Def. Studies Centre 1991) pp.2–19; Neville Brown, *The Strategic Revolution: Thoughts for the Twenty-First Century* (London: Brassey's 1992); Victor Utgoff, 'Military Technology: Options for the Future', in Barry Blechman *et al.* (eds.) *The American Military in the Twenty-First Century* (NY: St Martin's Press 1993) pp.143–95; W. Seth Carus, 'Military Technology and the Arms Trade: Changes and Their Impact', *The Annals* 535 (Sept. 1994) pp.153–74; Richard Garwin, 'New Applications of Nonlethal and Less Lethal Technology', in Arnold Kanter and Linton Brooks (eds.) *U.S. Intervention Policy for the Post-Cold War World: New Challenges and Responses* (NY: Norton 1994) pp.105–31; Williamson Murray, 'Thinking About Revolutions in Military Affairs', *Joint Force Quarterly* 16 (Summer 1997); Khalilzad and White (note 9); and Gray (note 7).

13. See Arquilla and Ronfeldt (note 10).

14. On the other hand, the RMA is promoting rising expectations about wars without death and destruction, lowering the threshold for 'acceptable' casualties not only for one's own forces but, in the West, for the enemy as well. In the US:

> '…as we have seen, that number evolves over time, depending in part on experience. If the military manages to come up with a solution…, it may simply generate new pressures to further reduce the time, treasure, and blood spent to secure military goals. …Eventually, technological solutions may cease to be able to provide an answer to the country's need for every more-overwhelming victories at an ever-diminishing cost'. See Shapiro (note 9) pp.141–2.

15. For a recent proposal along these lines see Dagobert Brito and Michael Intriligator, 'Deterring Nuclear Weapons Proliferation', UCLA Center for International Relations Working Paper No.16, June 1998.

16. Freedman (note 6) pp.76–7.

17. In the county where I live, in one long unsolved murder case the weapon was a crossbow.

18. Realistic cases of WMD-based deterrence today involve deterring either WMD attacks or attacks by more powerful conventional forces than the deterrer possesses. It is always possible to use WMD to deter any sort of attack and the US once used WMD deterrence against threats from distinctly weaker states (North Korea, China). But this seems to have disappeared today; it has become unacceptable to threaten to respond to a non-WMD attack that could be handled on just the conventional level by resorting to WMD.

19. The chief proponent of the view that nuclear weapons are outmoded and irrelevant has been John Mueller. See, for example, Mueller, 'The Escalating Irrelevance of Nuclear Weapons', in Paul *et al.* *Absolute Weapons* (note 7) pp.73–98.

20. Gray, 'Nuclear Weapons' (note 7).
21. See James Blight, *The Shattered Crystal Ball: Fear and Learning in the Cuban Missile Crisis* (Lanham, MD: Rowman & Littlefield 1992); and Ernest May and Philip Zelikow, *The Kennedy Tapes: Inside the White House During the Cuban Missile Crisis* (Cambridge, MA: Harvard UP 1997).
22. His remarks are cited in Barry Schneider, 'Nuclear Proliferation and Counter-Proliferation: Policy Issues and Debates', *Mershon International Studies Review* 38/2 (Oct. 1994) p.227.
23. The problem with CBW delivery systems is that the most suitable ones for a large attack are slow, not likely to penetrate serious defenses, etc. See International institute for Strategic Studies, *Strategic Survey 1996/97* (London: IISS 1997) pp.31–41 for discussion of this.
24. On Russia having too many nuclear weapons to maintain and deteriorating warning systems see the comments of Russian Deputy Prime Minister Yuri Maslyukov as reported in *NAPSnet Daily Report*, 6 Oct. 1998. Available at ftp://ftp.nautilus.org/napsnet/othnaps.html. On the implications for Russia strategic doctrine see Alexander Nikitin, 'Rethinking Russian Military Doctrine and Nuclear Policy', *Pugwash Newsletter* 31/1 (April 1998) pp.37–9.
25. See the comments of PRC Foreign Minister Tang Jiaxuan in the General Assembly, as reported in *NAPSnet Daily Report*, 30 Oct. 1998. Available at ftp://ftp.nautilus.org/napsnet/othnaps.html
26. It has launched efforts to upgrade its conventional forces but that will do little to erase inferiority *vis-à-vis* American forces for years, if ever. If the RMA works for the US as its proponents expect, China may end up even further behind.
27. Gary Millhollin, 'Made in America? How the U.S. is Fueling the South Asia Arms Race With Supercomputers and Other Assistance', *Washington Post National Weekly Edition*, 15 June 1998
28. One version of this argument can be found in David C. Gompert, 'Right Makes Might: Freedom and Power in the Information Age', in Khalilzad and White (note 9) pp.45–73.
29. See Martin van Creveld, *The Transformation of War* (NY: Free Press 1991).

8

The Methodology of Mass Destruction: Assessing Threats in the New World Order

JOHN MUELLER and KARL MUELLER

Over a decade after the fall of the Berlin Wall, euphoria about the end of the Cold War appears to have given way to anxiety about ominous perils lurking in the shadows of the New World Order. Western security concerns, once driven by the threat of apocalyptic war with the Soviet Union and the spread of communism, are now dominated by fears of terrorism, 'rogue states', and above all the acquisition of nuclear, biological, and chemical weapons by unpredictable potential enemies in the Third World. In fact, most of these dangers are neither as new nor as severe as much current rhetoric suggests.

The process of finding new nightmares to replace the old ones is exemplified by the widespread adoption of 'weapons of mass destruction' (WMD) as a blanket label to embrace not only nuclear weapons, but, often on a seemingly equal footing, arms that have thus far killed scarcely anyone (biological weapons), arms that are vastly less effective at killing (chemical weapons), and dramatic but costly and often ineffectual delivery devices (ballistic missiles). This can lead to excessive fears and costly overreaction.

In the meantime, an impressive method, if not exactly a weapon, for mass destruction has indeed matured in recent years: economic sanctions. As international cooperation grows in the post-Cold War era, the major powers have frequently employed this coercive device as an alternative to the unsavory use of military force, sometimes with what appear to be devastating results. Yet the casualties that can be inflicted by massive economic sanctions usually receive little attention.

These trends have converged dramatically in Western policy towards Iraq since the 1991 Gulf War. In a thus-far futile effort to drive its leader from office (and therefore from life), and in a more successful effort to keep him from building up his military and WMD capabilities, economic sanctions have probably already taken the lives of more people in Iraq than have been killed by all weapons of mass destruction in history. Unlike such weapons, however, indiscriminate economic sanctions, or more aptly economic warfare, generally kills quietly and statistically, and the severity of its effects often goes unappreciated as a result.

A serious reassessment of the impact of economic warfare, and of the dangers that are truly posed by states such as Iraq, suggests that it is time to find new strategies to deal with the serpents in the post-Cold War paradise. In the case of Iraq, a policy of deterrence and containment would seem to have been more sensible than one of slow motion destruction.

TERRORISM AND ROGUE STATES

For the most part, the impact of international terrorism has derived thus far much more from the fearful reaction it generates than from its actual physical effects. On average, far fewer Americans are killed each year by international terrorists than are killed by lightning or by auto accidents caused by deer or by peanuts.[1] To call this relatively minor problem a kind of warfare, as some have, is to stretch the language to the breaking point. And the popular declaration that terrorism in its present form poses a serious threat to national security is scarcely plausible.[2]

This is not to suggest that terrorism be ignored, of course. It is clearly an outrage that should be dealt with, but it is more reasonably seen as a form of crime than as a form of warfare, and it should be handled as such – with dogged, routine, unglamorous, patient police work.[3] And since it can be carried out by almost anyone with sufficient will, terrorism, like crime, can be reduced by good police work, but not eradicated.

For all the attention that terrorist attacks generate, it seems likely that the situation is improving, not deteriorating. Indeed, although there was a rise in 1991 at the time of the Gulf War, international terrorism has declined in frequency from late Cold War days thanks in part, perhaps, to enhanced prevention measures and better international police work.[4]

Since the effects of terrorism stem less from its actual consequences than from the fear and alarm it inspires, it might be better for governments, scholars, and the media to play terrorism for what it is, pathetic actions of the weak and desperate, instead of stoking popular fear and magnifying the destructive actions of terrorists to cosmic proportions. However dramatic and newsworthy, and however tragic to the innocent victims and their families, the damage done by these international criminals in the aggregate has thus far been quite low, and it is scarcely grounds for panic and hysteria.

Something similar can be said for 'rogue states'. When big problems go away, small problems tend to be elevated in perceived importance, and accordingly this concept has been recently invented and treated as if it were a new problem in international affairs. Yet there were plenty of such states during the Cold War, and some of these were engaged in devious complicity with the big, truly threatening rogues: the Soviet Union and China.

Sukarno's Indonesia, for example, was a problem for years as it engaged in a policy of military 'confrontation' with some neighbouring states, and it often obtained support and encouragement from one major Communist country or another.[5] Something similar was true of Nasser's Egypt and Castro's Cuba, to say nothing of the trouble and potential danger stirred by egomaniacal and sometimes deranged leaders in far more potent states like Stalin's Soviet Union and Mao's China. The problems posed today by such enfeebled, impoverished, and friendless states as Iraq and North Korea pale in comparison (indeed, North Korea is far less significant a threat than during the Cold War when it was variously backed by China and the USSR). Moreover, the 'rogue state' label falsely implies that they are too irrational to deterred by policies designed to deal with 'normal' countries.

WEAPONS OF MASS DESTRUCTION?

Terrorists and rogue states would present a considerably greater danger, of course, if they were to acquire 'weapons of mass destruction'. Apprehension about this possibility is understandable, though it too is not really all that new. The fear that terrorist groups or renegade states might obtain nuclear weapons has been around at least since the 1950s when it began to be possible to create small 'suitcase bombs'.

These concerns have been heightened of late, however, at least in part because fears of much larger dangers have dissipated with the demise of the Cold War. In the process, the phrase, 'weapons of mass destruction', has been embellished. Once taken to refer almost exclusively to nuclear arms, the WMD label in the 1990s has also come to be applied to biological and chemical weapons, and often to ballistic missiles as well. This escalation of language is highly questionable.

Nuclear Weapons

Nuclear weapons clearly deserve the 'weapons of mass destruction' designation because they can indeed destroy masses of people.

Even so, it is worth noting that any nuclear weapons acquired by terrorist groups or rogue states, at least initially, are likely to be of rather limited size compared to the thermonuclear weapons in the arsenals of the major nuclear countries. For example, contrary to Indian and Pakistani claims, independent analyses of their May 1998 nuclear tests find that the yields were of Hiroshima size or smaller.[6] The destruction such bombs can accomplish is very considerable of course, and concerns about them are fully justified. However, the damage is likely to be far from apocalyptic if such a bomb were dropped on a fire-resistant modern city, and against well-prepared, dug-in, and dispersed troops, the damage could actually be quite limited.[7]

This is not to deny, of course, that the consequences of an atomic explosion would be terrible. But if a single bomb or even a few were to fall into dangerous hands, this would hardly mean the end of civilization as much atomic rhetoric seems to imply.[8]

Biological Weapons

Biological weapons seem to be a promising candidate to join nuclear ones in the WMD club because, properly developed and deployed, they could indeed, if thus far only in theory, kill hundreds of thousands, perhaps even millions, of people. The discussion remains theoretical because biological weapons have scarcely ever been used even though the knowledge about their destructive potential as weapons goes back decades, even centuries in some respects (the British, for example, made some efforts to spread smallpox among American Indians in the eighteenth century French and Indian Wars).[9]

Belligerents have eschewed such weapons with good reason. Contrary to the popular image that they can be whipped up in a kitchen, biological weapons are extremely difficult to develop, to deploy, and to control. Terrorist groups or rogue states may be able to solve such problems in the future with advances in technology and knowledge, but the record thus far is unlikely to be very encouraging to them.

For example, Japan reportedly infected wells in Manchuria and bombed several Chinese cities with plague-infested fleas before and during World War II. These ventures may have killed thousands of Chinese, but they apparently also caused thousands of unintended casualties among Japanese troops and seem to have had little military impact.[10] In the 1990s, Aum Shinrikyo, a Japanese cult that had 10 or 20 scientists in its employ and estimated assets of $1 billion, reportedly tried at least nine times over five years to set off biological weapons by spraying pathogens from trucks and wafting them from rooftops, hoping fancifully to ignite an apocalyptic war. These efforts failed to create a single fatality – in fact, nobody even noticed that the attacks had taken place.[11]

For the most destructive results biological weapons need to be dispersed in very low-altitude aerosol clouds: aerosols do not appreciably settle, and anthrax (which is not easy to spread or catch and is not contagious) would probably have to be sprayed near nose level. Particles that are too large will likely be blocked before reaching the lungs, while ones that are too small are likely to be expelled.[12] Explosive methods of dispersion may destroy the organisms. Moreover, except for anthrax spores, long-term storage of lethal organisms in bombs or warheads is difficult, and, even if refrigerated, most of the organisms have a limited lifetime. The effects of such weapons can take days or weeks to have full effect, during which time they can be countered with civil defense measures. And their impact is very difficult to predict and may spread back on the attacker.[13]

Chemical Weapons

Like biological and nuclear weapons, chemical arms do have the potential, under appropriate circumstances, to panic people; killing masses of them in open areas, however, is beyond their modest capabilities.[14] Their inclusion in the weapons-of-mass-destruction category is highly dubious unless the concept is so diluted that bullets or machetes can also be included.[15]

Biologist Matthew Meselson calculates that it would take a ton of nerve gas or five tons of mustard gas to produce heavy casualties among unprotected people in an open area of one kilometer square. Even for nerve gas this would take the concentrated delivery into a rather small area of about 300 heavy artillery shells or seven 500-pound bombs,[16] and this would probably require a considerable amount of time, allowing many people to evacuate the targeted area.[17] A 1993 analysis by the Office of Technology Assessment of the US Congress finds that a ton of Sarin nerve gas perfectly delivered under absolutely ideal conditions over a heavily populated area against unprotected people could cause between 3,000 and 8,000 deaths. Under slightly less ideal circumstances – if there was a moderate wind or if the sun was out, for example – the death rate would be only one-tenth as great.[18] Nuclear weapons are considered weapons of mass destruction because a single bomb can generate great devastation. For chemical weapons to cause extensive damage, by contrast, many of them must be used, just like conventional ones.

Discussions of chemical weapons often stress their ability to cause casualties, both dead and wounded, glossing over the fact that historically most of these incapacitated by chemical weapons have not actually died.[19] Yet clearly, if they are to be classified as 'weapons of mass destruction', they must destroy, not simply incapacitate. In World War I only some 2 to 3 per cent of those gassed on the Western Front died while, by contrast, wounds caused by traditional weapons were some 10 or 12 times more likely to prove fatal.[20] Chemical weapons were used against substantially unprotected Iranians by Iraq in their 1980–88 war, but of the 27,000 gassed through March 1987, Iran reported that only 262 died.[21] Similarly, when Aum Shinrikyo abandoned its biological efforts in frustration and instead released 'deadly' Sarin nerve gas into a Japanese subway in 1995, the attack caused over a thousand casualties, but only 12 deaths.[22] Moreover, troops wounded by gas tend to return to combat more quickly than those wounded by bullets or shrapnel,[23] and to suffer less.[24] Against well-protected troops, gas is almost wholly ineffective except as an inconvenience.[25]

Although gas was used extensively in World War I, it accounted for less than one per cent of the battle deaths.[26] In fact, on average it took over a ton of gas to produce a single fatality.[27] In the conclusion to the official British history of the war chemical weapons are accordingly relegated to a footnote which asserts that gas 'made war uncomfortable, to no purpose'.[28] Defense analyst Thomas McNaugher considers this conclusion to be 'overly glib', but goes on to suggest that 'it is closer to the truth than the contention that chemical weapons are nearly magical devices that invariably cause large casualties and inspire panic'.[29]

Missiles

In recent years ballistic missiles have often been listed alongside explosive weapons of mass destruction in the litany of post-Cold War dangers. Once again, however, this concern is substantially misplaced when applied to terrorist groups and rogue states. Ballistic missiles are expensive and the kinds rogue states are likely to obtain will be rather unreliable and generally inferior to aircraft for delivering most any kind of weaponry.

Iraq's experience during the 1991 Gulf War is a case in point. Even though US-supplied Patriot interceptor missiles were largely ineffective, the 27 to 30 Scud missiles showered on Israel during the war caused one death directly (though this one may well have been caused by debris from a Patriot rather than by the Scud), and three by heart attack.[30] In addition, several people were reportedly suffocated by the gas masks they were wearing to protect themselves against the gas that, as it turned out, was not in the warheads. Missiles like the Iraqi Scuds are so inaccurate that it would require 3,700 of them armed with conventional weapons to achieve a 50 per cent chance of destroying a soft command center.[31] As US General Norman Schwarzkopf puts it, the Scud was the military equivalent of a mosquito.[32]

As delivery systems for chemical and especially for biological agents, ballistic missiles have further limitations. To deliver such weapons effectively the warhead cannot simply slam into the ground, but needs to disperse its contents in a spray at a very low altitude, something that requires a warhead of enormous sophistication.[33] In some ways, therefore, it may be wise to encourage rogue states and well-heeled terrorists to waste their money on expensive ballistic missiles instead of investing in cheaper and more effective aircraft, cruise missiles, or unmanned aerial vehicles.[34] More generally, UCLA's David Rapoport concludes after extensive historical study that terrorists and rogue groups tend to be more effective when they use familiar, conventional weapons because decisions about their use are easier and because accidents are less likely to happen in conditions of great uncertainty.[35]

ECONOMIC SANCTIONS AS ECONOMIC WARFARE

The dangers posed by chemical and biological weapons and by ballistic missiles, like those posed by rogue states and international terrorism, are far from new, are often exaggerated, and, for the most part, are still merely potential. They have been blown substantially out of proportion in the quest for things to be alarmed about in a relatively safe post-Cold War world. This may be a natural tendency – a similar pattern appeared in US domestic politics in the early 1990s as national security and economic problems receded, with politicians and the press consistently declaring crime rates, which were in fact falling dramatically, to be out of control.[36] Yet the exaggeration it is also potentially dangerous. It might be prudent to draw a cautionary lesson from the 1938 Munich crisis, when enormous overestimates of the potential destructiveness of German bombing contributed greatly to Great Britain's willingness to deliver an important Western ally into Hitler's clutches.[37]

By contrast, the dangers posed to human well-being by severe economic sanctions, are clear, present, and sometimes devastating. Yet they have been substantially overlooked by scholars, policymakers, and the media. Indeed, sweeping economic sanctions might better be designated by the older label of 'economic warfare'.[38]

Economic embargoes have often been devastating, frequently causing more deaths in wars than bombing or bombardment. For example, some estimates suggest that as many as 750,000 German civilians may have died as a result of the Allied naval blockade in World War I, a figure which does not include deaths in Austria, Turkey and Bulgaria, where conditions were even worse, or deaths after the war when the blockade continued until

Germany signed the Treaty of Versailles. By comparison, fewer than two million people have been killed by aerial bombing in all the wars of the twentieth century combined.[39]

During the Cold War, the effect of economic sanctions was generally limited because when one side imposed them, the other often undermined them. However, in the wake of the Cold War sanctions are far more likely to be comprehensive and thus effective in causing harm if not necessarily in achieving their intended political objective. In their new era of comparative harmony, the big countries have at their disposal a credible, inexpensive, and potentially potent weapon for use against small and medium sized foes. The dominant countries have shown that they can inflict enormous pain on them at remarkably little cost to themselves or the global economy. Indeed, in a matter of months whole economies can be devastated, as happened in Iraq in 1990, in Haiti in 1991, and in Serbia in 1992.

SANCTIONS IN IRAQ

The destructive potential of economic sanctions can be seen most clearly, albeit in an extreme form, in Iraq. That country seems to have been peculiarly vulnerable because so much of its economy was dependent on the export of oil and because the effects of sanctions have been enhanced by the destruction of much of Iraq's rather advanced infrastructure during the 1991 Gulf War. Moreover, the country's leadership often seems more interested in maximizing the nation's suffering for propaganda purposes (especially with an eye toward getting the sanctions removed) than in relieving it.

A 1999 United Nations report stresses that 'the gravity of the humanitarian situation of the Iraqi people is indisputable and cannot be overstated'. The country experienced 'a shift from relative affluence to massive poverty'.[40] No one knows with any sort of precision how many Iraqi civilians have died as a result, but various agencies of the UN, which is in overall charge of the sanctions on Iraq, have estimated that the sanctions contributed to the deaths of hundreds of thousands of people there as well as extensive malnutrition. The deaths are attributed to inadequate food and medical supplies (between 1990 and 1996 pharmaceuticals were allowed in at only 10 per cent of 1989 levels) as well as breakdowns in sewage and sanitation systems and in the electrical power systems needed to run them. These systems were destroyed by bombing in the Gulf War and have often gone unrepaired due to sanctions-enhanced shortages of money, equipment, and spare parts.[41] It was not until 1998, nearly eight years after sanctions began, that Iraq was allowed to buy material for rebuilding its agricultural sector, water supply facilities, oilfields, and once-impressive medical system.[42]

Imports of some desperately needed materials were often delayed or denied because of concerns that they might contribute to Iraq's WMD programs. Supplies of syringes were held up for half a year because of fears they might be used in creating anthrax spores.[43] Chlorine, an important water disinfectant, was not allowed into the country because it might be diverted into making chlorine gas,[44] the first chemical weapon used in World War I but later abandoned when more effective ones were developed.[45] Cancer soared because requested imports of radiotherapy equipment, chemotherapy drugs, and analgesics were blocked.[46] Medical diagnostic techniques that make use of radioactive particles, once common in Iraq, have been banned under the sanctions, and plastic bags needed for blood transfusions have been restricted.[47] The sanctioners have been wary throughout about allowing the importation of fertilizers and insecticides, fearing their use for WMD production, and as a result, disease-carrying pests that might have been controlled have proliferated.[48]

Although humanitarian exceptions to some of the restrictions have been available all along, Iraq has sometimes been slow to take advantage of them – sometimes, it seems, deliberately – and they have been plagued by administrative chaos and delays.[49] Some relaxation of the sanctions took place at the end of the 1990s, and this, together with higher oil prices, helped alleviate some of the suffering, but the problem remained considerable.[50]

Some casualty estimates have been questioned because they rely on Iraqi reports and because the government of Iraq clearly has an interest in exaggerating its losses in order to engender sympathy which could lead to the removal of the sanctions. On the other hand, it is likely that estimates are low in some areas. In particular, many deaths of infants may have gone unreported because ailing babies are not taken to hospitals which have become inadequate to the task of saving them. The UN also suspects an underreporting of deaths because survivors can then collect an additional food ration.[51] Some studies have been based on data gathered by foreign (and presumably independent) researchers in Baghdad and then extrapolated to the rest of the country. This process, however, probably understates the destruction because Baghdad is generally in better shape than other areas, particularly the South which is being neglected, or punished, by the regime for rebellions in 1991.[52]

These statistics are often lamented by the sanctioning governments, but usually not denied.[53] Instead, it is pointed out that the sanctions on Iraq have been designed to accomplish several desirable objectives. One is to keep Iraq from developing weaponry with which it can once again threaten its neighbours.

Another is to remove Saddam Hussein from office. For example, one of the UN measures accompanying the sanctions, Security Council Resolution 688, passed shortly after the Gulf War on 5 April 1991, condemns the repression in Iraq and demands that it be ended, a policy that Hussein doubtless realizes would result in his removal from the office that protects him.[54] At the same time, President George Bush announced that the economic sanctions would be continued until 'Saddam Hussein is out of there', and his deputy national security adviser declared that 'Iraqis will pay the price while he remains in power'. In 1997, Secretary of State Madeleine Albright stated that sanctions would not be lifted even 'if Iraq complies with its obligations concerning weapons of mass destruction'.[55]

Unlike many dictators, such as Somoza, Marcos, or Batista, Saddam Hussein has no other place to go. He is reasonably safe only in office and in control in Iraq. Therefore, the rather mild-sounding notion that he should be removed from office, that he should 'step aside' in Bush's words, is effectively a death sentence to him.

Not surprisingly, Saddam has been uncooperative about allowing the sanctions to have this effect, regardless of the cost to the Iraqi people. He has also sought to rebuild his military capabilities, including, it appears, his chemical and biological arsenals: these weapons must seem to offer the best deterrent against potential invaders who appear to be obsessed with such weapons. In particular, he has been wary of any threats to his 'sovereignty' and of arms inspectors and other outsiders whose activities could used to fix his whereabouts. Disclosures that the arms inspection teams have indeed been used to harbor spies are unlikely to enhance his enthusiasm for having them around.[56]

In an important sense, therefore, the costs of the sanctions have been caused by Saddam's policies, not by the sanctioners. This is an argument the latter often make in defense of the policy.[57] If the Iraqi dictator would only do as they demand, they argue, the sanctions would be removed. In effect, however, the sanctioners are demanding that Saddam commit suicide or at least take measures which he feels will put his life at notable and further risk. Moreover, as noted above, senior officials of the United States have at times rather clearly indicated that the sanctions will not be removed while he is still in office, proclamations Saddam probably takes very seriously. Thus, while the impact of the sanctions on the Iraqi people – Saddam's hostages, in effect – may ultimately be his fault, they are also a predictable, and arguably inevitable, consequence of the sanctions policy. If sanctions had not been instituted, it is likely that the country would have moved back toward the relative prosperity – including an able medical system – it enjoyed before the 1991 Gulf War and that death and suffering would have been far less.

It is easy to support, even to laud, the sanctioners' objectives: Saddam Hussein is a monster whose removal from the planet would doubtless make it a better place, above all for the tyrannized and victimized citizens of Iraq. And his even partial rearmament could pose a threat to other countries in the area. Yet the sanctions do not seem to have loosened his control, and it seems exceedingly unlikely that he will become enticed to relinquish leadership, and life, over concern about the sufferings that have been inflicted upon the Iraqi people by economic sanctions and by his policies.

The sanctioners hope that their policy will encourage or help facilitate a coup, an assassination, an army revolt, a popular uprising, or a rebellion or invasion by armed dissidents. However, while such an undertaking is certainly possible, the prospects do not appear very bright, at least at present.

Saddam Hussein does not need the loyalty of major portions of the Iraqi population to remain in power. Rather it is essential for him to have the dedicated support of a relatively small band of followers and sycophants including the Special Republican Guard, the Special Security Organization, and the Martyrs of Saddam. To maintain their loyalty, he does not need to inspire love but to carry out two policies.

First, he needs to give them privileges they would lose if he were removed from office. Ironically, the sanctions may make this task easier by creating artificial shortages and driving up prices for scarce commodities, demands that can be serviced only by smugglers and sanctions-busters. In so far as Saddam can control this highly lucrative market, he can funnel the considerable benefits of such enterprises to his followers. Moreover, the system of food rationing, made necessary by the sanctions, has been used by the government to strengthen its control. As one Iraqi puts it, 'I have to pledge loyalty to the party. Any sign of disobedience and my monthly card would be taken away.' And key supporters are rewarded with extra rations.[58] For sanctions to be effective, it is axiomatic that they weaken, rather than strengthen, the ties of the leader's core support group.[59]

Second, Saddam must instill in his supporters an awareness that if he dies, in all probability so will they. This task, crucial to his survival, does not appear to be difficult. Any forceful deposition of Saddam by Iraqis is likely to lead to a bloodbath as old scores are savagely settled. One Iraqi notes of a local official, 'If there were a revolution, that guy would be chopped into a thousand pieces and thrown into the river'.[60] And regime supporters are fully aware of this; as one puts it, 'I know the guy across the street hates me for being in the party' and a struggle with rebels would be 'very very bloody'.[61] He may be remembering the fate of one of Hussein's favorite poets who was caught in one of the 1991 uprisings. His captors dressed him in women's clothing, cut off his ears and tongue, demanded he try to recite some of his poetry, and then hacked him to death.[62]

Saddam might meet his demise by being violently deposed in a coup or by assassination. There reportedly have been several such efforts since the 1991 Gulf War: among them, planned attacks on Saddam's motorcade in 1991 and in 1994, an attempted poisoning by one of his cooks in 1994, shots fired by an army lieutenant acting alone in 1994, and aborted conspiracies in 1993 and 1996. The 1996 effort, by military officers and other defectors aided by the CIA, was undone, it seems, by agents planted among the conspirators, and resulted in 800 arrests and between 68 and 100 executions.[63]

To evade such efforts, Hussein warily travels in road convoys of at least six identical vehicles, flies only in military helicopters and selects his landing sites at the last minute, and holes up in various residences which are surrounded by 20-foot high fences.[64] Even his senior ministers do not know where he is at any particular time.[65]

And his retaliation against opponents is lethal, prompt, ruthless, and often sadistic. The two 1993 conspirators were executed by having dynamite jammed into their mouths and then detonated.[66] Deserting soldiers have had their ears amputated and have been branded with X's between the eyes. And thousands of people are believed to have been 'disappeared'.[67]

There have also been attempts by the military to depose Saddam: two in 1991, as well as a rising by a battalion of his Republican Guards in 1995.[68] Saddam's wariness of a repetition is suggested by the fact that the army is not allowed to bring heavy weapons anywhere near Baghdad due to fears that regular troops might turn and use it against his government.[69] Moreover, to counter possible defection or attack, the planes in his air force do not seem to have much fuel in them.[70]

A popular uprising is also possible, but that prospect appears rather slim. There were very substantial rebellions against Hussein and his government in 1991 in the immediate wake of the Gulf War – in no less than 15 of the country's 18 provinces. These were poorly coordinated and became associated with elements supporting Iran, and they were put down with tremendous brutality and with massive and indiscriminate executions.[71] The memory of this experience provides a strong disincentive to a repetition. Moreover, many observers have noted that the years of sanctions against Iraq have tended to sap the energies of the population as the quest for personal survival becomes paramount.

There have also been proposals for organizing an invasion by rebels, something that carries with it unsettling echoes of the Bay of Pigs. Like the 1961 effort to depose Castro, it would involve seeking to coordinate and to arm fractious opponents, probably over several years, and to provide them a base from which to attack.[72] Of course, Saddam Hussein is not without defenses in all this, and the opposition, both within the country and outside it, is splintered and infiltrated by agents. A cell of dissidents run by the Central Intelligence Agency was destroyed in September 1996 when it was betrayed by one of the Kurdish leaders, Massoud Barzani, as part of his power struggle with a rival in northern Iraq, an area that is being protected by the militaries of the sanctioning countries.[73]

A conventional military invasion by foreign forces could probably eliminate Saddam and his regime, and it seems entirely possible that Iraq's ill-led and demoralized army, which fought almost not at all when challenged in the Gulf War, would put up little armed resistance to such an attack.[74] Moreover, an invasion by an international force holds out a reasonable prospect that a bloodbath, seemingly nearly inevitable in any Iraqi civil conflict, can be avoided. As Germans in World War II found it safe to surrender to Western forces and as Iraqis were quite willing to surrender in huge numbers to coalition forces in the Gulf War, so Saddam's core defenders might be willing to abandon him to an invader that could credibly guarantee their safety.

Yet the sanctioning countries seem to consider such a venture to be a political non-starter because of the potential cost to their own troops. Moreover, an invasion would have to be based in some neighbouring host country, and there does not seem to be an abundance of willing potential candidates. Such political obstacles to an invasion would likely vanish, however, if Saddam were to launch another military attack or even a major military provocation in the area. This is something he probably understands.

None of the means by which Saddam Hussein might be removed from office at present appears to be a very likely prospect. Iraq's army and people already have plentiful incentives to oust their dictator; what they lack is sufficient prospects for success to make serious efforts to overthrow him appear worthwhile. The sanctions do little to solve this fundamental problem other than further weakening the country's decrepit armed forces.

WEIGHING THE VALUE OF HUMAN LIFE

How do the human costs of the Iraqi sanctions compare to the number of deaths caused thus far by weapons of mass destruction? The atomic bombings of Hiroshima and Nagasaki together killed over 100,000 people, and a high estimate suggests that some 80,000 died from chemical weapons in World War I. If one adds to this the deaths from other, later uses of chemical weapons in war or warlike situations (excluding the deaths of noncombatants in Nazi gas chambers), as well as deaths caused by the limited intentional or accidental use or release of biological weapons and ballistic missiles, the resulting total could be well under 300,000. If estimates of human damage are even roughly correct, economic sanctions on Iraq, designed in part to keep the country from developing weapons of mass destruction, may have been a necessary cause of the deaths of more people than have been slain either intentionally or accidentally, by nuclear, chemical, and biological weapons and by ballistic missiles in all of history.

The central question then becomes, 'Is the policy worth such costs?' One might wonder, with former UN Secretary General Boutros Boutros-Ghali, 'whether suffering inflicted on vulnerable groups in a target country is a legitimate means of exerting pressure on political leaders whose behavior is unlikely to be affected by the plight of their subjects'.[75] The question is asked of policy makers all too rarely. In 1996, however, on her country's most popular television news program, *60 Minutes*, it was put to Madeleine Albright that the sanctions had taken the lives of half a million Iraqi children, and she was bluntly asked if the price was worth it. Without denying the numbers, she acknowledged that 'this is a very hard choice', then firmly concluded, 'we think the price is worth it'.[76]

It is impressive that this loss of human life has failed to make a greater impression in the West. Americans do not blame the people of Iraq for that country's actions: even at the height of the Gulf War, fully 60 per cent said they held the Iraqi people to be *innocent* of *any blame* for Hussein's policies.[77] Yet, although the sanctions policy has been condemned by such prominent figures as the Pope, the massive death toll has stirred little perceptible public protest, or even much notice. In a letter published in the *New York Times* in 1998, a man who had traveled to Iraq and had seen 'hospital wards filled with dying children, Baghdad streets flooded with raw sewage, and doctors fighting diseases without adequate medicine', expressed the view that 'if the news media would only broadcast the intolerable suffering I have witnessed, I am convinced a genuine debate would begin'.[78] In fact, the news media *have* covered the story, albeit limitedly, but stories that do not incite much response from their audiences tend not to be followed up (so much for the famed 'CNN effect').[79]

Some of this inattention may derive from a lack of concern about foreign lives. Although Americans are extremely sensitive to American casualties, they, like others, often seem to be remarkably *in*sensitive to casualties suffered by foreigners, whether military or civilian. Extensive news coverage of civilian casualties resulting from an attack on a Baghdad bomb shelter during the 1991 Gulf War had no impact on support for the war or for such bombing policies.[80] Moreover, the images of the 'highway of death' and official estimates that 100,000 Iraqis had died in the war[81] did not dampen enthusiasm at the subsequent victory parades and celebrations.

However, much of the inattention may also be due to the fact that, in contrast to deaths caused by terrorist bombs, those inflicted by sanctions are dispersed rather than concentrated and statistical rather than dramatic. The same phenomenon helps explain why extremely infrequent multiple shootings in US schools and workplaces lead to frenzied outcries for gun control or media censorship, while most people accept with little comment the murder of several dozen Americans per day in ones and twos.

DETERRING AND CONTAINING SADDAM

Principally, however, it is likely that the sanctions have been supported because they are designed to accomplish a desirable goal: to force a tyrant from office and to keep him from menacing his neighbours. However, if sanctions have caused great human damage in Iraq, if the prospects for a deposition of Saddam Hussein by Iraqi forces are at best highly questionable, and if there is little likelihood of a foreign invasion, it seems reasonable to suggest that another policy might be in order.

To begin with, it is important to assess how much of a threat Iraq has actually posed to the area and to the world.

Some analysts posit that Saddam still harbors an 'ambition to dominate the Middle East'.[82] Whatever his present fancies on this score, it is difficult to see how he could carry out this presumed ambition, surrounded by hostile neighbors (two of which he invaded during his tenure in office) and watched over by wary countries representing virtually all the military strength in the world. Moreover, such 'dominance' could only be accomplished with the support of his army, whose reliability is, as already noted, very low.

It is also flatly predicted by some that if Saddam prevails in the standoff with his glowering enemy in Washington, 'other aggressors in the world will follow his example'.[83] It is not entirely clear who those other would-be aggressors are, nor is it clear that one would find much encouragement in the process by which Saddam led his country into ruin, impotence, and devastation, and himself into deep personal danger.

In contrast to such Napoleonic images, Saddam Hussein seems actually to be a rather pathetic creature. A prisoner in his own country, he seeks to maintain control in that shattered, impoverished place, and ruthlessly persecutes a population which lives in terror and in loathing of him.[84] For all that, however, he does seem to be rather good at staying in office. A policy to handle Saddam should acknowledge his potential for political survival, and it should be cost-effective and sustainable for the long term.

The confrontational approach has been expensive not only in Iraqi lives, but also in military readiness and in financial cost of over US$1 billion a year. The sanctions could be restructured to concentrate on important military issues, while easing considerably the restrictions that have brought so much hardship to Iraqi civilians. Saddam might crow about this as a great victory, but then he also proclaimed the 1991 Gulf War to be a great victory for Iraq. Few are likely to be impressed.

In place of sweeping trade sanctions, an export control process could be established to minimize Iraq's ability to import goods that will substantially contribute to its rearmament, and especially to its development of nuclear weapons, the true weapons of mass destruction. Precedent for such a scheme exists: the West sustained a strategic embargo of high technology exports against the Soviet Union and its allies with reasonable success for more than 40 years during the Cold War, and more limited arms embargoes have often been employed against other states.[85] Such an arrangement could not be airtight, and it would not entirely prevent Iraq from regaining military strength and from becoming more of a military threat in the region. Indeed, it must be anticipated that Saddam's first priority would remain his own physical safety – though it seems likely that, if only to curry a degree of favor from his beleaguered people, he would also seek to return the country to the relative prosperity it once enjoyed. Yet such controls would constrain his rearmament, and they would do so at a financial and human cost that could be easily borne, for decades if necessary. Perhaps as important, the process would not appear to be a humiliating lifting of the existing sanctions, merely a restructuring of them.

It would be impossible to stop Iraq from developing some biological and chemical weapons no matter what policy is pursued, particularly since weapons inspection was aborted after the December 1998 air attacks.[86] Therefore, the West must recognize that preventing their use ultimately depends on deterrence, just as it did during the 1991 Gulf War. If, as many argue, the specter of retaliation successfully deterred Iraq from launching chemical attacks during that conflict, it can do so again. Now, instead of exaggerating the threat posed by Iraq's biological and chemical arsenal, Washington should simply explain that Iraq will not be allowed to use these weapons without facing cataclysmic punishment, to include, most ominously, an invasion, actions that would strike at Saddam Hussein, not just at his long-suffering people.

Deterrence and containment have a rather good track record as policies for dealing with menaces far more significant than that posed by Saddam Hussein. When George Kennan called for containment against the Soviet Union in a famous article in 1947, he intended the policy to be long-term, patient, and vigilant.[87] Centrally, it was a policy designed to handle the situation at a bearable cost until Josef Stalin, the monster-kingpin of the Soviet Union, died. Kennan posited that containment might have to last some 10 to 15 years. This estimate seems to have been based on the fact that Stalin was approaching 70 at the time, and it anticipated that the power struggle after Stalin's demise might well facilitate the demise of the Soviet communist system. Kennan was wrong, of course, about the difficulties of the Soviet succession, but Stalin was at least replaced by individuals who were milder and less dangerous.

A similar approach could be applied to Iraq's monster-kingpin. He can be ringed by an alliance of convenience made up of neighbouring countries which have extremely good reason to distrust him deeply, while US and allied forces can be kept at the ready and in the neighbourhood. If some Iraqi groups seem to show real and credible promise of being able to overthrow the dictator, they might be given support. But for the most part, the policy would involve letting nature and history take their course while working to alleviate the suffering of the Iraqi people by allowing the country gradually to recover to its previous state of relative prosperity.

Considering the weakness of Iraq and the hostility of its neighbours (and of just about all the countries in the rest of the world), it seems likely that Saddam could be adequately deterred and contained by such a policy. Even assuming that his demoralized and unreliable army would obey such a patently disastrous order (especially after its experiences in Kuwait and Iran), another attack anywhere or even a major military provocation, certainly any including chemical, biological, or nuclear weapons, would essentially be suicidal.[88] And survival, not suicide, seems to be Saddam Hussein's chief goal.

SANCTIONS OF MASS DESTRUCTION

Much as nuclear weapons bound the upper end of the spectrum of military force, the United Nations sanctions against Iraq represent an extreme case of mass destruction through economic warfare. Iraq is unusually vulnerable to such an attack, yet the sanctions have largely failed because Saddam Hussein considers the stakes to be high and is essentially indifferent to the suffering of his people as long as he remains more or less securely in control. In most other cases the death toll from even such extensive trade sanctions would be lower. And economic warfare may be more effective, and thus less prolonged, when directed against states whose leaders are more concerned with their popular support (as in the case of Serbia after 1992), or when less vital interests are at stake (as in the recently successful effort to coerce Libya to deliver the PanAm 103 bombing suspects for trial).

Yet the Iraqi sanctions case provides an important cautionary lesson for Western leaders. Statistical deaths are nevertheless real ones. A sanctions policy that leads to an increase in infant mortality or a reduction in life expectancy kills its victims as assuredly, even if not so visibly, as a bomb or missile. A policy that effectively encourages Saddam to kill his own people by resisting Western demands may be less morally unsettling than directly killing them, but its effects on his Iraqi hostages are no more humane as a result.

An indiscriminate Western bombing campaign against Iraq that killed tens of thousands of civilians a year in the pursuit of only moderately important objectives would soon be changed if it produced only marginal results. In fact, it is unlikely that such a campaign would ever be launched due, among other reasons, to international legal proscriptions against inflicting disproportionate or indiscriminate harm against civilians. Indeed, it would be illegal for US Air Force officers to comply with an order to conduct an air campaign that would inflict the same sort of damage that has been caused by sweeping trade sanctions.[89] A campaign of economic warfare that has caused great loss of life with little prospect of major success should have been reassessed long ago, especially since alternative policies are available to contain the limited threat presented by Iraq.

At a broader level, the seemingly universal belief that the use of deadly military force ought to be a last resort in foreign policy, while economic sanctions are a kinder and gentler instrument, must be reexamined. Economic warfare has the potential to be every bit as indiscriminately destructive as naval blockades or urban area bombing, and it can inflict more damage than some 'weapons of mass destruction'. At the other end of the spectrum, economic sanctions can also be applied as precision weapons under appropriate conditions, targeting key leaders or powerful domestic interests and achieving notable coercive successes at relatively low cost.[90] Unfortunately, in the past few decades far greater attention has been devoted to honing the precision of Western military power than to the refinement of tools and techniques for economic warfare.

NOTES

1. In almost all years fewer than 10 American civilians die at the hands of international terrorists: US Dept. of State, *Patterns of Global Terrorism, 1997*, April 1998, p.85. Over the last 37 years, an average of 90 people have been killed each year by lightning in the United States: National Safety Council (Chicago), *Accident Facts*, 1997, p.120. About 100 Americans die each year from accidents caused by deer: Andrew C. Revkin, 'Coming to the Suburbs: A Hit Squad for Deer', *New York Times*, 30 Nov. 1998, p.A1.

2. Terrorism of course differs from some of the other risks listed here: it potentially threatens everyone (unlike peanut allergies), and governmental action can mitigate the danger it poses (unlike lightning). Note, however, that Americans are substantially more likely to be killed by a comet or meteorite than by lightning, let alone terrorism, yet very little is spent on deep space tracking systems that could dramatically reduce this risk. See John R. and Mary Gribbin, *Fire on Earth* (NY: St Martin's 1996).

3. Although, as Barry Buzan and Eric Herring suggest, it might be questioned whether the $5 billion per year that the US Department of Defense spends on terrorism policing and protection is justified by the small amount of damage that terrorism inflicts. See Buzan and Herring, *The Arms Dynamic in World Politics* (Boulder, CO: Lynne Rienner 1998) p.190.

4. For trend data, see US Dept. of State, p.81.

5. See Roger Hilsman, *To Move a Nation* (NY: Delta 1967) Part 8.

6. See Brian Barker, Michael Clark *et al.*, 'Policy Forum: Seismology: Monitoring Nuclear Tests', *Science* 281/5385 (1998) pp.1967–8; Raj Chengappa, 'Is India's H-Bomb a Dud?' *India Today* 8/41 (1998) pp.22–8.

7. On the effects of the 1945 atomic bombings, see US Army, Manhattan Engineer District, *The Atomic Bombings of Hiroshima and Nagasaki* (Washington DC 1946). US Strategic Bombing Survey, *The Effect of Atomic Bombs on Hiroshima and Nagasaki* (NY: Garland, 1946). Los Alamos Scientific Laboratory, *The Effects of Atomic Weapons* (NY: McGraw-Hill 1950). Ralph E. Lapp, *Must We Hide?* (Cambridge, MA: Addison-Wesley 1949) Ch.7. Alexander P. de Seversky, *Air Power: Key to Survival* (NY: Simon & Schuster 1950) Chs.9, 10.

8. Nor have nuclear weapons been proliferating at anywhere near the alarming rate that has often been held to be inevitable. Indeed, one of the most interesting developments in the postwar world has been the slow pace with which nuclear weapons have proliferated. In fact, several nations – Brazil, Argentina, South Africa, South Korea, Taiwan – have actually backed away from or reversed nuclear weapons programs. Mitchell Reiss, *Bridled Ambition: Why Countries Constrain Their Nuclear Capabilities* (Washington DC: Woodrow Wilson Center Press 1995). And three countries that inherited nuclear weapons, Belarus, Ukraine, and Kazakhstan, have abandoned them.
   At best, nuclear weapons seem to have only a kind of 'naughty child' effect: nuclear

behavior can attract notice. Thus North Korea can get people to pay more attention to it if it seeks to develop a bomb than if it does not, and Russia's nuclear arsenal perhaps causes people to be concerned about its destiny more than they would if it had no bombs. But this phenomenon hardly generates real status or import, and it is nothing compared to the kind of respect either country would attract if it were to become an important economic player – rather than a beggar – on the world scene. To enhance this process, a sensible reaction to the very noisy and very public atomic testing by India and Pakistan in 1998 might be the pointed admission of the non-nuclear but economically impressive states of Japan and Germany to prestigious permanent seats in the Security Council. On these issues, see also John Mueller, 'The Escalating Irrelevance of Nuclear Weapons', in T.V. Paul, Richard J. Harknett and James J. Wirtz (eds.) *The Absolute Weapon Revisited: Nuclear Arms and the Emerging International Order* (Ann Arbor: U. of Michigan Press 1998) pp.73–98.

 9. George W. Christopher *et al.*, 'Biological Warfare: A Historical Perspective', *JAMA*, 6 Aug. 1997, p.412; David C. Rapoport, 'Terrorism and Weapons of the Apocalypse', *National Security Studies Quarterly* 5/3 (Summer 1999) pp.53–4.

10. Office of Technology Assessment [hereafter OTA] US Congress, *Proliferation of Weapons of Mass Destruction: Assessing the Risks*, OTA-559 (Washington DC: US GPO, Aug. 1993), p.60; Peter Williams and David Wallace, *Unit 731: Japan's Secret Biological Warfare in World War II* (NY: Free Press 1989) Ch.6; Christopher *et al.* (note 9) p.413; Ralph Blumenthal and Judith Miller, 'Japanese Germ-War Atrocities: A Half-Century of Stonewalling the World', *New York Times*, 4 March 1999, p.A10; Rapoport (note 9) p.54.

11. William J. Broad, 'How Japan Germ Terror Alerted World', *New York Times*, 26 May 1998, p.A1. Rapoport (note 9) p.57. For an assessment of press and official exaggerations of Aum's capabilities, see Milton Leitenberg, 'Aum Shinrikyo's Efforts to Produce Biological Weapons', *Terrorism and Political Violence* 11/4 (Winter 1999).

12. Matthew Meselson, 'How Serious is the Biological Weapons Threat?' Defense & Arms Control Studies Program Seminar, Massachusetts Institute of Technology, 29 Nov. 1995. Don Terry, 'Treating Anthrax Hoaxes With Costly Rubber Gloves', *New York Times*, 29 Dec. 1998, p.A10. Jonathan B. Tucker and Amy Sands, 'An Unlikely Threat', *Bulletin of the Atomic Scientists* (July/Aug. 1999) p.51. Harvey Sokolski, 'Rethinking Bio-Chemical Dangers', *Orbis* 44/2 (Spring 2000) pp.207–19.

13. OTA (note 10) pp.48–9, 62. William J. Broad and Judith Miller, 'Iraq's Deadliest Arms: Puzzles Breed Fears', *New York Times*, 26 Feb. 1998, p.A1; Tucker and Sands (note 12).

14. On the rise of the sentiment that killing by gas is peculiarly wicked and immoral (as opposed to killing by bullets and shrapnel), see Richard M. Price, *The Chemical Weapons Taboo* (Ithaca, NY: Cornell UP 1997) and Frederic J. Brown, *Chemical Warfare: A Study in Restraints* (Princeton UP 1968).

15. For a recognition of this point, see OTA (note 10) p.9; also p.46. See also Richard K. Betts, 'The New Threat of Mass Destruction', *Foreign Affairs* 77/1 (Jan./Feb. 1998) pp.30–31.

16. Matthew Meselson, 'The Myth of Chemical Superweapons', *Bulletin of the Atomic Scientists* (April 1991) p.13.

17. Thomas L. McNaugher, 'Ballistic Missiles and Chemical Weapons: The Legacy of the Iran-Iraq War', *International Security* 15/2 (Fall 1990) p.31.

18. OTA (note 10) p.54. Another estimate is that some 300 kilograms of Sarin delivered under ideal circumstances might kill between 200 and 3000, a figure that drops by 90 per cent if there is civil defense. Steve Fetter, 'Ballistic Missiles and Weapons of Mass Destruction: What is the Threat? What Should Be Done?' *International Security* 16/1 (Summer 1991) p.22.

19. For example, see Brad Roberts, *Chemical Disarmament and International Security*, Adelphi Paper 267 (London: IISS 1992) pp.75–84.

20. McNaugher (note 17) p.19n. For the United States 2 per cent of gas casualties died while 24 per cent of those wounded by other weapons died. The rates for Germany were 2.9 per cent and 43 per cent, and for the British they were 3.3 per cent and 36.6 per cent. H.L. Gilchrist, *A Comparative Study of World War Casualties from Gas and Other Weapons* (Washington

DC: US GPO 1928) pp.7–8, 48.

21. McNaugher (note 17) p.19n.
22. Broad (note 11) p.A10. Tucker and Sands (note 12) p.48. A more skilful attack might have killed more, but it would also greatly increase the chance that the attacker would be killed or detected: see Rapoport (note 9) p.57.
23. McNaugher (note 17) p.20n.
24. Gilchrist (note 20) p.47.
25. OTA (note 10) pp.8, 58. Meselson, 'The Myth' (note 16) p.13. Roberts (note 19) p.81.
26. Gilchrist (note 20) p.7.
27. Fetter (note 18) p.15.
28. Sir James E. Edmonds and R. Maxwell-Hyslop (eds.) *Military Operations: France and Belgium, 1918*, Vol.5 (London: HMSO 1947) p.606.
29. McNaugher (note 17) p.21. Gas was apparently used in rather limited amounts in the 1930s by Italy in Ethiopia and by Japan in China, as well as by Egypt in the civil war in Yemen the mid-1960s and during the Iran–Iraq War of 1980–88: Brown (note 14) p.185n; Price (note 14) Chs.5, 6; McNaugher (note 17); Fetter (note 18) p.15.
30. Theodore A. Postol, 'Lessons of the Gulf War Experience with Patriot', *International Security* 16/3 (Winter 1991/92) p.140. In addition, a Scud killed 28 American troops when it hit a barracks in Saudi Arabia. Germany's V-2 missile program in World War II, which consumed vast resources, also achieved little of any military value. See Michael J. Neufeld, *The Rocket and the Reich* (NY: Free Press 1995), esp. pp.272–75. Neufeld points out that the German missile program, proportional to the economy, cost the Germans as much as the development of the atomic bomb did to the United States. It consumed enough resources to build 24,000 additional fighter aircraft in 1944–45, when German production was 36,000. 'In short', he concludes, 'German missile development shortened the war, just as its advocates said it would, but in favor of the Allies'.
31. Even if the missiles had the accuracy of the sophisticated (and extremely expensive) Pershing II, it would still take 16 attempts to reach the 50 per cent level against a hard command center and 50 to achieve the 90 per cent level. Postol (note 30) p.168.
32. H. Norman Schwarzkopf, *It Doesn't Take a Hero* (NY: Bantam 1992) p.417.
33. OTA (note 10) p.52. Buzan and Herring (note 3) p.63. Fetter (note 18) pp.17–18.
34. McNaugher (note 17) pp.32–3. On this issue, see also Fetter (note 18) pp.9–12, and Jeffrey N. Renehan, *Unmanned Aerial Vehicles and Weapons of Mass Destruction* (Maxwell AFB, AL: Air University Press 1997). It is possible to make a similar argument even about nuclear weapons. If a potentially dangerous country expends scarce resources on expensive nuclear weapons, it will not have nearly as much money to spend on conventional ones. It would now have the capacity, perhaps, to scare the easily traumatized major countries (whose fondest desire, of course, is to continue to spend resources on these weapons monopolistically), but it might be less able to cause actual trouble. Thus, if Saddam Hussein had been allowed happily to fritter away his oil money on nuclear weapons in 1979, he might have been less able to attack Iran. In fact, Hussein's nuclear weapons program may have helped to divert his military from purchasing the Global Positioning System, a device that would have been of great benefit to it during the Gulf War: see John Mueller, 'The Perfect Enemy: Assessing the Gulf War', *Security Studies* 5/1 (Autumn 1995) p.100.
35. Rapoport (note 9) pp.51, 57–8. See also Jessica Stern, 'Apocalypse Never, but the Threat is Real', *Survival* 40/4 (Winter 1998–99) p.177; Tucker and Sands (note 12) p.49. See also Ehud Sprinzak, 'The Great Superterrorism Scare', *Foreign Policy* (Fall 1998) pp.110–24.
36. Federal Bureau of Investigation, *Uniform Crime Reports for the United States* (Washington DC: GPO 1995).
37. Williamson Murray, *The Change in the European Balance of Power, 1938–1939* (Princeton UP 1984) Chs.6–7; Uri Bialer, *In the Shadow of the Bomber* (London: Royal Historical Society UP 1980) pp.157–9.
38. Technically, economic warfare refers to the use of economic means to cause or contribute to the military defeat of a current or potential enemy. It can be seen as a subset of economic

sanctions, but economic warfare is usually unconditional, while most economic sanctions are intended to be lifted if specific demands are met. For discussion, see David A. Baldwin, *Economic Statecraft* (Princeton UP 1985) pp.33–40, and also Klaus Knorr, *The Power of Nations* (NY: Basic Books 1975) Ch.6.

39. Philip S. Meilinger, 'Winged Defense: Airwar, the Law, and Morality', *Armed Forces and Society* 20/1 (Fall 1993) pp.112, 104.

40. United Nations, Report of the second panel established pursuant to the note by the president of the Security Council of 30 January 1999 (5/1999/100), 30 March 1999 [hereafter UN 1999], Paras. 43, 49. On the outlier status of the Iraq case, see Daniel W. Drezner, *The Sanctions Paradox* (Cambridge UP 1999) p.1.

41. Omar A. Obeid and Abdul-Hussein Al-Hadi, 'Sanctions against Iraq', *Lancet*, 347/8995, 20 Jan. 1996, pp.198–9. Lesley Stahl, co-host, 'Punishing Saddam', 60 Minutes (CBS television), 12 May 1996. Maggie O'Kane, 'The Wake of War', *Guardian* (London), 18 May 1996, p.T34. Barbara Crossette, 'Unicef Head Says Thousands of Children Are Dying in Iraq', *New York Times*, 29 Oct. 1996, p.A8. Storer H. Rowley, 'Iraq's Kids Pay Tragic Price Under 6 Years of UN Sanctions', *Chicago Tribune*, 24 Nov. 1996, p.8. Geoff Simons, *The Scouring of Iraq: Sanctions, Law and Natural Justice* (NY: St Martin's 1996) Ch.3. Richard Garfield, 'The Impact of Economic Embargoes on the Health of Women and Children', *JAMWA* 52/4 (Fall 1997) p.182. Maggie O'Kane, 'Another Day in Babylon', *Guardian* (London), 7 March 1998. Julian Borger, 'Iraq élite rides high despite sanctions', *Guardian Weekly*, 8 March 1998, p.4. 'War on Sanctions', The NewsHour with Jim Lehrer (PBS television), 13 March 1998. Patrick Cockburn, 'Poisoned Tigris Spreads Tide of Death in Iraq', *Independent* (London), 25 April 1998, p.16. UNICEF Report, 'Situation Analysis of Children and Women in Iraq', 30 April 1998. Tim Weiner, 'Response to Baghdad: Military Muscle May Not Suffice', *New York Times*, 12 Nov. 1998, A12. Stephen Kinzer, 'Iraq's Sad Cultural Elite Pines for Good Old Days', *New York Times*, 23 Dec. 1998, p.A10. Stephen Kinzer, 'The Misery of Babylon In the Age Of Hussein, *New York Times*, 24 Dec. 1998, p.A6. Denis J. Halliday, 'Iraq and the UN's Weapon of Mass Destruction', *Current History*, Feb. 1999, pp.65–8. Judith Miller, 'UN Panel Seeks to Ease Suffering of Iraq's People', *New York Times*, 31 March 1999, p.A6. Scott Ritter, *Endgame: Solving the Iraq Problem – Once and for All* (NY: Simon & Schuster 1999) pp.147–50. Andrew Cockburn and Patrick Cockburn, *Out of the Ashes: The Resurrection of Saddam Hussein* (NY: HarperCollins 1999) Ch.5. David Sharrock, 'Iraq is falling apart. We are ruined', *Guardian* (London) 24 April 1999, p.14. 'Life and Death in Iraq', *Seattle Post-Intelligencer*, 11 May 1999. Larry Kaplow, 'Consequences of Kuwait: Sanctions Have Iraq Withering', *Atlanta Journal and Constitution*, 13 June 1999, p.2F. Drezner (note 40) pp.1, 8n. Richard Garfield, 'Morbidity and Mortality Among Iraqi Children from 1990 to 1998', Kroc Inst. for Int. Peace Studies, University fo Notre Dame, March 1999.

42. Vernon Loeb, 'Oil-for-Food Program Continues as Key Facet of U.S. Policy on Iraq', *Washington Post*, 14 Nov. 1998, p.A16. Eric D. K. Melby, 'Iraq', in Richard N. Haass (ed.) *Economic Sanctions and American Diplomacy* (NY: Council on Foreign Relations Press 1998) p.121.

43. John Sweeney, 'The truth about Iraq's dying babies', *Guardian Weekly*, 15 March 1998, p.7.

44. 60 Minutes (note 41). Cockburn and Cockburn (note 41) p.131.

45. Brown (note 14) pp.4, 38.

46. Karol Sikora, 'Cancer services are suffering in Iraq', *BMJ* 318 (16 Jan. 1999) p.203.

47. Maggie O'Kane, 'Iraqi Rich Make Mockery of Sanctions', *Guardian* (London) 21 Nov. 1998, p.18. Similarly restricted at times have been cotton, ambulances, and pencils: Borger (note 41).

48. Maggie O'Kane, 'Sick and Dying in Their Hospital Beds, the Pitiful Victims of Sanctions and Saddam', *Guardian* (London) 19 Feb. 1998, p.1.

49. Barbara Crossette, 'Iraq Is Said to Shun Vital Food and Medicine It Could Import Under U.N. Sanctions', *New York Times*, 13 Jan. 1999, p.A6. UN 1999 (note 40) paras.37, 45, 57.

50. O'Kane, 'Iraqi Rich' (note 47). Cockburn and Cockburn (note 41) p.135. Kinzer, 'Iraq's Sad'

(note 41) Halliday (note 41) pp.65–6. Kaplow (note 41). UN 1999 (note 40), paras.29–47, 58. Robert Corzine, 'Aid chief attacks UN's policy on Iraq', *Financial Times*, 17 Feb. 2000, p.16. Barbara Crossette, 'U.N. Chief Assesses Benefits to Iraq of Oil-for-Food Program', *New York Times*, 15 March 2000, p.A13. 'When Sanctions Don't Work', *Economist*, 8 April 2000, pp.23–5.

51. UNICEF (note 41) p.42.
52. On these issues, see Obed and Al-Hadi (note 41); Mary C. Smith Fawzi and Sarah Zaidi, 'Sanctions against Iraq', *Lancet*, 347/8995 (20 Jan. 1996) p.198; UN 1999 (note 40) Paras.10, 49; Eric Herring, 'Between Iraq and a Hard Place', *Review of International Studies*, forthcoming.
53. One commentary briefly takes issue with some of the results, arguing unclearly that some have been based on a dubious extrapolations, unspecifically that no 'independent' sources of health data are available, and irrelevantly that many of the deaths may be due to unrepaired infrastructure breakdowns caused by bombing in the 1991 Gulf War: Daniel W. Drezner, 'Serious About Sanctions', *National Interest*, Fall 1998, pp.70–1.
54. On the essential intention of the sanctions to inspire efforts in Iraq to bring down Saddam Hussein, see Drezner (note 40) p.1; Melby (note 42) pp.118, 123.
55. Cockburn and Cockburn (note 41) pp.43, 263; see also p.98.
56. Since chemical and biological weapons can be made and stored in very small places, it is logical that the inspectors should have the complete run of the country at all times. Not surprisingly, he is most notably resentful when arms inspectors have demanded visits to his presidential sites and party headquarters purportedly to discover if he had perhaps been hiding germ or gas bombs there. See Peter J. Boyer, 'Scott Ritter's Private War', *New Yorker*, 9 Nov. 1998, p.72. Boyer also discusses the zealous hostility of some of the arms inspectors to Saddam Hussein who he, apparently not without some justification, sees as spies.
     The security apparatus used to conceal weapons is the same as the one used to protect Saddam: Tim Weiner, 'US Spied on Iraq Under UN Cover, Officials Now Say', *New York Times*, 7 Jan. 1999, p.A1; Thomas W. Lippman and Barton Gellman, 'UN "Helped US to Spy on Saddam"', *Guardian Weekly*, 17 Jan. 1999, p.17.
57. See, for example, Milton Leitenberg, 'Sanctions against Iraq', *Lancet* 347/8995, 20 Jan. 1996, pp.199–200; Madeleine K. Albright, letter to 60 Minutes (CBS television) 19 May 1996; Drezner (note 41) p.71. For a nuanced assessment, see Joy Jordan, 'A Peaceful, Silent, Deadly Remedy: The Ethics of Economic Sanctions', *Ethics and International Affairs* 13 (1999) pp.123–42.
58. Richard Downes, 'Saddam's men use sanctions to secure their grip', *Independent* (London) 12 Dec. 1998, p.17. See also Sharrock (note 41); UN 1999, Para.27.
59. See Jonathan Kirshner, 'The Microfoundations of Economic Sanctions', *Security Studies* 6/3 (Spring 1997) pp.32–64; Drezner (note 40).
60. Downes (note 58).
61. Maggie O'Kane, 'We Want Saddam Gone', *Guardian* (London), 17 Nov. 1998, p.1.
62. O'Kane, 'Another Day' (note 41). The current Poet Laureate keeps his job by penning such verses as 'Be happy, my President/Your light is coming and theirs is passing away in vain./When our horse stumbled in the confusion you led the way...'. or 'You are the Sword of all the earth, whose pride refused to be sheathed./The world rose against you but you were the one who rattled their little chains'. Hussein's biographer introduces the 19 volumes of 'The Life and Struggle of Saddam Hussein' with these generous and self-preserving words: 'He has honored me with my revolutionary pen which is dipped in the love of Saddam Hussein and that has completed the most holy and honorable writing in the history of literature'. Various volumes bear such titles as *Days from the Life of Saddam Hussein*, *A Trip with Saddam Hussein as a Person and as a Leader*, *Saddam Hussein Away from Politics*, *Glances into his Comprehensive Thoughts*, and *Statements on Science, Technology and Development*.
63. O'Kane, 'Another Day' (note 41). Cockburn and Cockburn (note 41) Ch.7.
64. Maggie O'Kane, 'Saddam Wields Terror – and Feigns Respect', *Guardian* (London) 25 Nov.

1998; O'Kane 'Wake of War' (note 41).

65. Cockburn and Cockburn (note 41) p.256.

66. O'Kane, 'Another Day' (note 41). One of Hussein's sons-in-law defected together with his brother. They were persuaded to come back in Jan. 1996 by promises of pardon and were executed within 24 hours of their return: Cockburn and Cockburn (note 41) Ch.8.

67. O'Kane, 'Wake of War' (note 41).

68. O'Kane, 'Another Day' (note 41). James Risen and Barbara Crossette, 'Even US Sees Iraq Opposition As Faint Hope', *New York Times*, 19 Nov. 1998, p.A1.

69. O'Kane, 'Saddam Wields Terror' (note 64). Relatedly, government officials are often wary of journeying south of Baghdad, particularly to such hostile cities as Karbala and Najaf. Maggie O'Kane and Ian Black, 'Saddam deputy escapes assassination attempt', *Guardian* (London) 24 Nov. 1998, p.2.

70. Robin Wright, 'US Pilots Fire on Iraq Jets in "No-Fly" Zone Confrontation', *Los Angeles Times*, 6 Jan. 1999, p.A1.

71. See Cockburn and Cockburn (note 41) Ch.1.

72. See Daniel Byman, Kenneth Pollack, and Gideon Rose, 'The Rollback Fantasy', *Foreign Affairs* 78/1 (Jan./Feb. 1999) pp.24–41. Ritter (note 41) pp.202–3.

73. Tim Weiner, 'Opponents Find That Ousting Hussein Is Easier Said Than Done', *New York Times*, 16 Nov. 1998, p.A10. Cockburn and Cockburn (note 41) Ch.7.

74. On the incapacity and low morale of the Iraqi army in the Gulf War, see Mueller, 'Perfect Enemy'(note 34). On the abilities of the Iraq army, see also Ritter (note 41) pp.199–201. A comparison might be made with US policy toward Manuel Noreiga's Panama. Sanctions against the country failed to loosen Noriega's grip for much the same reasons as in Iraq, and he was removed only by a US invasion in 1989. For a discussion, see Kirshner (note 59) pp.50–6.

75. Quoted, O'Kane, 'Wake of War' (note 41).

76. 60 Minutes (note 41). This statement has become famous in the Arab world: Cockburn and Cockburn (note 41) p.263.

77. John Mueller, *Policy and Opinion in the Gulf War* (U. of Chicago Press 1994) p.316.

78. *New York Times*, 11 Nov. 1998, p.A30.

79. On this phenomenon more generally, see Mueller, *Policy and Opinion* (note 77) pp.129–34, 334n9. A contrast can be made with the ill-fated 1993 assault on a religious sect at Waco, Texas, in which some 80 cult members died. In both cases, action was directed against outlaw 'rogue' actors, and, like Saddam, the cult leader in Waco was unwilling to sacrifice himself for the good of his people. In both cases the US government was not deliberately trying to harm civilians, but adopted policies that did so. However, the Iraqi death toll has been vastly greater, civilian casualties there were far more clearly foreseeable, and the prospects for success were much smaller than at Waco. Yet concern about the unintended deaths at Waco still looms large, while few have expressed serious concern about those in Iraq.

80. Ibid. p.79. On this issue more generally, see John Mueller, 'The Common Sense', *National Interest*, Spring 1997, pp.81–8; John Mueller, 'Fifteen Propositions about American Foreign Policy and Public Opinion in an Era Free of Compelling Threats', paper given at Annual Convention of the International Studies Association, San Diego, CA, 19 April 1996.

81. This figure is almost certainly much too high, probably by a factor of more than 10: see Mueller, 'Perfect Enemy' (note 34).

82. Melby (note 42) p.119.

83. William Kristol and Robert Kagan, 'Bombing Iraq Isn't Enough', *New York Times*, 30 Jan. 1998, p.A19.

84. On this terror and loathing, see in particular O'Kane, 'Another Day' (note 41). Also, Cockburn and Cockburn (note 41) p.290.

85. On the CoCom export control system, see Michael Mastanduno, *Economic Containment* (Ithaca, NY: Cornell UP 1992).

86. See Rod Barton, 'Iraq Is Down But Not Out', *New York Times*, 23 Dec. 1998, p.A27.

87. X [George F. Kennan], 'The Sources of Soviet Conduct', *Foreign Affairs* 25/4 (July 1947) pp.566–82.
88. For a rare consideration of this elemental issue, see Tom Clancy, 'Know the Answers Before Going to War', *New York Times*, 13 Feb. 1998, p.A27.
89. US Air Force regulations specifically require that an attack be cancelled or suspended if it 'may be expected to cause incidental loss of civilian life, injury to civilians, damage to civilian objects, or a combination thereof which would be excessive in relation to the concrete and direct military advantage anticipated'. Department of the Air Force, *AFP 110-31: International Law – The Conduct of Armed Combat and Air Operations*, 19 Nov. 1976, pp.5–9.
90. See Kirshner (note 59) pp.56–63, and Jonathan Kirshner, *Currency and Coercion* (Princeton UP 1995) pp.63–82, 95–9, 228–35.

9

Rogue Rage:
Can We Prevent Mass Destruction?

ERIC HERRING

The concept of 'rogue states' is now well established and used frequently in world politics but with little critical examination of the various perspectives on its meaning. The perspectives considered below are that the label 'rogue state':

- is appropriate for the very serious threats to the United States and its allies and is not applicable to the United States or its allies (the conservative perspective).

- exaggerates threats and is not applicable to the United States or its allies (the liberal perspective).

- exaggerates threats and is applicable also or even primarily to the United States and some of its allies (the left-wing perspective).

- can be understood less in terms of facts than on the basis of asserted values and identities which determine the construction and interpretation of the facts (the interpretivist perspective).

This set of perspectives is an organising device. Its main value is that it stakes out a set of positions broadly shared by groups of politically relevant actors. It shows that there is no single, natural and inevitable way of looking at the issue. This organising device has the limitation of obscuring the nuances of the position of any particular individual. That is an acceptable cost because my objective here is not principally to work out precisely where any individual stands.[1] Having said that, I do discuss the positions of individuals. After all, in claiming the existence of general perspectives, I have to show that some specific individuals adhere to major elements of those perspectives, even if the particular combinations and weightings of those elements vary.

This essay, explores a range of perspectives of the extent of the threat posed by rogue states. It spends a significant amount of time on the issues of the use or sponsorship of terrorism, violations of international norms or international law, and involvement in the spread of what are normally regarded as weapons of mass destruction (WMD) – that is, nuclear, biological and chemical weapons – and related delivery systems. There are two reasons for this.

First, such actions may be interpreted as indirect evidence that rogue states would be more willing than others to violate the norm against the use of WMD in general and nuclear weapons in particular.

Second, my concern is with preventing mass destruction by any means, be it conventional war, terrorism, economic sanctions or whatever. A focus on mass destruction inflicted only through WMD is inadequate. Hence the subtitle is 'Can we prevent mass destruction?' not 'Can we prevent the use of weapons of mass destruction?' I consider the policy recommendations that are linked to the various perspectives on the concept of rogue states. The conservative line on rogue states has dominated both perceptions and policies thus far in the West. Those writing from the conservative and liberal perspectives simply ignore the left. Ironically, the left's position is found to be the most persuasive of the three. However, it is also argued that one's position on this issue is driven less by the facts than by one's own values and identity. These underly one's construction and interpretation of the facts (the interpretivist perspective). The conclusion proposes the development of 'radical security studies', not only as an approach to the issue of rogue states but as an approach to the study of security generally. Radical security studies aims to integrate and map out the common ground between the perspective of the left and that of intepretivism.

THE CONSERVATIVE PERSPECTIVE: IT'S SOME OF THE WEST'S OPPONENTS, AND THEY'RE VERY DANGEROUS

Rogue states are portrayed by conservatives with great hostility and in emotive terms as wilful violators of the international rules of the road who thus deserve drastic counter-action. All blame is attached to the other party. Any suggestion that both parties share some of the blame for the situation, that both sides are violators of the international rules of the road, that conservatives have double standards in not seeing this, or that some of the motivations of the 'rogue' could be defensive and reactive tends to be treated with scorn and suspicion. This is what I mean by the phrase 'rogue rage'. Fear of their potential or actual ability to inflict mass destruction is given as justification for preparations to inflict mass destruction on them through limited nuclear war or for the actual infliction of mass destruction on them through conventional war and economic sanctions, as in the case of Iraq.[2] By mass destruction I mean large-scale death and injury among people and large-scale damage to property.

Although rogue states are represented by conservatives in the West as the most important military security threat of the post-Cold War world, the concept of the 'rogue state' has been the subject of relatively little analytical attention. Furthermore, the conservative and liberal analyses that do focus on this issue more or less agree on which are the rogue states with occasional disputes about the precise extent of the threat or the required response.[3] The possibility that Western states could be categorised as rogue states is rarely considered: it is just assumed that they could not.

The idea of rogue states is much older than the label. It is the latest in a long series of labels used by Western decision-makers to distinguish themselves from their perceived opponents. Notable examples have been the labels civilised versus barbarian states,[4] moderate (including fascist and Nazi) versus Bolshevik states,[5] *status quo* or moderate versus renegade, revisionist or revolutionary states,[6] and normal versus paranoid or pariah states.[7]

The concern with rogue states is very reminiscent of the fears of US (and Soviet) leaders in the late 1950s and early 1960s about China's efforts to acquire nuclear weapons. In 1963 President Kennedy expressed the view that the Chinese attached a lower value to human life and he dwelled on their supposed fanaticism. In July 1963 he contacted the Soviet Union about the possibility of US, Soviet or joint US-Soviet military, and possibly nuclear, action to prevent China from acquiring nuclear weapons.[8] The idea of using force to prevent a potentially hostile state from acquiring nuclear weapons has persisted in US policy circles.

As the Cold War drew to a close, Pentagon and conservative civilian analysts began to argue that the new threat was from less industrialised regional powers with (or seeking to acquire) large high-tech conventional forces and WMD. Such states were portrayed as having hostile intentions towards their weak or even defenceless neighbours and as being engaged in serious rivalries with similar rising powers close by. US military planners considered the military potential of a whole range of states – China, Taiwan, India, Pakistan, North Korea, South Korea, Iran, Iraq, Syria, Turkey and Egypt.[9] Ever since, the Pentagon has claimed to plan in terms of the capabilities of all regional powers, ostensibly on the grounds that they might have or develop hegemonic ambitions and WMD. This planning baseline has been set even if those countries are friendly to or allies of the United States, and even though military clashes with other states are more likely. Much of the threat assessment is based on concern about Third World states with actual or potential First World military capabilities. However, this has also been supplemented by a barrage of labels implying malign intentions and behaviour. Such states are referred to variously as 'rogues', 'outlaws', 'mavericks', 'renegades', 'backlash states' (as Anthony Lake, Clinton's Special Assistant for National Security Affairs, put it) and even 'demons' (as Colin S. Powell, Bush's Chairman of the Joint Chiefs of Staff, put it).[10] US politicians have tended to focus principally on North Korea, Iraq, Iran, Libya, Syria, Cuba and occasionally rump Yugoslavia as possible or actual rogue states.

In 1990, the United States began to plan to fight two such rogue states simultaneously.[11] Iraq had already invaded Iran, had used conventionally-armed ballistic missiles and chemical weapons against Iran,[12] and had a record of brutal domestic repression (including the use of chemical weapons). Its WMD and ballistic missile programmes were well known. The US military had already been using Iraq as a paradigmatic rogue state in training. However, US leaders had downplayed it as a rogue state and had actively assisted it with money, intelligence and technology. It was seen as a useful ally against Iran and it was not seen as particularly threatening to US interests elsewhere in the Middle East. Only once Iraq invaded Kuwait on 2 August 1990 did the US government portray it publicly as a rogue state. Particular emphasis was placed on the danger of Iraq having or developing WMD, and destruction of these capabilities became a high priority for the US government and US public opinion.[13]

Events in the Gulf were portrayed by the Bush administration as vindication of its claim that the new threat was from rogue states and of its military strategy for dealing with two of them simultaneously and unilaterally.[14] The Pentagon argued that Iraq was enormously militarily capable, that the conflict with Iraq known as Operation 'Desert Storm' was the model for future conflicts with rogue states, and that there was a need for substantial expenditure on high technology and force mobility for such conflicts. In the subsequent debate on US military requirements, the participants even calculated in terms of Desert Storm Equivalents (DSEs), with the two main options being either one and a half or two DSEs.

Although (or perhaps because) the Clinton administration is a Democratic one, it has asserted the conservative perspective on rogue states even more strongly than the Republican Reagan and Bush administrations. A typical characterisation of rogue states is that of Toby Gati, Assistant Secretary for Intelligence and Research in the Clinton administration:

> 'rogue' states threaten us by maintaining programs for weapons of mass destruction, sponsoring terrorism, often targeted specifically at Americans, and by their hostility toward and active opposition to our political and social systems and those of our friends and allies.[15]

Clinton's Bottom-Up Review (BUR) of US military requirements published in September 1993 agreed with the Bush administration that the United States needed to be prepared to fight two Iraq-sized regional powers simultaneously and unilaterally – in other words, it needed two DSEs.[16] The administration is also investing in capabilities for counter proliferation which include the development of options to use conventional weapons to destroy the NBC capabilities of rogue states.[17] The Clinton administration sees a role for nuclear weapons in deterring or retaliating against NBC use by rogue states against the United States or against other states deemed important to US interests.[18] One of the concerns is also to show that possession of WMD would not deter a US conventional response to regional conventionally-armed 'aggression' by a rogue state. The US government has funded research into very low yield nuclear weapons for battlefield use. The United States decided in 1997 to increase expenditure on the design and development of new nuclear warheads by $4 billion per year, using computer simulation testing rather than underground explosions in order to stay within the letter of the Comprehensive Test Ban Treaty.[19] The nuclear war plans adopted by the United States in December 1997 include options for nuclear attacks on states identified as rogues which have 'prospective access' to WMD.[20]

In similar vein, although Britain is planning to cut its Trident nuclear warheads unilaterally by 50 per cent and has scrapped its other nuclear weapons,[21] efforts are being made to make it more flexible and usable in what the Ministry of Defence labels 'sub-strategic' roles.[22] Rogue states are seen as targets of such weapons.

The Clinton administration has taken a much tougher line on attempts by its designated rogue states to acquire WMD. The most notable example of this was during the crisis in the summer of 1994 when a preventive (probably conventional) attack by the United States to destroy North Korea's nuclear facilities seemed like a substantial possibility. Late in 1998, the United States deliberately leaked war plans in which it envisaged responding to a North Korean invasion of South Korea by invading North

Korea, overthrowing the regime there, and reunifying the country.[23] Overall, the US military posture is increasingly geared towards dealing with what it deems to be rogue states.

The only substantial study of the rogue states issue from a conservative perspective has been written by Raymond Tanter, formerly a member of the US National Security Council under Reagan. He defines rogue states or leaders as ones that 'have large conventional military forces and that condone international terrorism and/or seek weapons of mass destruction, including nuclear, biological, chemical armaments' and defines rogue behaviour vaguely as 'unacceptable international conduct'.[24] Note that even conservatives would have to accept that the United States and some of its allies fulfil two out of three of these criteria for a rogue state: it has large conventional forces and has WMD. As discussed later, the left argues that the United States has condoned, sponsored and carried out acts of international terrorism. The definition of 'international terrorism' and the assessment of the content of the historical record are crucial political battlegrounds.[25] He asserts that the United States practices what it preaches about acceptable international conduct, that rogue behaviour is clearly identifiable and that, once identified, it creates an obligation to respond to it. If the left had anything to do with it, these words would come back to haunt him. But first I wish to explore the much more mild dissent contained in the liberal perspective.

THE LIBERAL PERSPECTIVE: IT'S SOME OF THE WEST'S OPPONENTS, AND THEY'RE QUITE DANGEROUS

Liberals argue that such an exaggerated sense of threat has led to extreme actions such as those against Iraq and the closing off of otherwise useful policy options.[26] Are the states seen by the United States as actual or potential rogues worthy of the name in terms of military capabilities? Liberals think not. Tables 1 and 2 draw upon and extend the analysis of Michael Klare, who has a liberal perspective on the issue of rogue states. Although the United States would prefer to fight with allies, the DSE as a planning device is based on the United States fighting alone.

Table 1 summarises the position with regard to potential rogue states as defined by US military planners. All of them would require at least or vastly more than a DSE were the United States to fight them single handedly. With the exception of Turkey, they also possess or are pursuing WMD and ballistic missiles. However, a survey of their neighbours leaves us with a highly improbable list of states for which the United States would launch a

TABLE 1

THE STRATEGIC POSITION OF SUPPOSED POTENTIAL ROGUE STATES

Potential rogue states as defined by US military planners	Conventional military capabilities requiring a US Desert Storm Equivalent?	Possessing/ pursuing WMD and ballistic missiles?	Have militarily weak neighbours?
China	Yes	Yes	Yes (Burma, Laos, Mongolia, Vietnam) No (Taiwan)
Egypt	Yes	Yes	Yes (Libya, Sudan) No (Israel)
India	Yes	Yes	Yes (Bangladesh, Nepal, Burma, Sri Lanka) No (China, Pakistan)
Pakistan	Yes	Yes	Yes (Afghanistan)
South Korea	Yes	Yes	No (North Korea)
Turkey	Yes	No	Yes (Armenia, Bulgaria) No (Iraq, Greece)

TABLE 2

THE STRATEGIC POSITION OF SUPPOSED ACTUAL ROGUE STATES

Rogue states as defined by US leaders	Conventional military capabilities requiring a US Desert Storm Equivalent (assumes US fighting alone)?	Possessing/ pursuing WMD and ballistic missiles?	Have militarily weak neighbours?
North Korea	No, but close	Yes, but does not have nuclear weapons	No (South Korea, China)
Syria	No, but close	Yes, but does not have nuclear weapons	No (Israel) Yes (Lebanon)
Iran	No, but potentially in the longer term	Yes, but does not have nuclear weapons	No (Iraq, Pakistan, Turkey)
Iraq	No, but potentially in the longer term	Yes, but does not have nuclear weapons	No (Iran, Syria, Turkey) Yes (Kuwait, Jordan)
Libya	No, and not potentially	Yes, but does not have nuclear weapons	No (Egypt) Yes (Chad)

lone DSE – Burma, Laos, Mongolia or Vietnam if invaded by China; Libya and Sudan if invaded by Egypt; Bangladesh, Nepal, Burma or Sri Lanka if invaded by India; Afghanistan if invaded by Pakistan; and Armenia or Bulgaria if invaded by Turkey. At least on this point Klare bends over backwards to be fair to conservatives in giving some limited credence to the scenario of a Turkish bid for hegemony in the Middle East which leads it to clash directly with the United States.[27]

If the criteria used by the planners really are just military capability and potential, then countries like Germany and Japan should be on the list. They are not, possibly for fear of causing political offence. Russia is also not on the list, partly for the same reason and partly also because it is seen in the Pentagon as requiring a return to a baseline much larger than a DSE. Although Israel should also figure on the list, it is omitted, according to Klare, because 'Israel's military posture is so closely aligned with that of the United States ... and the probability of Israel ever severing its links to Washington is so low'.[28] This is putting it rather delicately, and Klare does not address the argument that Israel itself looks in many ways like a rogue state (with the obvious exception of the hostility to the United States criterion).

Table 2 illustrates Klare's claim that one of the basic weaknesses of the DSE as a planning assumption with regard to the supposedly existing rogue states is that none of them fulfil the combined criteria which would require a DSE.

First, among the supposed rogue states, only two come close to having the requisite conventional military capabilities (North Korea and Syria), two are a long way off such a capability (Iran and Iraq), and the last has no chance of acquiring it (Libya).

Second, and more important, the militarily strongest of them generally face militarily strong neighbours. For example, North Korea faces China and South Korea. Hence planning based on the United States effectively fighting alone is in most cases invalid and likely to remain so. What we are left with is extremely improbable – the United States going it alone to defend Lebanon from Syrian invasion, or Chad from Libyan invasion – or (Klare maintains) very unlikely – the United States going it alone to defend Kuwait or Jordan from Iraqi invasion.

Overall, Klare is unequivocal: 'The probability of US troops engaging in even one replay of Desert Storm appears to be very low; that of a two-DSE scenario, close to zero.'[29]

Furthermore, Klare rightly argues, contrary to the Pentagon and BUR position, that victory in the Gulf was critically dependent on allies for funding, bases, petroleum products and political support, and that the circumstances of the victory were unlikely to be repeated.[30] On the latter issue, he points out that the United States had technological superiority, a nuclear monopoly, established logistical facilities in Saudi Arabia and favourable desert terrain. In contrast, Iraq had many military weaknesses, virtually no allies, Saddam Hussein's incompetent leadership, and domestic rebellion in the north and south to cope with. Rather than Iraq being the archetypal rising rogue state brought to heel by US technological superiority, Iraq was an unlikely to be repeated case of a highly vulnerable and badly led regional power brought (only partly) to heel due to a combination of many favourable circumstances.

Although Klare sees 'rogue state' as an appropriate label for North Korea, Iran, Iraq, Libya and Syria, the central thesis of his book is that the threat posed by them has been exaggerated by the Pentagon in order to prevent its post-Cold War budget from being cut.[31] To support this claim he would need to have shown that those in the Pentagon believed the threat to be low, that they agreed to exaggerate it deliberately, and that they did so for the sole or at least primary purpose of budget protection. Klare has not provided the evidence necessary to sustain any of these three claims, yet all three are necessary to bear out his thesis. Instead, he conducted his own threat assessment, decided that the Pentagon one was too high, and jumped to his conclusion. However, the same evidence can be read very differently.

First, it is possible that Pentagon planners are influenced by motivated bias; they sincerely see a relatively high level of threat because they are seeing what they want to see. This motivated bias could be caused unconsciously by a desire to prop up their military budget; self-deception rather than the deliberate deception Klare hints at. Demonisation of the opponent (which tends to be characteristic of those who perceive the existence of rogue states) is seen by Ralph White to be a very negative misperception produced by the workings of political psychology. He argues that things go wrong when decision-makers have a demonised enemy image, an idealised self-image, are overconfident or underconfident, and fail to have empathy with opponents or other parties. He asserts: 'The demonized enemy image (defined here as an exaggeration of the actual evil in an adversary's character) is with little doubt the most common concomitant of war and probably the most important direct cause of offensive action.'[32]

Note that to call it misperception requires one to be able to sort out true perception from false perception, no easy task. Those who fear rogue states would insist that the demons are actually demonic, and that liberals are the ones who are misperceiving, but in the other direction by projecting their positive image onto the opponent in a situation in which the opponent is actually proactive and so on.

Second, and even more problematic for Klare's thesis, is the fact that conservatives could even agree that another DSE is unlikely and two simultaneous DSEs extremely unlikely, but could still argue for maintaining or increasing the Pentagon's budget. This is because conservatives are wedded to military strength as a basic prudential principle. Threat assessment and peering dimly into the future can only get you so far. The other half of the equation is your values, interests and objectives. Conservatives regard lack of current evidence of a likely military threat as being less important than the potential of events to spring very large, very dangerous and very improbable surprises. No amount of liberal analysis can change that. There are different ways of being prudent: you pay as much of your money as you feel you have to and you choose your risks.

THE PERSPECTIVE OF THE LEFT:
IT'S THE WEST AS MUCH AS (OR MORE THAN) ANY OF THE WEST'S
OPPONENTS, AND THE WEST IS DANGEROUS

Left-wing critics of the policies of the United States and its allies provide evidence and arguments in support of their claim that, in effect, they are rogue states. Some of them would argue that the United States is the most rogue-like state of all. As John Pilger has written: 'If we are to speak of truly "rogue" powers, the US leads the pack.'[33] Some on the left focus on what they see as the double standards of the United States and its allies while others on the left couch the arguments in terms of an underlying single standard of doing whatever is in their perceived interests. Together, they claim that the West engages in the very behaviour which it condemns in supposed rogue states: use of and support for terrorism, violations of international law, defiance of the international community, and assisting the spread of WMD and related delivery systems:

First, the left claims that the United States and its allies condone, sponsor and use terrorism.[34] I take terrorism to mean the threat or use of violence by states or non-state actors targeted against civilians for political purposes. The cases they cite in support of their position include the following:

• The US Army School of the Americas (SOA) at Fort Benning in Georgia is the target of a campaign to close it down because of the continuing involvement of some of its Latin American graduates in state terrorism against citizens of their countries.[35]

- The United States condemned Libya for not handing over for trial two Libyans suspected in the blowing up of a Pan Am airliner over Lockerbie in Scotland in 1988, yet it continues to shield Cuban exile CIA operative Luis Posada Carriles linked to the blowing up of a Cuban airliner in 1976 and US CIA operative John Hull indicted by Costa Rica in connection with a bomb attack at a press conference in Nicaragua in 1984.[36]

Second, the United States and its allies are portrayed by the left as violating international norms and international law, and defying the will of the international community.[37] Examples they see as relevant include these:

- The International Court of Justice (ICJ) concluded on 27 June 1986 that the war the United States was sponsoring was an illegal war of aggression against Nicaragua, and ordered the United States to stop and to pay compensation to Nicaragua. The United States simply ignored the judgement yet turned to the ICJ in support of its case against Libya over the Lockerbie bombing.[38]

- The economic sanctions enforced unilaterally by the United States against Cuba since 1961 are causing widespread suffering and unnecessary deaths among the civilian population, in spite of extensive efforts by the Cuban government.[39] The embargo, which includes food and medicine, is opposed by many individuals, groups and governments around the world. In October 1998, 157 states in the UN General Assembly voted for an end to the US sanctions: only the United States and Israel opposed the resolution, and 12 other countries abstained.[40] Cuban research scientists announced in December 1998 that they had found a vaccine for meningitis B. A team of British medical researchers immediately went to Cuba to assess the vaccine. In other words, British children may benefit from Cuban medical research while Britain does little to end US sanctions which deny Cuban children vital medical treatment.

- UN sanctions, combined with the after-effects of the US-led UN war against Iraq in 1991, have resulted in an increase of around 90,000 deaths per year compared with 1989.[41] If this figure is accurate, 720,000 Iraqis died due to this policy between 1991 and 1998 inclusive. The UN Children's Fund (UNICEF) calculated in April 1998 that the deaths have disproportionately hit children under five years of age (an increase of around 40,000 deaths per year compared with 1989). This works out at 320,000 children under five between 1991 and 1998 inclusive. This policy has been kept in place by US and British pressure, although widespread international disquiet has meant that some movement in the US and especially British position could be detected in 1999.

The economic sanctions are ostensibly aimed at ensuring Iraqi compliance with UN resolutions passed during and after their expulsion from Kuwait in 1991. Iraq is required, among other things, to dismantle its capabilities to produce WMD and related delivery systems and to submit to long-term UN monitoring of its WMD capabilities. Iraq is entitled to sell some oil in order to pay for things such as food and medicines.

Those in favour of the sanctions argue that all moral responsibility for the fate of ordinary Iraqis is thereby transferred to Saddam Hussein: if he complies, the sanctions will be lifted, they maintain.

However, the critics of the sanctions on the left argue that the sanctions are in violation of the Geneva Conventions and the Convention on the Prevention and Punishment of the Crime of Genocide.[42] They argue that, in violation of the relevant UN resolutions, the United States has indicated its intention to keep the sanctions in place until Saddam Hussein is overthrown even if Iraq complies with the UN's demands; that Iraq has complied extensively if not fully with disarmament and monitoring requirements; that the oil sales programme is totally inadequate to the task of reducing the rate of death and suffering among ordinary Iraqis; and that the United States and Britain have frequently blocked UN approval of humanitarian supplies.

- In February 1998, the United States was seeking the use of force against Iraq (without UN explicit authorisation) for refusing to allow UN inspectors access to certain sites and for objecting to US and British membership of the UN inspection teams. Iraq objected that the US and British inspectors would be hostile rather than neutral and might engage in spying (an accusation which turned out to be true – US personnel were spying under the cover of UNSCOM and passing the information on directly to the United States, which also shared it with Israel).

At precisely the same time, the United States was passing legislation which codified exactly the same exceptions regarding the Chemical Weapons Convention (CWC).[43] Clause 307 of the legislation stated that 'The president may deny a request to inspect any facility in the United

States in cases where the president determines that the inspection may pose a threat to the national security interests of the United States.' Another clause stated that 'any objection by the president to any individual serving as an inspector ... shall not be reviewable in any court'. Furthermore, private companies are to be exempt from inspection. In 1997, the United States refused to cooperate with two members of the Organisation for the Prohibition of Chemical Weapons (one Cuban and one Iranian) which has the task of monitoring compliance with the CWC. The left point out that no-one called for the bombing of the United States for this rogue behaviour.

Third, support for the spread of WMD and related delivery systems is deemed to be a characteristic of a rogue state, and the left argues that Western countries have been extensively involved in this process. For example:

- The United States has shown itself very willing to allow Israel to acquire technology from US manufacturers which is vital to its nuclear weapon programme.[44]

- Germany is funding three *Dolphin*-class submarines to give Israel an undersea platform for nuclear-armed sea-launched cruise missiles (SLCMs) being developed under the bizarre name Popeye Turbo. Israel had scrapped plans to deploy SLCMs. The project was only saved by the German intervention. The objective of the programme is supposedly to give Israel a secure retaliatory nuclear capability should Iran develop a nuclear arsenal of its own.[45]

The left construes Israel as being a rogue state on all three counts of terrorism, violating international law and norms, and spreading WMD and related delivery systems. It has persistently defied UN Security Council resolutions, has secretly built up a substantial nuclear arsenal, was involved in assisting the acquisition of nuclear weapons by South Africa, officially approves of torture in its jails, invaded Lebanon in 1982, has occupied and terrorised much of southern Lebanon ever since, and uses terrorist tactics against Palestinians. Frequently Israel has been able to avoid international censure due to the threatened or actual veto of the United States on the UN Security Council.

Social scientists try to adjudicate between the three perspectives outlined thus far by assessing their internal logical coherence and their fit with empirical evidence. We can all do better or worse at engaging in the social science exercise. In particular, claims about rogue states can be tested in their own terms: criteria have been specified for what constitutes a rogue state and claims have been made about which states fulfil them. By social science standards, Tanter's conservative perspective fails. Klare's liberal perspective fares better but still falls at the basic hurdle of failing to provide the evidence and connected arguments necessary to support the claim that the Pentagon's concern to prop up its budget is behind its position that rogue states are a major threat. The liberal perspective also does not consider the possibility that the United States or its allies could be considered rogue states. In contrast, much plausible evidence can be gathered in support of the position of the left that the United States and its allies can be classified as rogue states too, using the criteria laid out by conservatives and accepted by liberals.

Conservatives do not give a response to the left although I am sure they could think of one. They refuse to engage, and act as if the left-wing perspective simply does not exist. In the manuscript of the forthcoming revised edition of *Rogue Regimes*, Tanter responds to what he sees as my arguments in an earlier version of this study.[46] First, he asks: 'Is it unreasonable to fear the potential and actual ability of hostile states to inflict mass destruction?' My answer is of course not, and that was not my point, which is that we should not have double standards – we should oppose rogue behaviour, whoever it is that carries it out – and that Western states indulge in rogue behaviour. Tanter does not address this argument and continues:

> the present study contrasts sharply with the critical approach. The alternative outlook argues that the Pentagon manufactured a rogue state threat. That approach claims that the US policy of containment of the USSR shifted to containment of rogue states simply to maintain approximate levels of defense spending in the post-Cold War days.

Note that Tanter refers to 'the critical approach' in the singular, with the critical approach being that of Klare, even though in the introduction of the earlier version of this work I criticised the work of Tanter and Klare specifically as follows: 'The possibility that Western states could be rogue states is simply never considered: it is just assumed that they could not.' The liberal-conservative dispute is a cosy one because it leaves a shared positive image of the United States and its allies intact.[47] Left-wing arguments are defeated not through engagement and social scientific disconfirmation but non-engagement and marginalisation.

It is not simply that some of the debate is about potential, future threats. It is also that the analyst's own values and objectives will to a substantial degree be what drives the outcome rather than theoretical and empirical evidence. A conservative will tend to plump for larger military investment as they best way to hedge against uncertainty whereas a liberal will tend to fall back on a general scepticism about the threats touted by armed forces and politicians. And so on.

In other words, the analysis can have a pre-determined outcome and everyone will continue to occupy their usual positions and feel vindicated. Yet their claims of vindication will be presented as being based on the general truth of their world views combined with 'the facts', and those who continue to hold an alternative position will tend to be dismissed as stupid, malign or both. I have no illusion (or, as will become clear below, desire) that self-appointed adjudication by any individual will close the debate.

THE INTERPRETIVIST PERSPECTIVE: THREAT ASSESSMENT IS AS MUCH ABOUT ASSERTING VALUES AND IDENTITIES AS ASSESSING THREATS

As a means of trying to be better social scientists we have a great deal to learn from what might be called 'interpretivism'.[48] Interpretivists claim to reject the political game of asserting and imposing single supposed truths. The aim is not finding answers to win and end the debate but finding answers in such a way that debate can still exist. It is an ethic which values contestation highly. Following on from the work of Michel Foucault and others, its principal exponent in the field of international security studies is David Campbell.[49] I present here my take on interpretivism, with the aim of offering a version of it which is easy to grasp and which can be readily applied to the issue of rogue states.

Interpretivism is not interested in the truth or falsity of knowledge claims, but in the relationship of knowledge claims to power, and argues that knowledge is inseparable from power. When a question is posed, such as 'To what extent is our security threatened by potential or actual rogue states?', social scientists seek to provide the best single answer based on the most objective theory and evidence possible, while accepting (I hope!) that it may be supplanted subsequently by better theory or new evidence.

Interpretivists do not try to provide a single answer to the question. Instead, they seek to develop several answers and ask 'What exercise of power is served by the question and the various answers to the question?'

Simplifying interpretivism into six separate points allows me to generate the following analysis of the rogue state issue:

- Deconstruction involves 'unsettling concepts and conceptual oppositions which are otherwise taken to be settled'.[50] The rogue versus non-rogue state distinction is widely (though not unanimously) taken to be settled. The conservative perspective is the dominant one among the United States and its allies. Liberals and the left argue over who is to be labelled a rogue or how serious is the threat but they tend not to challenge the basic conceptual opposition.

- The purpose behind deconstruction is to reveal the effects of conceptual oppositions. If you accept the rogue versus non-rogue state distinction, you are more likely to take action against those states labelled 'rogue' and to act leniently towards states not so labelled, even if they do the same things. Hence the infliction of mass destruction on Iraq through economic sanctions and the planning for possible use against rogue states of those things more usually classified as WMD. At the other end of the political spectrum, the left is trying to mobilise against the United States and its allies.

- Conceptual oppositions are not natural. They are a product of power rather than of the inherent characteristics of the phenomena the concepts purport to describe. The rogue-non-rogue state distinction did not simply emerge from the neutral, progressive, universal and scientific study of world politics but in the context of promoting the power of the United States and its allies as the Cold War drew to a close.

- Conceptual oppositions are not neutral but hierarchical, with one claimed to have good characteristics the other lacks. Rogue states are assumed to be bad states, non-rogue states good ones.

- Totalisation or closure (i.e. the conclusive achievement of clearly separate oppositions) is impossible, in spite of great efforts to achieve it. It is not that objective reality does not exist but that we cannot apprehend it directly. Facts are inevitably imbued with value and only take on meaning through interpretation. Effort is put into lambasting supposed rogue states and lauding supposed non-rogue ones, and those who dissent are seen as flying in the face of 'reality'. Yet the pesky awkward squad which persists in seeing it differently never quite goes away and cannot be proven wrong decisively.

- Technologies (i.e. power-knowledge combinations) of normalisation (e.g. conceptions of prison, psychiatry, military intervention, economic sanctions) are supposedly neutral ways of eliminating or at least minimising the number of or danger from deviants (criminals, the insane, sexual perverts, terrorists, rogue states), when what they actually do is define into existence these deviants and thus ensure their existence. The existence of these deviants is primarily about defining who 'we' are (identity politics): whether or not there is a real threat from them is secondary. Interpretivists argue that what is needed is an understanding of how difference becomes represented as dangerous other-ness. Social scientific commentaries on rogue states are invariably permeated with assertions of a particular, morally superior, 'us'. The entry price of being part of conservative, liberal and left-wing discussions of rogue states is buying into a particular identity involving the assertion of 'our' moral superiority: that matters more than scepticism about the extent of threat from rogue states. This may be the moral superiority of the West in the eyes of conservatives and liberals or the moral superiority of those opposing Western hegemony in the eyes of the left.

Reactions from social scientists to interpretivism tend to take two highly contrasting forms. One objection is that intepretivism is dramatically different from social science, and that interpretivism leads to morally and intellectually paralysing relativism, with an inability to judge between moral claims or truth claims. The opposite objection is that interpretivism is merely saying what social scientists can already say and can say more clearly: from this viewpoint, interpretivism is merely social science dressed up in fancy continental clothes. This is a question that goes way beyond the scope of this analysis: it is a vast, sprawling debate on the whole nature of moral and intellectual endeavour. I will limit my response here to two points.

First, interpretivism does not have to lead to relativism. It is striking, and it is a point made frequently by interpretivists, that some social scientists tend to base their greater willingness to rely on facts (even while accepting in principle their constructedness) not on the reliability of facts but on the fear of the moral consequences of taking the position that meaning cannot flow directly from facts but is a product of interpretation. Interpretivism is a product not of a lack of moral commitment but of a different moral commitment. From an interpretivist perspective, the rogue-non-rogue state dichotomy is an expression of the broader phenomenon of 'biopolitics', namely, the process of pervading all aspects of human activity with economy (efficiency), order (government) and measures of normality (and hence unacceptable abnormality), ostensibly to ensure the survival, health and happiness of the population.[51] From the perspective of interpretivism, the shared biopolitical outlook of conservatives and liberals (but to a much lesser extent the left, with whom interpretivists tend to have an affinity), their division of what it means to be into the right and wrong way to be with related notions of control, underlies the will to mass destruction. And nothing less than the rejection of biopolitics becomes necessary to the avoidance of mass destruction.

Second, different epistemological emphases (different views of how we know what we know) have substantially different political and ethical consequences. John Mueller and Karl Mueller argues that chemical and biological weapons are not really WMD because they have not been and still are not very effective at killing masses of people, whereas economic sanctions can be WMD because they can bring about the deaths of masses of people.[52] Similarly, one of my students, Vanja Buljina, who describes herself as 'a southern Slav', argues that nationalism is a WMD. Should one rule this claim in or out?

To give another example, there were 600,000 tobacco-related deaths in China in 1990. With the marketing skills of Western tobacco firms which are gaining access to China, that death toll is predicted to rise many fold to the point where it will eventually kill one in three of the 300 million Chinese men currently alive under the age of 29.[53] Those who sell tobacco could be construed as inflicting mass destruction on the Chinese people.

Another characteristic often attributed to WMD is that only small numbers of them are needed to inflict mass destruction. This is another reason Mueller and Mueller give for not counting chemical and biological weapons as WMD. With current (though, I would argue, possibly not future) technology, large numbers of them would be needed to inflict large numbers of casualties. Yet it is difficult to know how to apply the small numbers criterion to economic sanctions: the phrase is plural but how many of them are needed for economic sanctions to cease to be a WMD in Mueller and Mueller's terms? Ought tobacco to be categorised as a WMD? Is it singular (tobacco) or plural (billions of cigarettes)? What about intentions? Tobacco firms do not want smokers to die, because then they can not make money from them. For every smoker that dies, another must be hooked if tobacco firms are even to stand still. Then again, whether or not the tobacco firms intend it, it is a knowable consequence of their profitmaking. Hence Chomsky's labelling of them as the real narcotraffickers.[54] One more point: should tobacco be left out of the WMD category because it does not wreak its destruction at high speed?

Social scientists try to sort this sort of question out by pointing to the facts of the phenomena being investigated and by using theories to try to extract further meaning from those facts. Mueller and Mueller argue for the recategorisation of chemical and biological weapons as not being WMD and economic sanctions as being WMD on this basis. They attribute what they see as the current miscategorisation to the distortions introduced by professional pessimists. Their writing has a tone which implies deliberate deception on the part of those professional pessimists: the use of words of mass deception about weapons of minimal destruction.

In the debate over what constitutes WMD and use of WMD, social science protagonists often aim to show that they have the objectively right definition of concepts and categorisation of activities. They see those with whom they disagree as offering knowledge that is inaccurate because it has been corrupted by power. Knowledge is presented as something which can and should be separable from power.

Similarly, White's approach to the issue of demonisation is premised on an ability to separate correct perception from misperception – that demons are not actually demons, for example. And he asserts that there is little room for doubt that his conclusions are right.

In contrast, an interpretivist approach is concerned to a greater extent with viewing all claims to knowledge as power moves. This allows for a more reflexive position even on those views with which one agrees. I tend to be persuaded by the basic argument of the left that the United States and its allies operate on the basis of double standards, underlying which there is a systematic single standard of serving perceived US interests. However, interpretivism reminds me that the facts that have so persuaded me could be reinterpreted by conservatives and liberals to show that the double standards do not exist because differences between the paired examples means that the apparent double standards are actually an illusion.[55] This does not mean that anything goes, but that finality and certainty are unachievable, that imposition of a single perspective on all is a form of political oppression, and that arguments about fact are often really arguments about value. We need to proceed not only on the basis of what we think is correct, but also on the basis that what we think is correct may be wrong.

BEYOND ROGUE RAGE: RADICAL SECURITY STUDIES

Some may see what they define as Western interests as being best served by violating international norms as often as they think they can get away with it while imposing them (through means which often violate the same or other international norms) upon perceived enemies. Some Western conservatives will frankly simply not care about analyses which argue that they have double standards in that they define as rogue behaviour things done by other states, but do not call those same things rogue behaviour when done by their state or their allies. For them, this is justified as part of a propaganda battle in a war of national interests. In other words, if there is a way of delegitimising their opponent's violations of international law but not their own, then they are happy. Their moral imperative is the defence of what they call the national interest. Hence, they are only interested in rogue states and rogue behaviour which they perceive as threatening to themselves. Indeed, they might argue that drawing attention to the existence of their double standards is short-sighted and dangerous because it makes harder for them to defend the national interest.

However, rogue rage is a form of demonisation. While demonisation can serve to mobilise people in defence of norms worth defending, it can have substantial costs. It can lock you into an unnecessarily high level of conflict. It can cause you to impose higher costs upon everyone, including third parties, than you would otherwise have done. It can encourage you to feel morally and prudentially justified in violating the very norms you are supposedly defending. You can assume that you are right simply because you are you. All of these costs have been associated with the demonisation of some states as rogue states.

Rogue rage has brought about mass destruction by the United States and its allies in the name of preventing mass destruction by others, and the focus on preventing the use of WMD by supposed rogue states has distracted attention from the actual mass destruction taking place in the world. Accusing the United States and its states of double standards in their behaviour does not have to be the same thing as asserting their moral equivalence with other actors or states. The opposite can be the case. Western states claim to be morally superior, and in accusing them of having double standards, some people may be hoping that they will act in accordance with their asserted higher standards more often. In other words, to accuse someone of having double standards can be indicative of some faith in them.

Equally, asserting that the United States and its allies are not morally equivalent to states such as Iraq is not an adequate justification for double standards. It is precisely because they claim not to be morally equivalent that they must have at the very least consistent standards. In addition, the 'rogue state' label should be ditched altogether. Interestingly, not all opponents are demonised, and so it might be valuable to analyse when opponents are demonised and when they are not. This could be done at a host of levels. For example, individual cases could traced for when demonisation begins and when it ends.[56] Particular countries could be examined for the pattern of their tendencies to demonise or not. Different countries could be compared for when they demonise at the same time or in the same way, and when they do not.

There is much to be learned from existing work on norms in international relations.[57] However, we should listen also to the sceptical voices of the interpretivists and the left, who in their different ways would caution us about the potential for promotion of norms to turn into the infliction of mass destruction on the demonised rogue other in new, more respectable clothes. Many on the left think this is already happening through the much-vaunted norm of humanitarian intervention as exemplified by NATO's military action against Yugoslavia in relation to Kosovo.[58]

This engagement with the issue of rogue states illustrates my wider belief that there is much to be said for a general approach to security studies which I would label 'radical security studies'.[59] This would combine the left's detailed empirical engagement and insistence that the United States and its allies be held to account for the vast amount of destruction they inflict on other societies, with interpretivism's problematisation of the implicit claim of some that their position is a product of facts which can be perceived by those who are not ideologically blinkered.

Those on the left delve into the nasty detail of the foreign and security policies of liberal democracies. They offer direct engagement with the issues of the day in a way which is generally comprehensible to a wider audience. Their work also involves a fundamental critique of the limitations of liberal democracy, of the antipathy to liberal democracy contained within realism, of the importance of material forces in world politics, and of the importance of money and power in the role played by the media in undermining real democratic control of policy.

It might be objected that the approaches of the left and the interpretivists are simply incompatible. However, a metatheoretical middle ground which can be used to bring them together not only is possible but already exists.[60] Radical security studies has the potential to combine the problematisation of knowledge with a serious engagement with the detail of policy in the service of common humanity rather than any supposed national interest.[61] Without this combination, it may be that mass destruction in the future cannot be prevented and the mass destruction which is already being inflicted cannot be brought to an end.

NOTES

I am very grateful to Noam Chomsky, Lene Hansen, Carolyn James, Pat Morgan, Yannis Stivachtis and those who participated in the discussion when I presented this study as a paper at the Pan European International Relations – International Studies Association annual conference in Vienna on 16 September 1998 for their valuable comments. The opinions expressed in this contribution are solely those of the author.

1. Nevertheless, that would be a worthwhile research objective. If one developed a more complex picture based on cross-pressured, ambivalent preferences, one might grasp how coalitions of preferences could play an important role in influencing how perspectives on rogue states shape world politics. For the application of this kind of approach to the politics of nuclear weapons policy, see James DeNardo, *The Amateur Strategist. Intuitive Deterrence Theories and the Politics of the Nuclear Arms Race* (Cambridge: CUP 1995).
2. See John Mueller and Karl Mueller, 'The Methodology of Mass Destruction: Assessing Threats in the New World Order', this volume. See also Geoff Simons' polemic *The Scourging of Iraq. Sanctions, Law and Natural Justice* 2nd ed. (Basingstoke: Macmillan 1998).
3. Alexander L. George, *Bridging the Gap. Theory and Practice in Foreign Policy* (Washington DC: United States Inst. of Peace Press 1993). Michael Klare, *Rogue States and Nuclear Outlaws. America's Search for a New Foreign Policy* (NY: Hill & Wang 1995). Raymond Tanter, *Rogue Regimes. Terrorism and Proliferation* (NY: St Martin's Press 1998). For left-wing critiques, see Stephen Zunes, 'The Function of Rogue States in US Middle East Policy'. <http://www.mepc.org/zunes56.htm> and John Pilger, '"Humanitarian Intervention" is the Latest Brand Name for Imperialism as it Begins a Return to Respectability', *The New Statesman*, 28 June 1999.
4. Gerrit W. Gong, *The Standard of 'Civilization' in International Society* (Oxford: Clarendon Press 1984).
5. Noam Chomsky, *Deterring Democracy* (London: Vintage 1992) pp.27–45.
6. Barry Buzan, *People, States and Fear. An Agenda for International Security Studies in the Post-Cold War Era* 2nd ed. (Hemel Hempstead: Harvester Wheatsheaf 1991) pp.297–311; Stephen Chan and Andrew J. Williams (eds.) *Renegade States. The Evolution of Revolutionary Foreign Policy* (Manchester UP 1994); Eric Herring, *Danger and Opportunity: Explaining International Crisis Outcomes* (ibid. 1995) pp.47–9; Randall L. Schweller, 'Bandwagoning for Profit: Bringing the Revisionist State Back In', *International Security* 19/1 (Summer 1994) pp.72–107; and Charles L. Glaser, 'Political Consequences of Military Strategy. Expanding and Refining the Spiral and Deterrence Models', *World Politics* 44/4 (1992) pp.497–538.
7. Richard K. Betts, 'Paranoids, Pygmies, Pariahs and Nonproliferation', *Foreign Policy* 26 (1977) pp.157–83. Robert Harkavy, 'Pariah States and Nuclear Proliferation', *International Organization* 35 (1981) pp.135–63.
8. Gordon H. Chang, 'JFK, China and the Bomb', *Jnl of American History* 74 (1988) pp.1287–310. The Soviet Union and United States also shared concerns over the possibility of a revanchist Germany or Japan with nuclear weapons, and of the potential for nuclear use by Britain and France.
9. Klare, *Rogue States* (note 3) pp.16, 19–20, 24, 133.
10. Debra von Opstal and Andrew C. Goldberg, *Meeting the Mavericks: Regional Challengers for the Next President* (Washington DC: Center for Strategic and Int. Studies 1988); Anthony Lake, 'Confronting Backlash States', *Foreign Affairs* 73/2 (March–April 1994) pp.45–55; and Klare, *Rogue States* (note 3) p.24.
11. Ibid. pp.28–37.
12. There is much less awareness of the fact that Iran used chemical weapons against Iraq. See Carolyn C. James, 'Iran and Iraq as Rational Crisis Actors: Dangers and Dynamics of Survivable Nuclear War', this volume.
13. John Mueller, *Policy and Opinion in the Gulf War* (U. of Chicago Press 1994) pp.20, 23, 39–42, 118, 142.

14. Klare, *Rogue States* (note 3) pp.41–2, 62–85, 104.
15. Toby I. Gati, *Assessing Current and Projected Threats to U.S. National Security*, Statement by Assistant Secretary for Intelligence and Research before the Senate Select Committee on Intelligence, Washington, DC, 5 Feb. 1997. <http://www.state.gov/www/global/terrorism/970205.html>. See also Lake 'Confronting Backlash States'(note 10). Lake's list of backlash (i.e. rogue) states is Iran, Iraq, North Korea, Libya and Cuba.
16. Klare, *Rogue States* (note 3) pp.97–116.
17. See James Wirtz, 'Counterproliferation, Conventional Counterforce and Nuclear War', this volume.
18. Klare, *Rogue States* (note 3) pp.119–25; Martin Kettle, 'US Strategy on Nuclear War', *The Guardian*, 9 Dec. 1997.
19. Ed Vulliamy, 'US Building Up New Nuclear Arsenal', *The Guardian*, 19 Aug. 1997.
20. Kettle, 'US Strategy on Nuclear War' (note 18).
21. Ian Black and Richard Norton-Taylor, 'Trident Warheads to be Cut By Half', *The Guardian*, 18 June 1998.
22. David Fairhall, 'Nuclear Deterrent Aimed at Third World Dictators', *The Guardian*, 9 Jan. 1996.
23. Richard Halloran, '... But Carry A Big Stick', *Far Eastern Economic Review* 161/49 (3 Dec. 1998) pp.26–27, and John Gittings, 'US Threat to Invade North Korea', *The Guardian*, 26 Nov. 1998. This has strong and not very reassuring echoes of the US invasion of North Korea in 1950. The fact that starvation and malnutrition is rife in North Korea makes conservatives worry that it will attack South Korea conventionally or develop nuclear weapons and create a nuclear crisis. In contrast, liberals and the left argue that the dire situation in North Korea makes such a war or crisis less likely. They also argue that the hardliners in North Korea and the United States are in a symbiotic relationship (officially they may exist to eliminate each other, but the existence of the other is vital to their identity, mission and status). See John Gittings, 'An Enemy Already Defeated', *The Guardian*, 26 Nov. 1998.
24. Tanter, *Rogue Regimes* (note 3) pp.ix, xi, 40. Unacceptable to whom, one might ask.
25. Tanter's list of rogue states is Iran, Iraq, North Korea, Libya and Syria (with Sudan as its surrogate). Unusually among conservatives, Tanter does not see Cuba as a rogue state because he sees it as no longer exporting terrorism or revolution and no longer seeking WMD. Ibid. Ch.6.
26. See James, 'Iran and Iraq', this volume, and Mueller and Mueller, 'Methodology of Mass Destruction', this volume.
27. Klare, *Rogue States* (note 3) p.161.
28. Ibid. p.3.
29. Ibid. p.206.
30. Ibid. pp.85–96, 116–19.
31. Ibid. p.22.
32. Ralph K. White, 'American Acts of Force: Results and Misperceptions', *Peace and Conflict: Jnl of Peace Psychology* 4/2 (1998) p.114. For more on the psychological bias of portraying oneself as reactive, defensive, benign, and directed towards no-one in particular, and the opponent as pro-active, offensive, malign and directed against you, see Wirtz, 'Counterproliferation', this volume, and Robert Jervis, *Perception and Misperception in International Politics* (Princeton UP 1976) Chs.8–10.
33. Pilger, '"Humanitarian Intervention"' (note 3). Brief discussions by Chomsky of the issue of 'rogues' can be found in *World Orders, Old and New* (London: Pluto Press 1994) pp.72–3, and 'The Current Bombings: Behind the Rhetoric' May 1999 <http://www.zmag.org/chomsky/index.cfm>. See also Phyllis Bennis, *Calling the Shots. How Washington Dominates Today's UN* (Brooklyn, NY: Olive Branch Press) pp.159–73.
34. For many claims from the left of examples, see Noam Chomsky and Edward S. Herman, *The Political Economy of Human Rights* (Boston, MA: South End Press 1979) 2 volumes; Noam Chomsky, *Pirates and Emperors: International Terrorism in the Real World* (NY: Claremont 1986); Noam Chomsky, *The Culture of Terrorism* (London: Pluto Press 1989); Alexander George (ed.) *Western State Terrorism* (Cambridge: Polity Press 1991); and Zunes, 'Function of Rogue States' (note 3).

35. See Jack Nelson-Pallmeyer, *School of Assassins* (Maryknoll, NY: Orbis Books 1997) and the SOA Watch website http://www.soaw.org/. For a response by the SOA, see its website http://www.benning.army.mil/usarsa/main.htm.

36. Zunes, 'Function of Rogue States' (note 3). In April 1999, Libya did hand over the two suspects to face trial in The Netherlands unders Scottish Law.

37. For additional examples, see Geoff Simons, *Vietnam Syndrome. Impact on US Foreign Policy* (Basingstoke: Macmillan 1998) and *Scourging of Iraq* (note 2).

38. Chomsky, *Deterring Democracy* (note 5) p.315 and, on Libya, Zunes, 'Function of Rogue States' (note 3).

39. Victoria Brittain, 'Children Die in Agony as US Trade Ban Stifles Cuba', *The Guardian*, 7 March 1997 and Stephen Bates and Martin Kettle, 'US Under Fire for Cuba Ban', *The Guardian*, 28 April 1998.

40. *New York Times*, 'UN Call To End Block on Cuba', *The Guardian*, 16 Oct. 1998,

41. UNICEF *Situation Analysis* summarised by the Iraqi Action Coalition (IAC) <http://leb.net/IAC/main.html>. See also CASI [Campaign Against Sanctions on Iraq] *Starving Iraq: One Humanitarian Disaster We Can Stop* (Cambridge: Campaign Against Sanctions on Iraq, Feb. 1999) <http://linux.clare.cam.ac.uk/casi>.

42. Simons, *Scourging of Iraq* (note 2).

43. Ed Vulliamy, 'US Law Blocks Weapons Inspectors', *The Guardian*, 12 Feb. 1998.

44. Zunes, 'Function of Rogue States' (note 3).

45. Julian Borger and Martin Kettle, 'Israel Goes Underwater to Counter Arab Bomb', *The Guardian*, 2 July 1998. Note the topsy-turvy perspective of *The Guardian*: German assistance for the Israeli nuclear weapon programme is presented as countering an Arab bomb, even though there is at present no Arab bomb to counter, and serious dispute over whether Iran is actually seeking nuclear weapons.

46. Tanter, *Rogue Regimes* (note 3) forthcoming rev. ed., Ch.7.

47. Samuel Huntington made a similar move. He wrote that 'While the United States regularly demonises various countries as "rogue states", in the eyes of many countries it is becoming the rogue superpower.' However, the rogue behaviour he has in mind is anodyne stuff – merely leaning a bit too hard on allied governments. The much more robust rogue accusations made by the left are omitted from his discussion. See Samuel P. Huntington, 'The Lonely Superpower', *Foreign Affairs* 78/2 (March/April 1999) p.42. In the same issue Gary Wills presents a slightly tougher version of the same line as that of Huntington. See Gary Wills, 'Bully of the Free World', *Foreign Affairs* 78/2 (March/April 1999) pp.50–9.

48. The same sort of ideas tends to be labelled post-structuralism, post-positivism or post-modernism. Of course, this is just a broad cluster of ideas, and there are deep disputes among those who might be categorised with these labels. Tanter also does not engage with the interpretive perspective on rogue states outlined in my Vienna paper.

49. David Campbell, *Writing Security. United States Foreign Policy and the Politics of Identity* (Manchester UP 1998) rev. ed., and *National Deconstruction: Violence, Identity and Justice in Bosnia* (Minneapolis: U. of Minnesota 1998).

50. Richard Devetak, 'The Project of Modernity and International Relations Theory', *Millennium: Jnl of International Studies* 24/1 (1995) pp.27–51.

51. On biopolitics see, for example, Paul Rabinow (ed.) *The Foucault Reader* (London: Penguin 1994).

52. Mueller and Mueller, 'Methodology of Mass Destruction', this volume.

53. Trish Saywell, 'Death Sentence', *Far Eastern Economic Review* 161/50 (10 Dec. 1998), pp.54–6 and Sarah Bosely, 'Tobacco Will Kill 1 in 3 Chinese Men', *The Guardian*, 20 Nov. 1998. Although the US tobacco industry agreed to hand over $120 billion to various US authorities to compensate for the mass destruction they cause, with US government help they are using international trade regulations to gain access to people in less industrialised countries to replace this lost profit.

54. Chomsky, *Deterring Democracy* (note 5) pp.123–7.

55. For a fascinating application of this kind of thinking to a debate over whether or not US behaviour contradicts its professed principles, see Toby Robertson, Stephen Reicher, 'An Analysis of the Construction and Contestation of Contradictions in a Debate Between Noam

Chomsky and Lord Jenkins on the Gulf War', *British Journal of Social Psychology* 37 (1998) pp.287–302.

56. For example, Chomsky argues that 'Typically, the thugs and gangsters whom the US backs reach a point in their careers when they become too independent and grasping, outliving their usefulness.' At this point, he claims, they become demonised by the United States and treated as foes to be crushed. *Deterring Democracy* (note 5) pp.161, 201–02.

57. For diverse contributions, see Martha Finnemore, *National Interests in International Society* (Ithaca, NY: Cornell UP 1996); Peter J. Katzenstein (ed.) *The Culture of National Security. Norms and Identity in World Politics* (NY: Columbia UP 1996); Keith Krause and Michael C. Williams (eds.) *Critical Security Studies. Concepts and Cases* (London: UCL Press 1997); Barry Buzan, Ole Wæver and Jaap de Wilde, *Security. A New Framework for Analysis* (Boulder, CO: Lynne Rienner 1998); and Campbell, *National Deconstruction* (note 49).

58. Pilger, '"Humanitarian Intervention"' (note 3), Chomsky, 'Current Bombings'(note 33).

59. Michael Sheehan also uses the phrase 'radical security studies'. The extent to which he and I mean the same thing by it remains to be seen.

60. For a statement of the common ground between social science and interpretivism, see Georg Sørensen, 'IR Theory After the Cold War', *Review of International Studies* 24/3 (1998) pp.83–100. One of the many virtues of Campbell's interpretivist work is its detailed engagement with empirical material. However, Campbell is intent mainly but not exclusively upon emphasising what divides him from those working from a social science perspective: see Barry Buzan and Eric Herring, *The Arms Dynamic in World Politics* (Boulder, CO: Lynne Rienner 1998) pp.193–8. Chomsky's position is that social science already fully accepts that interpretation is unavoidable, that there can be no such thing as an unintepreted fact, and that, in this sense, a social science-interpretivism dichotomy is false. I agree that social science generally accepts this in principle: what I have in mind is are spectra in which interpretivists tend to be more or differently preoccupied with the difficulties and pitfalls of choosing one interpretation over another.

61. On the processes by which national interests get constructed while appearing to be natural (and hence non-constructed), see Jutta Weldes, 'Constructing National Interests', *European Journal of International Relations* 2/3 (1996) pp.275–318, and idem and Diana Saco, 'Making State Action Possible: The United States and the Discursive Construction of "The Cuban problem", 1960–1994', *Millennium* 25/2 (1996) pp.361–95.

Abstracts

Counterproliferation, Conventional Counterforce and Nuclear War
JAMES J. WIRTZ

This essay examines an increasingly important element of US defense policy, counterproliferation. It explains how US security strategy is no longer constrained by Mutual Assured Destruction: American strategists now contemplate using precision conventional weapons to deny proliferants nuclear capabilities. The study also suggests that US nuclear deterrent capabilities backstop counterproliferation policies. It explores the risks inherent in counterproliferation and how US escalation dominance helps to reduce these risks. In concluding, the analysis questions whether or not new counterproliferation strategies are superior to arms control or deterrence in countering nuclear-armed states.

NATO's Non-Proliferation and Deterrence Policies: Mixed Signals and the Norm of WMD Non-Use
HENNING RIECKE

Since 1994, the member states of the North Atlantic Treaty Organization (NATO) have run a campaign to stem the spread of WMD. NATO tries to raise the costs and to reduce the benefits of WMD proliferation. The alliance, however, still utilises its nuclear posture to deter the use of all classes of WMD. The sobering status of proliferation indicates that the usual suspect states have not renounced the use of WMD at all. How is this possible? Neoliberal and constructivist hypothesis are applied to consider the effects of NATO's non-proliferation campaign on other states' decisions to use WMD. While NATO assists several non-proliferation regimes, it points to the strategic relevance of WMD and legitimacy of their use. States in NATO's vicinity might be successfully deterred from using WMD against the alliance, but they do not change their beliefs about the applicability of such weapons.

Iran and Iraq as Rational Crisis Actors: Dangers and Dynamics of Survivable Nuclear War
CAROLYN C. JAMES

This essay will develop and analyze propositions about the behavior of 'mini-arsenal' nuclear dyads in crisis situations. 'Mini- arsenal' is a concept developed to describe more effectively a minimal nuclear capability. The guiding principle of the research is that *the dynamics of nuclear strategy are expected to be different within mini-arsenal,third-,second-and first-level dyads*. The specific objective of this study is to present a paradigm of crisis interaction that (a) encompasses these respective types of nuclear states, concentrating on mini-arsenals in this treatise; and (b) indicates whether preferences and behavior adhere to te assumptions of Classical (or Rational) Deterrence Theory.

Beliefs, Culture, Proliferation and Use of Nuclear Weapons
BEATRICE HEUSER

A state-focused analysis is insufficient in explaining why countries have in the past acquired nuclear weapons or chosen not to do so This can only be understood if one factors in the analysis of beliefs specific to the predominant culture in the respective states. Even taking these into consideration, it is not always possible to predict a state's behavior in times of war as can be demonstrated by past decisions to resort to large-scale city bombing (with conventional ordnance or with nuclear weapons). These decisions were functions of personal convictions of individual key decision-makers, and did not necessarily reflect the overall beliefs of the culture from which they sprang. In-depth analysis of cultures and even individual key decision-makers' beliefs is thus vital.

The International System and the Use of Weapons of Mass Destruction
YANNIS A. STIVACHTIS

This study examines the relationship between the type of international system and the use of WMD. Comparing the Cold War and post-Cold War international systems, it argues first, that as long as anarchy remains the basic ordering principle the structure of international system is irrelevant to the use of WMD. Second, it is relatively unclear whether the power structure of the system is related to the use of WMD although multipolarity seems to increase the chances that WMD might be used in wars between secondary powers. And third, the possibility of the use of WMD depends on the actors involved, the relevant strategic factors, the technical conditions related to WMD, the systemic processes in which the actors are involved and the rules and norms that regulate their behavior in the system.

The Impact of the Revolution in Military Affairs
PATRICK MORGAN

This contribution begins by discussing what makes for a revolution in military affairs (RMA), the components of the of the current one, and its probable effects on warfare in the future. Then it speculates on how the revolution will affect the future importance and use of weapons of mass destruction. It notes that the RMA has already encouraged efforts to put WMD in the background and strengthened efforts to eliminate those weapons, but that it has also incited some states to develop or rely more heavily on WMD because they fear US or Western dominance in conventional forces.

The Methodology of Mass Destruction: Assessing Threats in the New World Order
JOHN MUELLER and KARL MUELLER

The label, 'weapons of mass destruction' has lately been applied not only to nuclear weapons, but, often on a seemingly equal footing, to arms that have thus far killed scarcely anyone (biological weapons), to arms that are vastly less effective (chemical weapons), and to costly and often ineffectual delivery devices (ballistic missiles). Meanwhile, in a thus-far futile effort to drive out, and essentially kill, its leader, economic sanctions have probably already taken the lives of more people in Iraq than have been killed by all weapons of mass destruction in history. A reassessment of economic warfare and of the limited dangers posed by 'rogue states' is overdue. For Iraq, deterrence and containment are preferable.

Rogue Rage: Can We Prevent Mass Destruction?
ERIC HERRING

For many, 'rogue' states are the most worrying kind of state when it comes to the potential for WMD use. For conservatives, the label 'rogue' state is appropriate for the very serious threats to the West which exist. For liberals, it exaggerates the threats but is still appropriate. For the left, it exaggerates the threats to the West and is applicable to the United States and some of its allies. For interpretivists, one's position on this issue is driven to a great extent by one's own values and identity. The essay argues that the perspectives of the left and the interpretivists are the most persuasive.

About the Contributors

Eric Herring is a Lecturer in International Politics at the University of Bristol, England. He has been a Visiting Scholar at George Washington University, Washington DC and Social Science Research Council MacArthur Fellow in International Peace and Security at Columbia University, New York. His publications include the following books: (co-author Ken Booth) *Keyguide to Information Sources in Strategic Studies* (Mansell 1994); *Danger and Opportunity: Explaining International Crisis Outcomes* (Manchester UP 1995); (co-editors Geoffrey Pridham and George Sanford) *Building Democracy? The International Dimension of Democratisation in Eastern Europe* (Leicester UP 1994, rev. ed. 1997); and (co-author Barry Buzan) *The Arms Dynamic in World Politics* (Lynne Rienner 1998).

James J. Wirtz is an Associate Professor of National Security Affairs at the US Naval Postgraduate School, Monterey, California. He is the author of *The Tet Offensive: Intelligence Failure in War* (Cornell UP 1991) and co-editor of *The Absolute Weapon Revisited: Nuclear Arms and the Emerging International Order* (Michigan UP 1998). His work has been published in *Air Power Journal, Defense Analysis, Intelligence and National Security, International Journal of Intelligence and Counterintelligence, International Security, International Studies Notes, Orbis, Political Science Quarterly, Security Studies, Strategic Review, Studies in Intelligence*, and *The Journal of Strategic Studies*.

Henning Riecke is a Post-Doctoral Fellow at the Weatherhead Center for International Affairs, Havard University. In his dissertation, he examined US non-proliferation campaigns and their impact on the nuclear non-proliferation regime. He has been research assistant at the Center for Transatlantic Foreign and Security Policy Studies, Free University of Berlin, and Visiting Fellow at the Center for Science and International Affairs, Harvard University He has published on non-proliferation, European security and international relations theory.

Carolyn C. James is a Research Fellow at the International Institute for Theoretical and Applied Physics at Iowa State University, USA. She is the author of articles and book chapters on the subjects of international relations and civil-military relations. Among the honors and awards received by Dr James are the Taft Fellowship from the University of Cincinnati and grants from the Earhardt Foundation and John F. Kennedy Library. Her most recent research focuses on the management of nuclear proliferation.

Beatrice Heuser is Professor of International and Strategic Studies at King's College, London. She taught temporarily at the University of Reims, and has been an SSRC-MacArthur Foundation post-Doctoral Fellow. She is the author of several books, including *Western Containment Policies in the Cold War* (Routledge 1989); *Nuclear Strategies and Forces for Europe* (Macmillan 1997), *Nuclear Mentalities?* (Macmillan 1998) and many articles. Among the books she has edited is *Haunted by History: Myths in International Relations* (Berghahn 1998), with Cyril Buffet. Her most recent book is *The Bomb: Nuclear Weapons in their Historical, Strategic and Ethical Context* (Longman 1999).

Yannis A. Stivachtis is Assistant Professor of International Relations at Schiller International University (The American College of Switzerland) and Senior Analyst at ARIS, Research and Consulting Office for Security Studies (Vienna), Austria. Until recently, he was Research Fellow at the United Nations Institute for Disarmament Research (UNIDIR). He holds a PhD and an MA from Lancaster University. He is author of *The Enlargement of International Society: Culture versus Anarchy and Greece's Entry into International Society* (London: Macmillan and New York: St Martin's Press 1998); *The Limitations of Non-Offensive Defence: The Greco-Turkish and Middle East Cases*, forthcoming (Frankfurt, Vienna: Peter Lang Winter 2000); *Demography, Development and Security*, forthcoming (Frankfurt, Vienna: Peter Lang Spring 2000) and co-author of *Non-Offensive Defence in the Middle East* (Geneva, New York: UN Publications 1998). He has also published articles on Balkan and Middle Eastern Security in various journals.

Patrick M. Morgan was appointed Thomas and Elizabeth Tierney Chair in Peace and Conflict Studies, and Professor of Political Science, at the University of California, Irvine in 1991. Prior to that he had been at Washington State University since 1967. During 1985–97 he was also a faculty member at the College of Europe in Bruges, and a regular lecturer at Katholieke Universiteit Leuven, in Belgium. In 1992–98 he was Director of the Global Peace and Conflict Studies Program at UC Irvine. He is the author or editor of *Deterrence: A Conceptual Analysis*, 2nd ed. (1983); *Strategic Military Surprise* with Klaus Knorr (1983), *Regional Orders: Building Security in a New World* with David Lake (1997); and *Security and Arms Control* with Edward Kolodziej (1989) as well as other books plus many chapters and articles.

John Mueller is a Professor of Political Science at the University of Rochester, New York. He is the author of *War, Presidents and Public Opinion, Retreat from Doomsday: The Obsolescence of Major War, Policy and Opinion in the Gulf War, Quiet Cataclysm: Reflections on the Recent Transformation of World Politics*, and articles in *International Security, American Political Science Review, Orbis, American Journal of Political Science, National Interest, British Journal of Political Science, International Studies Quarterly*, and *Foreign Policy*, as well as many editorial page columns in the *Wall Street Journal, Los Angeles Times*, and *New York Times*. Mueller is an elected member of the American Academy of Arts and Sciences, has been a John Simon Guggenheim Fellow, and has received grants from the National Science Foundation and the National Endowment for the Humanities. His latest book is *Democracy, Capitalism, and Ralph's Pretty Good Grocery*, will be published by Princeton University Press.

Karl Mueller is Associate Professor of Comparative Military Studies at the US Air Force's School of Advanced Airpower Studies, at Maxwell Air Force Base, Alabama. He has written articles about deterrence theory, coercion, air strategy, and US defense policy, and is one of the authors of the recently released Air University Balkans Air Campaign Study. He is currently completing a project on space weaponization and a book about the asymmetric deterrence strategies of European middle powers. The opinions he expresses in his paper in this volume are his own and do not reflect the views of the US Air Force or the US Government.

Index

[Note:The Editor and contributors would like to thank Patricia Owens for doing a characteristically swift and thorough job of compiling the index. The suffix n refers to a page with endnote material of significance.]